THE HISTORY OF AL-ṬABARĪ

AN ANNOTATED TRANSLATION

VOLUME II

Prophets and Patriarchs

The History of Al-Ṭabarī

SUNY

SERIES IN NEAR EASTERN STUDIES

Said Amir Arjomand, Editor

Bibliotheca Persica
Edited by Ehsan Yar-Shater

The History of al-Ṭabarī
(*Ta'rīkh al-rusul wa'l-mulūk*)

VOLUME II

Prophets and Patriarchs

translated and annotated
by
William M. Brinner
University of California, Berkeley

State University of New York Press

The preparation of this volume was made possible by a grant from the Translation Program of the National Endowment for the Humanities, an independent federal agency; and by the Persian Heritage Foundation.

Published by
State University of New York Press, Albany

Printed in the United States of America

For information, address State University of New York
Press, State University Plaza, Albany, N.Y., 12246

Library of Congress Cataloging in Publication Data

Ṭabarī, 838?—923.
Prophets and patriarchs.

(The history of al-Ṭabarī = Ta'rikh al-rusul wa'l-mulūk; v. 2)
(Bibliotheca Persica) (SUNY series in Near Eastern studies)
Translation of extracts from: Ta'rīkh al-rusul wa-al-mulūk.
Bibliography: p.
1. Prophets, Pre-Islamic. I. Brinner, William M. II. Title.
III. Series: Ṭabarī, 838?—923. Ta'rīkh al-rusul wa-al-mulūk.
English; v. 2. IV. Series: Bibliotheca Persica (Albany, N.Y.)
v. Series: SUNY Series in Near Eastern Studies.
BP137.T33 1987 84-97
ISBN 0-87395-921-3
ISBN 0-88706-313-6 (pbk.)

10 9 8 7 6 5 4 3 2 1

Acknowledgements

In 1971 the General Editor proposed to the UNESCO to include a translation of al-Ṭabarī's *History* in its Collection of Representative Works. UNESCO agreed, but the Commission in charge of Arabic works favored other priorities. Deeming the project worthy, the Iranian Institute of Translation and Publication, which collaborated with UNESCO, agreed to undertake the task. After the upheavals of 1979, assistance was sought from the National Endowment for the Humanities. The invaluable encouragement and support of the Endowment is here gratefully acknowledged.

The General Editor wishes to thank sincerely also the participating scholars, who have made the realization of this project possible; the Board of Editors for their selfless assistance; Professor Franz Rosenthal for his many helpful suggestions in the formulation and application of the editorial policy; Professor Jacob Lasner for his painstaking and meticulous editing; and Dr. Susan Mango of the National Endowment for the Humanities for her genuine interest in the project and her advocacy of it.

Preface

The History of Prophets and Kings (*Ta'rīkh al-rusul wa'l-mulūk*) by Abū Jaᶜfar Muḥammad b. Jarīr al-Ṭabarī (839–923), here rendered as the *History of al-Ṭabarī*, is by common consent the most important universal history produced in the world of Islam. It has been translated here in its entirety for the first time for the benefit of non-Arabists, with historical and philological notes for those interested in the particulars of the text.

Ṭabarī's monumental work explores the history of the ancient nations, with special emphasis on biblical peoples and prophets, the legendary and factual history of ancient Iran, and, in great detail, the rise of Islam, the life of the Prophet Muḥammad, and the history of the Islamic world down to the year 915. The first volume of this translation will contain a biography of al-Ṭabarī and a discussion of the method, scope, and value of his work. It will also provide information on some of the technical considerations that have guided the work of the translators.

The *History* has been divided here into 38 volumes, each of which covers about two hundred pages of the original Arabic text in the Leiden edition. An attempt has been made to draw the dividing lines between the individual volumes in such a way that each is to some degree independent and can be read as such. The page numbers of the original in the Leiden edition appear on the margins of the translated volumes.

Al-Ṭabarī very often quotes his sources verbatim and traces the chain of transmission (*isnād*) to an original source. The chains of transmitters are, for the sake of brevity, rendered by only a dash (—) between the individual links in the chain.

Thus, According to Ibn Ḥumayd—Salamah—Ibn Isḥāq means that al-Ṭabarī received the report from Ibn Ḥumayd who said that he was told by Salamah, who said that he was told by Ibn Isḥāq, and so on. The numerous subtle and important differences in the original Arabic wording have been disregarded.

The table of contents at the beginning of each volume gives a brief survey of the topics dealt with in that particular volume. It also includes the headings and subheadings as they appear in al-Ṭabarī's text, as well as those occasionally introduced by the translator.

Well-known place-names, such as, for instance, Mecca, Baghdad, Jerusalem, Damascus, and the Yemen, are given in their English spellings. Less common place-names, which are the vast majority, are transliterated. Biblical figures appear in the accepted English spelling. Iranian names are usually transcribed according to their Arabic forms, and the presumed Iranian forms are often discussed in the footnotes.

Technical terms have been translated wherever possible, but some, such as qāḍī and imām, have been retained in Arabic forms. Others that cannot be translated with sufficient precision have been retained and italicized as well as footnoted.

The annotation aims chiefly at clarifying difficult passages, identifying individuals and place-names, and discussing textual difficulties. Much leeway has been left to the translators to include in the footnotes whatever they consider necessary and helpful.

The bibliographies list all the sources mentioned in the annotation.

The index in each volume contains all the names of persons and places referred to in the text, as well as those mentioned in the notes as far as they refer to the medieval period. It does not include the names of modern scholars. A general index, it is hoped, will appear after all the volumes have been translated.

Ehsan Yar-Shater

Contents

Translator's Foreword

Like almost all other medieval Muslim historians and chroniclers, Ṭabarī begins his history with the creation of the world and the story of Adam. As he proceeds to follow the descendants of Adam, his point of view becomes clear. The two great civilizations to which the Arabs—and hence Islam—were heirs were the civilization of the ancient Israelites, as recorded in the Qur'ān and in Muslim tradition, and the civilization of ancient Iran. These two civilizations, in turn, must be connected with each other, must be shown as two strands which intertwine, genealogically and historically, and give rise to pre-Islamic civilization which was to be transformed by the coming of Islam.

This volume treats one part of that early history. Based on Qur'ān, on Muslim tradition of the Israelite past, and on a version of Iranian history very close to that found in the *Shāhnāmeh*, the national epic of Iran, it unfolds the stories of Noah, Abraham, the Arabian prophets—Hūd, Ṣāliḥ, Job and Shu'ayb—Lot, and Joseph. These tales form part of the literary genre of *qiṣaṣ al-anbiyā'* or tales of the prophets, namely stories of biblical figures regarded as prophets by Muslims. Unlike most such collections, these fascinating tales are treated by Ṭabarī with a certain scholarly detachment, making clear his own acceptance of or doubts about certain traditions such as which of his sons Abraham was commanded to sacrifice, Isaac or Ishmael, or exactly which sins of Lot's people brought about the destruction of Sodom. Together with this comes the interweaving of Iranian tradition as in the case of Bīwarasb—a legendary ruler—and

Noah, or of Nimrod, the persecutor of Abraham, and his role in Iranian history.

This is proto-history presented in fascinating detail and with the meticulous scholarship which Ṭabarī displays when he deals with more recent or contemporary history in later volumes.

The translator's thanks go to Dr. Mahmoud Omidsalar for his assistance with the Old Persian material; to Dr. Maurice Salib for reviewing the translation; and to Mr. Jeffrey Deboo for his assistance with the final revision and typing.

William Brinner
University of California, Berkeley

An Account of Bīwarasb, that is, al-Azdahāq[1]

The Arabs call him al-Ḍaḥḥāk, for they take the sound between the letters *s* and *z* in Persian to be a *ḍ*, the *h* to be *ḥ*, and the *q* to be *k*.[2] He is the one whom Ḥabīb b. Aws[3] had in mind when he said, "He did not accomplish merely what Pharaoh had accomplished in this world, nor Haman, nor Korah;[4] rather, he was like al-Ḍaḥḥāk in the greatness of his power over the world, and you are Afarīdhūn."[5] He was the one about whom al-Ḥasan b. Hāni'[6] boasted by claiming that al-Ḍaḥḥāk was from his people:

---

1. New Persian Bēwar.asp, another name for Zahhāk (al-Ḍaḥḥāk) in the *Shāhnāmeh*. A compound from *bēwar* "myriad, ten thousand" and *asp/asb* "horse", i.e., "master of ten thousand horses." See *Shāhnāmeh*, 44, verses 83–85. Al-Azdahāq, from Avestan *aži.dahāka-* who was a three-headed dragon king. This Avestan form was later Arabicized into al-Azdahāq and finally al-Ḍaḥḥāk (Zahhāk in New Persian). For a full discussion see Omidsalar, n. 9.

2. This is Ṭabarī's effort to explain the phonetic shift from what he considered a Persian form, Azdahāq (which, as we have seen above, is already Arabicized), to al-Ḍaḥḥāk.

3. Abū Tammām Ḥabīb b. Aws al-Ṭā'ī (808–842). This is found in his *Dīwān*, III, 321. There the name of the hero is Ifrīdhūn.

4. Fir'awn, Hāmān, Qārūn; in the Qur'an, 40:23–25, Moses was sent to these three with "our revelation and clear warrant," but they disbelieved and ordered the slaying of the sons of believers. The three became symbolic figures representing disbelief and tyranny in Islamic literature.

5. The name occurs as Farēdūn, Ferīdūn, Afrīdūn, and Āfarīdūn in New Persian. The hero who defeated Zahhāk and imprisoned him in Mount Damavand. (See below).

6. Muḥammad b. Hāni' b. Muḥammad b. Sa'dūn al-Azdī al-Andalusī, Abū al-Qāsim [326–362(938–973)]. See *al-A'lām*, VII, 354.

One of us was al-Ḍaḥḥāk whom
the madmen and jinns worshipped in their river beds.

[202] The Yemenites have claimed him as one of themselves. I have transmitted the following account from Hishām b. Muḥammad b. al-Sā'ib regarding this al-Ḍaḥḥāk: The Persians claim al-Ḍaḥḥāk, asserting that Jam[7] gave his sister in marriage to one of the nobles of his family and made him ruler over the Yemen, whereupon she bore him al-Ḍaḥḥāk. But the Yemenites claim him, asserting that he was one of them. They say that he was al-Ḍaḥḥāk b. ʿAlwān b. ʿUbayd b. ʿUwayj, and that he appointed his brother Sinān b. ʿAlwān b. ʿUbayd b. ʿUwayj as ruler over Egypt. The latter was the first Pharaoh and was ruler of Egypt when Abraham, the Friend of the Merciful, came there.

As for the Persians, they attribute to this al-Azdahāq a Yemenite genealogy different from the one given by Hishām. They say that he was Bīwarasb b. Arwandasb b. Zīnkāw b. Wīraw-
[203] shak b. Tāz b. Farwāk b. Sayāmak b. Mashā b. Jayūmart.[8] There are others who attribute this genealogy to him, but pronounce the names of his forefathers differently. They say that he is al-Ḍaḥḥāk b. Anduramasb b. Ranḥadār b. Wandarisaḥ b. Tāj b. Faryāk b. Sāhimak b. Mādhī b. Jayūmart. The Magians[9] assert that this Tāj was the ancestor of the Arabs, and they also claim that al-Ḍaḥḥāk's mother was Wadak bt. Wīwanjahān.[10] Also, they claim that he killed his father to curry favor with

---

7. Or Jamshīd; Avestan, Yima-. Fourth of the mythical kings of Iran, he appears as both Jam and Jamshīd in the *Shāhnāmeh.* He was overthrown and killed by Zahhāk after a reign of some seven hundred years. *Shāhnāmeh,* I, 49, verses 165–183, and I, 50, verses 184–186.

8. The genealogy as given in the *Bundahishn,* 293, is Ḍaḥḥāk son of Khrutāsp son of Zaingāw son of Avirashyang son of Tāj son of Farvāk son of Siyāmak [son of Mashya son of Gayōmart (Jayūmart), op. cit., line 1]. Ṭabarī is thus in general agreement with this early genealogy, although the individual names appear in greatly differing forms in various manuscripts. The next genealogy given below may be explained, in part at least, as being due to confusion of Arabic letters *r* for *z*, or substitution of *y* and *w*.

9. Al-Majūs, i.e., the Zoroastrians. See *Shorter Encyc.,* 298.

10. Not mentioned in the *Shāhnāmeh,* her name and genealogy are given in the *Bundahishn,* 293, as Uṭa (misreading by editor for Vadak) daughter of Tambayak of Ōwōikhm of Pairiurvo of Urvaēsm of Gadwithw of Drujaskān of Ganā Mīnūy.

the devils. He often lived in Babylon, and he had two sons, one of them named Sarnafiwār and the other Nafawār.[11]

Al-Sha'bī[12] used to say that he (al-Ḍaḥḥāk) was Qarishat, whom God had transformed into Azdahāq.

The Account of That Tale

According to Ibn Ḥumayd—Salamah b. al-Faḍl—Yaḥyā b. al-'Alā'—al-Qāsim b. Salmān—al-Sha'bī: Abjad, Hawwiz, Ḥuṭṭi, Kaliman, Sa'faṣ, and Qarishat[13] were tyrannical rulers. One day Qarishat became engrossed in thought and said, "Blessed [204] be God, the best of Creators," so God transformed him into Ajdahāq. He had seven heads and was the one who lived in Danbawand.[14] All the historians, both Arab and Persian, claim that he ruled over every clime and that he was a wicked sorcerer.

According to Hishām b. Muḥammad: Al-Ḍaḥḥāk reportedly reigned for one thousand years after Jam—but God knows better. Settling in the Sawād in a town called Nars[15] near the Kūfah Road, he ruled over all the earth, displaying tyranny and oppression. He killed excessively and was the first to enact (the punishments of) crucifixion and mutilation. He was also the first to levy tithes and to mint dirhams, and the first to sing and be sung to. It is said that there were two ganglia growing out of his shoulders, which caused pain to him. The pain be-

---

11. Not mentioned in any of the sources.

12. Abū 'Amr 'Āmir b. Sharāḥīl (640–721). An early traditionist, legal and literary scholar. See *GAS*, I, 277[5].

13. These names are actually combinations of the letters of the alphabet in the traditional order of the Semitic alphabet (*ḥurūf al-abjad*), combined in groups of four, three, three, four, and four from *aleph* to *taw*.

14. The highest summit of the Elburz Mountains in Iran. While the early Persian manuscripts show the spelling Danbavand, the word is today pronounced Damavand. The *nb* cluster > to *mb* and finally > *m*.

15. Nars, on the canal of the same name, which took its name from the Sassanian king Narses who came to the throne in A.D. 292 (LeStrange, *Lands*, 74) to the east of al-Kūfah. The latter was founded immediately after the Muslim conquest of Mesopotamia, about 17(636) during the caliphate of 'Umar. On the Arab, or desert, side of the Euphrates, it became 'Alī's capital city. (LeStrange, op.cit., 74–75).

came so intense for him that he would anoint them with the brains of human beings. For this purpose he killed two men each day and anointed his ganglia with their brains. When he did this, the pain would abate.

A man of the common people of Babylon rebelled against him; he set up a banner and many people rallied to him. When al-Ḍaḥḥāk learned of this he was alarmed and sent (the following message) to him, "What is the matter? What do you want?" The man replied, "Do you not claim that you are the ruler of the world, and that the world belongs to you?" Al-Ḍaḥḥāk replied, "Certainly." Whereupon the rebellious man said, "Then let your thirst be for all the world and not only for us, for you kill us alone of all the people." Al-Ḍaḥḥāk agreed with him
[205] about this and ordered that the two men whom he would slay each day should be divided among all the people and should not be taken specifically from one place rather than another.[16]

We have been told that the people of Iṣbahān[17] are descendants of that man who raised the banner, and that this banner is still preserved by the kings of Fārs[18] in their treasure-houses. According to what we have been told, it was the skin of a lion, which the kings of Fārs covered with gold and brocade and from which they drew good auguries.

Hishām continued: We have been told that al-Ḍaḥḥāk was Nimrod[19] and that Abraham, the Friend of the Merciful, was born during his era, and that al-Ḍaḥḥāk was Abraham's master who wanted to burn him. We have been told that Afarīdhūn (who was of the stock of Jam, the king before al-Ḍaḥḥāk—some claim that he was the ninth among his children and that

16. ee the Persian translation of the text by al-Balʿamī, which adds many details.

17. See LeStrange, *Lands* 202–207. Today generally known as Iṣfahān, the usual Arabic name was as given in the text. Located in the southwestern corner of the Jibāl province of Iran. Yāqūt, *Muʿjam*, I, 292–98.

18. The province of Fārs (southwestern Iran) was the home of the Achaemenian dynasty and the center of their government. Its name, Hellenized as Persia, became a common European name for the whole country. Shīrāz, founded by the Arabs after the conquest, became its capital. LeStrange, *Lands*, 248–298; Yāqūt, *Muʿjam*, III, 835–838, s.v. Fāris.

19. Namrūd, Namrūdh, Nimrūd. As in Jewish aggadic literature, though not in the Bible or explicitly in the Qur'ān, associated with the childhood of Abra-

his birthplace was Danbawand) went forth until he reached the residence of al-Ḍaḥḥāk while the latter was away in India. Afarīdhūn then took possession of the residence and of everything in it. News of this reached al-Ḍaḥḥāk, and he came back. But God deprived him of his power, and his rule was ended. Afarīdhūn attacked him, tied him fast, and led him to the mountains of Danbawand. The Persians claim that he is there to this day, fettered with iron, and still being punished.

Someone other than Hishām mentioned that al-Ḍaḥḥāk was not away from his residence, but that Afarīdhūn b. Athfiyān came to a dwelling of his in a fortress called Zaranj[20] (during the month of) Māh Mihr, (on the day of) Rūz Mihr[21] and married two of his women, one called Arwanāz and the other Sanwār. Bīwarasb was frightened when he discovered this, and fell down speechless and uncomprehending. Afarīdhūn struck [206]
his head with an iron mace—he had one with a curved top[22]—and Bīwarasb became more terrified and confused. At this, Afarīdhūn made off with him to Mount Danbawand where he tied him up securely. He ordered the populace to adopt Mihr Māh, Mihr Rūz, the day on which Bīwarasb was tied up, as a holiday (*ʿīd*)—it is today called al-Mihrjān.[23] Then

ham. The Muslim tales hinge on the verses in *sūrah* 2, which are attributed to Nimrod's speech although he is not mentioned by name. Muslim legend derives the name from *tamarrada* "he who rebelled" (against God). See *Shorter Encyc.*, 437–438. See also n. 52 below.

20. Zaranj/Zarang. The capital of Sijistān/Sistān (present-day Zahedan) on the Afghan frontier in eastern Iran, destroyed by Timur. LeStrange, *Lands*, 335; Yāqūt, *Muʿjam*, I, 926.

21. Lit. "the month of Mihr, the day of Mihr," here in its Arabic form. In the Sassanian calendar each month had thirty days, each one named after a deity, as were the months. When the name of the day coincided with the name of the month in which it fell, there was a festival. The 16th day of every month was called *Mihr Rūz* (or Rōz), "day of Mihr" (Old Iranian, Mithra-), the god of contracts and protector of the Iranian peoples. The name of the seventh month was also Mihr. Thus the 16th day of the seventh month, when the day-name and the month-name coincided, was called Mihrgān (Arabic, Mihrjān/Mahrjān) and was an important festival. It fell on the autumnal equinox, and was the harvest festival.

22. *Jurz*, for Persian *gurz*, club or mace . After preparing to attack Zahhāk, Fereydun ordered a great mace topped with a bull's head to be made for him. See *Shāhnāmeh*, I, 75, verse 429, and 66, verses 261–265.

23. See n. 21, above.

Afarīdhūn ascended the throne. It is mentioned that when al-Ḍaḥḥāk reigned and the crown was set upon him, he said, "We are rulers of this world, possessors of all therein." The Persians claim that rule will belong only to the clan from which Awshhanj, Jam, and Ṭahmurat came,[24] and that al-Ḍaḥḥāk had been a rebel who had seized the people of the land with witchcraft and deceit and had completely terrified them with the two serpents which had been on his shoulders. They also said that he had built a city in the land of Babylon and named it Ḥawb,[25] and that he made the Nabateans[26] his companions and courtiers. The people were subjected to every kind of pressure by him, and he slew the young boys.

Many of those who are learned in books say that the things on his shoulders were two long, swollen pieces of flesh, each of which looked like the head of a serpent, and that in his wickedness and cunning he hid them with his clothing. In order to cause terror he let it be known that they were two snakes which demanded food from him and moved under his garment when he was hungry, just as the organ of a person moves when he burns with hunger or anger. However, there are some people who say that they really were two snakes. I have mentioned what is related on the authority of al-Shaʿbī regarding that, but God knows better concerning its truthfulness and accuracy.[27]

According to some authorities on the genealogies of the Persians and their affairs: People went on suffering greatly from
[207] this Bīwarasb until God decided to destroy him. At that time a

24. Awshhanj, for Persian Hūshang, the second mythical king of the *Shāhnāmeh* and the father of Jam and Ṭahmūrath (here, Ṭahmūrat; Avestan, Taxmū.urupi-), the third of the mythical kings.

25. *Bundahishn* XXXII:4. "One is that which Zahhāk erected in Babylon which they call Kvirinta Duzita." If this is the same as Ḥawb, the latter was probably spelled *khawb/khub/khʷab*.

26. Nabateans: in the early Arab chronicles, usually applied to peoples who inhabited areas of Iraq; later applied to people of mixed stock (i.e., Arab and non-Arab) and the lowest level of society—probably because of their being distinguished for agriculture. See Lane, VIII:2759–60, s.v . nbṭ.

27. Some variations on this story occur in the Persian version by al-Balʿamī, who records that these actions of al-Ḍaḥḥāk the Arab went on for two hundred years and almost caused the world to be depopulated. See al-Balʿamī, 144.

common man of Iṣbahān, named Kābī,[28] attacked him. He did this because two of his sons had been seized by Bīwarasb's messengers for the two serpents on his shoulders. It is said that when grief for his sons overtook this Kābī, he took a staff which he had and hung a leather bag on its end. He set this up as his banner and called upon the people to come out against Bīwarasb and engage him in combat, since they shared his great distress and felt oppressed as he did. When Kābī was victorious, the people looked upon the banner as a good omen. They bestowed more and more honor upon it until it became the greatest banner of the kings of Persia. They sought blessing through it and named it Darafsh Kābiyān.[29] They brought it out for travel only in the most important campaigns, and raised it only for princes who were being sent on important missions.

From the account of Kābī we learn that he left Iṣbahān with his original followers and with those who joined him on his way. When he drew near to al-Ḍaḥḥāk and looked over his position, al-Ḍaḥḥāk became terrified and fled from his encampments, abandoning his place to the Persians who were able to capture whatever they wanted from him. They gathered round Kābī and argued. Kābī told them that he did not want to be king because he was not of royal lineage. He ordered them to take one of the sons of Jam as king because Jam was the son of the great king Awshhanq b. Farwāk,[30] who had been the first to design the institution of kingship and had preceded all others in carrying it out.

Afarīdhūn b. Athfiyān,[31] who was off in some other region [208]
hiding from al-Ḍaḥḥāk, appeared before Kābī and those who were with him. The people took his arrival to be a good omen because, according to a tradition of theirs, Afarīdhūn was a

---

28. Kābī is an Arabic rendering of the New Persian, Kāva; Middle Persian, Kāvag. Not mentioned in Avestan material, he figures prominently in the Classical Persian sources.

29. Lit. "banner of Kābī."

30. Jam, son of Hūshang, was the first king to sit on a throne, and he began many important institutions of kingship, according to Iranian tradition. See *Shāhnāmeh*, I, 41, verses 48–49 , and 42, verses 50–52.

31. Athfiyān. (Middle Persian, Aspyān) was Ferēydūn's father. See *Bundahishn* XXXV, line 8. In the *Shāhnāmeh* his name appears as Ātbīn or Ābtīn; see *Shāhnāmeh*, I, 57, verse 117.

candidate for rule. They then made him king, and Kābī and the notables became aides to Afarīdhūn in his affairs. Afarīdhūn assumed control and did everything necessary to consolidate his rule. Having also taken possession of al-Ḍaḥḥāk's dwellings, he pursued him and made him a prisoner in the Danbawand mountains. Some Magians claim that he took al-Ḍaḥḥāk captive and imprisoned him in those mountains, putting a group of jinn in charge of him; others assert that he killed him.

They assert that only one thing that could be considered good was ever said of al-Ḍaḥḥāk. When his affliction became great, his tyranny prolonged, and his days lengthened, the people felt that they were suffering so badly under his rule that their notables discussed the situation and agreed to travel to al-Ḍaḥḥāk's gate. When the notables and powerful men from various districts and regions reached his gate, they argued among themselves about coming into his presence and complaining to him and achieving reconciliation with him. They agreed that Kābī al-Iṣbahānī would approach him to speak on their behalf. When they were traveling toward al-Ḍaḥḥāk's gate, al-Ḍaḥḥāk was told that they were coming and permitted them to enter, which they did, with Kābī leading them. The latter appeared before al-Ḍaḥḥāk but refrained from greeting him. He said, "O king! What greeting should one give you? The greeting for one who rules all these climes or the greeting for one who rules only this clime—meaning Babylon?" Al-Ḍaḥḥāk replied, "Nay, but the greeting for one who rules all these climes, for I am king of the earth." Then al-Iṣbahānī said
[209] to him, "If you rule all the climes and your sway extends to all of them, why then have we in particular been assigned the burden of you, your intolerance, and your misdeeds out of all the peoples of the climes? Why then do you not divide such-and-such a matter between us and the other regions?" Speaking the truth boldly, he addressed the issue and enumerated to al-Ḍaḥḥāk the ways in which the latter would be able to lighten their burdens. His words pierced al-Ḍaḥḥāk's heart, and he kept working on him in that way until the king ended by admitting his wrongdoing. He talked intimately with the people and promised them what they wanted. Then he commanded them to leave so that they might go to their camps and remain

calm. They were to return to him to fulfill their needs before going back to their towns.

They claim that his mother Wadak was worse than he, and more wicked, and that while the people were remonstrating with him she was nearby, following what they were saying to him. When the people left she entered, burning with anger. Disapproving of al-Ḍaḥḥāk's patience with the people, she said to him, "I have been told of everything that happened and of these people's boldness toward you, that they frightened you in such-and-such ways and reviled you in such-and-such ways. Would you not destroy them and unleash your wrath on them or cut off their hands?" When this became too much for al-Ḍaḥḥāk he said to her, in spite of his haughtiness, "O you! You have not thought of anything that I had not thought of before, but the people surprised me with the truth and frightened [210]
me with it. When I was about to assail them harshly and attack them, the truth presented itself and appeared between me and them like a mountain. So I was unable to do anything against them." Thus he silenced her and sent her away. Then, after some days, he held audience for the people of the provinces and fulfilled his promises to them. He thus warded them off, having become gentle with them, and met most of their needs. This was the only good deed which is said to have been done by al-Ḍaḥḥāk.

The lifespan of this al-Ajdahāq was reportedly a thousand years. He actually ruled for six hundred years, while during the rest of his life he was like a king because of his power and the authority of his command. Some have said that he ruled for one thousand years and lived for one thousand one hundred years, until Afarīdhūn rebelled against him and overthrew and killed him. Some of the Persian sages have said, "We do not know of anyone who lived longer, whose name was not mentioned in the Torah, than this al-Ḍaḥḥāk and Gomer b. Japheth b. Noah,[32] the father of the Persians—for it is [also] said that Gomer's lifespan was one thousand years."

---

32. Gomer: Jāmir, Jāmar, in the text, and Jawmar or Jūmar, Ṭabarī, I, 211. (The Arabic text by De Goeje is meant whenever Ṭabarī is cited, as here.) According to Gen 10:2–3, I Chron 1:5–6 , the first-born son of Japheth and the fa-

We have only mentioned the story of Bīwarasb at this point because some people claim that Noah lived during his reign and was, in fact, sent to him and to those people in his kingdom who gave him allegiance and followed him in spite of his insolence and insubordination towards God.[33] We have mentioned God's kindness and helpfulness to Noah. This was because of Noah's obedience to God and his steadfastness in the face of all the injury and unpleasantness which befell him in this world. God thus saved him and those of his people who believed with him and followed him. God peopled the world with his descendants and made his name a name to be praised for-
[211] ever, and stored up for him a life of everlasting pleasure and ease in the hereafter. All others He slew, because they had disobeyed Him and rebelled against Him, contradicting His command. He deprived them of the comforts they had and made an example of them for all those who came after them, along with the painful punishment He had stored up for them in the hereafter with Him.

Now let us return to Noah and the tales about him and his progeny, for they—as God has mentioned—are those who are alive today. The others to whom Noah was sent, save his children and descendants, perished as did their offspring; none of them or their descendants remained. We have mentioned earlier that God's messenger, referring to God's word, "And we made his seed the survivors,"[34] said that they (his seed) are Shem, Ham, and Japheth.[35]

According to Muḥammad b. Sahl b. ʿAskar—Ismāʿīl b. ʿAbd

ther of Ashkenaz, Riphath, and Togarmah. Also, in Ezek 38:6, the name of a nation, today associated with the Assyrian, Gi-mir-ra-a; Greek, Kimmerioi. See *Encyc. Judaica*, VII:768.

33. Illustrative of the effort by early Islamic chroniclers to connect the two ancient histories known to them, i.e., those of the Jews and the Persians, to serve as a unified history of revelation culminating in the final revelation to Muḥammad.

34. Qur'ān 37:77.

35. In the text, Sām, Ḥām, and Yāfith (rarely, Yāfit; see Ṭabarī, I, 222). Though alluded to in the Qur'ān, they are not mentioned by name there. According to Qur'ān 40:42–47, one son of Noah drowned in the deluge and three survived. Hence a fourth son is posited, sometimes (but not here) associated with Canaan, who in the Bible is a son of Ham. See *Shorter Encyc.*, 128, s.v. Ḥām; *EI*[2], s.v. Ham.

al-Karīm—ʿAbd al-Ṣamad b. Maʿqil—Wahb b. Munabbih: Shem b. Noah was the father of the Arabs, the Persians, and the Greeks; Ham was the father of the Blacks; and Japheth was the father of the Turks and of Gog and Magog[36] who are cousins of the Turks. It is said that the wife of Japheth was Arbasīsah bt. Marāzīl b. al-Darmasīl b. Mehujael b. Enoch b. Cain b. Adam, and that she bore him seven sons and a daughter. One of the sons she bore him was Gomer b. Japheth, who was the father of Gog and Magog as told by Ibn Ḥumayd—Salamah—Ibn Isḥāq. The other sons she bore him were Mariḥu b. Japheth, Wā'il b. Japheth, Ḥawwān b. Japheth, Tubal b. Japheth, Hawshil b. Japheth, and Tiras b. Japheth. Their daughter was Shabokah bt. Japheth. They also claim that among the sons of Japheth were Gog and Magog, the Slavs and the Turks. [212]
The wife of Ham b. Noah was Naḥlab bt. Mārib b. al-Darmasīl b. Mehujael b. Enoch b. Cain b. Adam. She bore him three offspring: Cush b. Ham b. Noah, Put[37] b. Ham, and Canaan b. Ham.[38] Cush b. Ham b. Noah married Qarnabīl, the daughter of Batāwīl b. Tiras b. Japheth, and it is asserted that she bore him the Abyssinians, Sindis and Indians. Put b. Ham b. Noah married Bakht, another daughter of Batāwīl b. Tiras b. Japheth b. Noah, and it is said that she bore him the Copts—that is, the Copts of Egypt. Canaan b. Ham b. Noah married Arsal, another daughter of Batāwīl b. Tiras b. Japheth b. Noah, and she bore him the Blacks, Nubians, Fezzan, Zanj, Zaghāwah, and all the peoples of the Sudan.

According to Ibn Ḥumayd—Salamah—Ibn Isḥāq in the ḥadīth: The people of the Torah claim that this was only because of an invocation of Noah against his son Ham. This was because while Noah slept his genitals were exposed, and Ham saw them but did not cover them. Shem and Japheth, on the other hand, saw them and the two of them threw a garment

36. Yājūj, Mājūj (also Ya'jūj, Ma'jūj); Gen 10:2, Qur'ān 21:96. Two peoples who belong to the outstanding figures of Jewish and Muslim eschatology. Connected with the peoples of the Northeast of the ancient world, the dwelling place of peoples who are to burst forth from their isolation in the last days, devastating the world southwards. *Shorter Encyc.*, 637.

37. Qūṭ throughout the Arabic text.

38. Kanʿān. See n. 35 above, as well as *Shorter Encyc.*, 216, s.v. Kanʿān.

over him and concealed his genitals. When he awoke from his sleep he knew what Ham had done as well as what Shem and Japheth had done. He said, "Cursed is Canaan b. Ham. Slaves will they be to his brothers!" Then he said, "May God my Lord bless Shem, and may Ham be a slave of his two brothers. May God requite Japheth and let him alight at the dwelling places of Shem, and may Ham be a slave to them."[39] The wife of Shem b. Noah was Ṣalīb bt. Batāwīl b. Mehujael b. Enoch b.
[213] Cain b. Adam, who bore him several male offspring: Arpachshad b. Shem, Asshur[40] b. Shem, Lud[41] b. Shem, and Elam b. Shem. Shem also had Aram b. Shem. I (Ibn Isḥāq) do not know whether Aram was from the same mother as Arpachshad and his brothers or not.

According to al-Ḥārith—Ibn Saʿd—Hishām b. Muḥammad—his father—Abū Ṣāliḥ—Ibn ʿAbbās: When Sūq Thamanīn became too confining for the children of Noah they moved to Babylon and built it. It is situated between the Euphrates and the Ṣarāt. It was twelve *farsakh*s (seventy-two km) by twelve *farsakh*s; its gate was situated in the place of today's Dūrān,[42] above the Kūfah Bridge to the left as you cross it. They multiplied there, and they had reached one hundred thousand when they became Muslims.

Returning to the account of Ibn Isḥāq: Lud b. Shem b. Noah married Shakbah bt. Japheth b. Noah, and she bore him Fāris, Jurjān, and the races (*ajnās*) of Fāris.[43] In addition to the Persians, Lud begat Ṭasm and ʿImlīq, but I do not know whether the latter was by the mother of the Persians or not. ʿImlīq was the progenitor of the Amalekites, who were dispersed throughout the land. The peoples of the East and those of ʿUmān, of the Ḥijāz, of Syria, and of Egypt are all descended from him. From

39. Note the shift of the object of the curse from Canaan to Ham. For differing versions of this curse in Jewish and Muslim tradition, see *Encyc. Judaica*, 7:1216–17; *EI*², s.v. Ham.

40. Ṭabarī, I, 213, has Ashūdh.

41. Ṭabarī, loc. cit., has Lāwudh.

42. See Yāqūt, *Muʿjam*, II, 615.

43. The significance of this genealogy is that the descendants of Shem and Japheth are here united—thus the two great peoples of Islam at the time of Ṭabarī, the Arabs and the Persians, may be of a common origin. Ṭabarī shows some doubts about this, however. See below, note 61.

them, too, came the giants in Syria who were called Canaanites, the Pharaohs of Egypt, and the people of Baḥrayn and ʿUmān from whom a nation (*ummah*) called the Jāsim is descended. The inhabitants of al-Madīnah are descended from them—the Banū Huff, Saʿd b. Hizzān, the Banū Maṭar, and the Banū al-Azraq. The people of Najd—the Badīl, the Rāḥil, and the Ghafār—were of them, and the same is true of the people of Taymā'. The king of the Ḥijāz in Taymā' was one of them (his [214] name was al-Arqam), but they were inhabitants of Najd nevertheless, while the inhabitants of al-Ṭā'if were the Banū ʿAbd b. Ḍakhm, a clan of the first ʿAbs.

The Banū Umaym b. Lud b. Shem b. Noah were the people of Wabār in the sandy land, the sands of ʿĀlij.[44] They had increased and multiplied there when God's vengeance struck them down because they were openly disobedient. As a result, they were destroyed; only a remnant of them survived, which are the ones called the Nasnās.

Having increased and multiplied in al-Yamāmah[45] and its surroundings, the Ṭasm b. Lud inhabited that area as far as (the borders of) al-Baḥrayn. The Ṭasm, the Amalekites, the Umaym, and the Jāsim comprised an Arab people (*qawm*); their language, to which they were predisposed, was an Arabic dialect. Fāris was of the people of the East in the land of Persia (Fārs), where they spoke Persian (*fārisiyyah*).

Aram b. Shem b. Noah begat Uz b. Aram, Gether b. Aram, and Hul b. Aram. Then Uz b. Aram begat Gether b. Uz (and ʿĀd b. Uz) and ʿUbayl b. Uz. And Gether b. Aram begat Thamūd b. [215] Gether, and Judays b. Gether; they were an Arab people speaking the Muḍarī tongue.[46] The Arabs would call these nations the *ʿāribah* Arabs because the Arabic language was their original language, whereas they called the children of Ishmael b.

---

44. For an explanation of the origin of this name and its location in Arabia, see Yāqūt, *Muʿjam*, III, 591; Brice, *Atlas*, 15.

45. A region of eastern Arabia southwest of the area known as al-Baḥrayn in early Islamic times, roughly equivalent to the regions of al-Ḥasā and al-Kharj in the Eastern Province of today's Saudi Arabia. See Brice, *Atlas*, 19.

46. Namely descendants of Muḍar, the ancestor of most of the North Arabian tribes, as distinct from the descendants of Rabīʿah and Qaḥṭān. See Wüstenfeld, *Genealogische Tabellen*, (1) Übersichts -Tabelle, and D.

Abraham the *muta'arribah* Arabs because they only spoke these peoples' languages after they had settled among them.[47] The ʿĀd, the Thamūd, the Amalekites, the Umaym, the Jāsim, the Judays, and the Ṭasm are the real Arabs. The ʿĀd dwelt in the sands all the way to Ḥaḍramawt and in the Yemen. The Thamūd occupied the rocky land between the Ḥijāz and Syria as far as the Wādī al-Qurā and its environs. The Judays followed the Ṭasm and lived with them in al-Yamāmah and its environs as far as Baḥrayn. The name of al-Yamāmah at that time was Jaww. The Jāsim inhabited ʿUmān and thus came to be situated there.

Others besides Ibn Isḥāq have said that Noah prayed that prophets and apostles would be descended from Shem and that he prayed that kings would be among the descendants of Japheth. He began with the prayer for Japheth and, in so doing, gave him precedence over Shem. He prayed that Ham's color would be changed and that his descendants would be slaves to the children of Shem and Japheth.

It is mentioned in the books that Noah took a milder attitude toward Ham afterwards and prayed that he should be granted compassion by his brothers. He also prayed for some of his children's children—for Cush b. Ham and Gomer b. Japheth b. Noah. That was because some of the grandchildren matured while Noah grew old, and served him as the sons of
[216] his loins had done. As a result, he prayed for a number of them.

To Shem were born Eber, Elam, Asshur, Arpachshad, Lud, and Aram. Shem's place was in Mecca. From the descendants of Arpachshad came the prophets and apostles and the Best of Mankind[48] and all the Arabs and the Pharaohs of Egypt. Descended from Japheth b. Noah were all the kings of the non-Arabs, such as the Turks, the Khazars, and others, as well as the Persians. The last to rule among them was Yazdajird b.

47. See below, Ṭabarī, I, 352, where Ṭabarī states that Ishmael was sent as a prophet to the Amalekites and the peoples of Yemen, i.e. the non-Muḍarī Arabs.

48. That is, Muḥammad the Prophet, who is often called by this epithet.

Shahriyār b. Abrawīz,[49] whose genealogy leads back to Jayū-mart b. Japheth b. Noah.

It is said that a people descended from Lud b. Shem b. Noah, and others descended from his brothers, went off to this Gomer, and that Gomer took them under his favor and his rule. Among them was Maday (Mādhay)[50] b. Japheth, the one to whom *mādhiyyah* swords are attributed. Cyrus the Mede,[51] the slayer of Belshazzar b. Evilmerodach b. Nebuchadnezzar, was reportedly descended from this Maday. Among the descendants of Ham b. Noah are the Nubians, the Abyssinians, the Fezzanites, the Indians, the Sindis and the peoples of the coastlands in the East and the West. Among them was Nimrod, that is, Nimrod b. Cush b. Ham.[52]

To Arpachshad b. Shem was born his son Qaynān, who is not mentioned in the Torah. He was the one of whom it was said that he was not worthy of being mentioned in the revealed scriptures, because he was a magician and called himself a god. The genealogies in the Torah reach to Arpachshad b. Shem and then continue with Shelah b. Qaynān b. Arpachshad, without mentioning Qaynān. That is because of what has been said.

It is (thus) said about Shelah that he was Shelah b. Arpachshad, among those born to Qaynān. To Shelah was born Eber, and to Eber two sons were born. One of these was Peleg, which in Arabic means Qāsim (one who divides, distributes); he was called that only because it was during his era that the earth was [217]
divided up into diverse regions and tongues became diversified. Eber's other son was named Joktan (Qaḥṭān), to whom were born Yaʿrub and Yaqṭān—the two sons of Joktan b. Eber b. Shelah. They settled in the land of Yemen. Joktan was the first to rule the Yemen and the first to be greeted with the kingly salute, "May you disdain the curse."

49. Yezdigrid III (r. 634–642), the last Sassanian ruler of Iran, was defeated by the Arabs at Qādisiyyah (637) and finally at Nehawend (642). He fled to Central Asia and was murdered in 651.

50. *Mādhī* in Arabic.

51. The text reads: Khayrash or Kīrash al-Mādhī.

52. See n. 19, above.

To Peleg b. Eber[53] was born Reu,[54] and to Reu Serug was born, and to Serug Nahor was born, and to Nahor was born Terah, whose name in Arabic is Āzar.[55] To Terah was born Abraham.

Arpachshad also had a son, Nimrod b. Arpachshad, whose dwelling was in the vicinity of al-Ḥijr. To Lud b. Shem were born Ṭasm and Judays, who dwelled in al-Yamāmah. Lud also begat ʿImlīq b. Lud whose dwelling place was the holy area (al-Ḥaram) and the outskirts of Mecca. Some of his descendants reached Syria; among these were the Amalekites, from whom the Pharaohs of Egypt came. To Lud too was born Umaym b. Lud b. Shem, who had many offspring. Some of these broke away to join Gomer b. Japheth in the East. To Aram b. Shem was born Uz b. Aram, whose home was al-Aḥqāf. To Uz was born ʿĀd b. Uz.

As for Ham b. Noah, to him were born Cush and Mizrayim and Put and Canaan. One of the offspring of Cush was Nimrod, the one who ruled tyrannically in Babylon. He was Nimrod b. Cush b. Ham. The rest of Ham's offspring came to reside in the coastlands of the East and West, and in Nubia, Abyssinia, and Fezzan. It is said that Mizrayim begat the Copts and Berbers and that Put journeyed to the land of Sind and Hind,[56] where he settled; the inhabitants there are said to be his descendants.

[218] As for Japheth b. Noah, to him were born Gomer, Magog,[57] Maday, Javan, Tubal, Meshech, and Tiras. Among the descendants of Gomer were the kings of Persia; the descendants of Tiras included the Turks and Khazars. Among the offspring of Meshech are the Ashbān;[58] descended from Maday are Gog and Magog, who are in the eastern part of the land of the Turks

53. The text reads: Fāligh b. ʿAbir.

54. The text reads: Arghū.

55. This name for Abraham's father occurs in Qur'ān 6:75. It has been suggested that it is based on the name of Abraham's servant Eliezer. See *Shorter Encyc.*, 49–50. Ṭabarī was aware of the problem; see below, Ṭabarī, I, 224.

56. That is, India, Sind being nearer India and Hind being further India.

57. Ṭabarī, I, 218 has Mawʿaʿ/Mūʿaʿ. Note that Ms. A has variant Mawghugh/Mūghugh.

58. Also Ishbān. According to Blachère, *Dictionnaire*, I, 126, an Iranian colony from Iṣfahān established in Syria, Egypt, North Africa, and Spain. Here, possibly Spain and the Spanish are meant.

and Khazars. Among the offspring of Javan are the Slavs and Burjān.[59] The Ashbān formerly lived in the land of the Byzantines before it was attacked by the descendants of Esau and others. Each of the three branches—Shem, Ham, and Japheth—set out for a land which it settled and from which it drove others away.

According to al-Ḥārith b. Muḥammad—Muḥammad b. Saʿd—Hishām b. Muḥammad b. al-Sā'ib—his father—Abū Ṣāliḥ—Ibn ʿAbbās: God revealed to Moses, "You, O Moses, and your folk and the people of the island[60] and of the high lands are descendants of Shem b. Noah." Ibn ʿAbbās continues: The Arabs, the Persians, the Nabateans, the Indians, and the Sindis are among the offspring of Shem b. Noah.[61]

According to al-Ḥārith—Muḥammad b. Saʿd—Hishām b. Muḥammad—his father: The Indians and Sindis are children of Buqayin b. Yaqṭān b. Eber b. Shelah b. Arpachshad b. Shem b. Noah, while Makran is the son of al-Band. Jurhum's name was Hadhram b. Eber b. Siba b. Joktan b. Eber b. Shelah b. [219]
Arpachshad b. Shem b. Noah. Hazarmavet was the son of Joktan b. Eber b. Shelah, and (this) Joktan was Qaḥṭān b. Eber b. Shelah b. Arpachshad b. Shem b. Noah, according to the words of whoever ascribed him to someone other than Ishmael.

The Persians are descendants of Fāris b. Nabras b. Nāsūr b. Shem b. Noah, while the Nabateans are children of Nabit b. Mash b. Aram b. Shem b. Noah. The people of the island and of the highlands are the offspring of Mash b. Aram b. Shem b. Noah. ʿImlīq—who is ʿUrayb—and Ṭasm and Umaym are sons of Lud b. Shem b. Noah. ʿImlīq is the father of the Amalekites, from whom came the Berbers, who are children of Thamīlā b. Mārib b. Fārān b. ʿAmr b. ʿImlīq b. Lud b. Shem b. Noah, with the exception of Sinhajah and Kitāmah who are offspring of Furayqish b. Qays b. Ṣayfī b. Sibā'. It is said that ʿImlīq was the

59. Probably the Bulgars, who settled in the Balkans in 678. See Blachère, *Dictionnaire*, I, 501.

60. Al-Jazīrah, the Arabic name for the Arabian Peninsula.

61. An example of the effort to link the major peoples of the early Islamic Empire in their genealogy, even though this conflicts with other genealogies given earlier. The name of Ibn ʿAbbās is often used to validate unusual and even forged traditions. See *Shorter Encyc.*, 171.

first to speak Arabic when they departed from Babylon. They and Jurhum were called the *ʿāribah* Arabs.

Thamūd and Judays were sons of Eber b. Aram b. Shem b. Noah, while ʿĀd and Ubayl were sons of Uz b. Aram b. Shem b. Noah. The Byzantines are descendants of Lanṭā b. Javan b. Japheth b. Noah while Nimrod was the son of Cush b. Canaan b. Ham b. Noah. He was the lord of Babylon and of Abraham, the Friend of the Merciful.

[220] In that era ʿĀd was called "ʿĀd of Iram," and when ʿĀd was destroyed, Thamūd was called Iram. When Thamūd in turn was destroyed, the remaining sons of Iram were called Armān—they are Nabateans.[62] All of them were of Islam while they lived in Babylon, until Nimrod b. Cush b. Canaan b. Ham b. Noah ruled over them and called on them to worship idols, which they did. Whereas one evening their speech was Syriac, the next morning God had confused their tongues, and thus they became unable to understand each other. As a result, the descendants of Shem came to have eighteen languages. The descendants of Ham also came to have eighteen languages, while the descendants of Japheth had thirty-six languages.[63]

God made ʿĀd, ʿUbayl, Thamūd, Judays, ʿImlīq, Ṭasm, Umaym, and the children of Joktan b. Eber b. Shelah b. Arpachshad b. Shem b. Noah able to understand Arabic. The one who flew these peoples' banners over Babylon was Būnāẓir[64] b. Noah.

According to al-Ḥārith—Ibn Saʿd—Hishām—his father—Abū Ṣāliḥ—Ibn ʿAbbās: Noah married a woman of the children of Cain and she bore him a son whom he named Būnāẓir.

62. Iram occurs frequently in early Arabic literature as the name of a tribe or place, usually connected with ʿĀd but also, as here, with Thamūd, Ḥimyar, etc. See *EI*^{2}, s.v. Ḥimyar. The name of the early Nabateans who inhabited Transjordan was connected, after the Arab conquest, with the people of Iraq.

63. Thus yielding 72, the supposed number of languages spoken in the world. The number 72 is also used for the number of sects of the children of Israel, while Islam was to be divided into 73 sects, 72 of which would be in Hell while one, that of the Prophet and his companions, would be the right one. See *Mishkat*, I, vi, 2.

64. A problematic reading. Possibly a variant on the name Nebuchadnezzar, which is usually Bukhtnaṣar in Arabic texts. Note that the story of this otherwise unknown son of Noah is again attributed to Ibn ʿAbbās.

He begat him in a city in the East called Maʿlūn Shamsā.[65]

The descendants of Shem settled al-Majdal, the navel of the earth, which is situated between Satidamā[66] and the sea between the Yemen and Syria. God bequeathed them prophecy, scripture, and beauty, and gave them complexions that were brown and white.

The descendants of Ham settled along the course of the south and west wind—this region is called al-Dārūm[67]—and God gave them brown complexions, though a few were white. He populated their land and their sky. He made them free of plague, and he placed in their land the tamarisk, the thornbush, the asclepias, the sweet-fruited trees, and the date-palm. The sun and the moon move in their heavens. [221]

The descendants of Japheth settled in al-Ṣafūn,[68] along the course of the north and east wind. There are ruddy-complexioned and blond people among them. God emptied their land, intensified its cold, and emptied its skies—none of the seven planets moves above them, because they came to be under (the constellation of) Ursa (Major), the North Star, and the two bright stars of Ursa Minor. There they were afflicted with the plague. After this, ʿĀd reached al-Shiḥr[69] and perished there in a valley called Mughīth.[70] Following that, Mahrah still reached them in al-Shiḥr. The ʿUbayl reached the site of Yathrib, while the Amalekites reached Sanʿāʾ before it had that name. Following that, some of them went to Yathrib and evicted ʿUbayl, who then settled in the site of al-Juḥfah. But a

65. Probably not an actual place but an Arabization of the Aramaic *Maʿal-enei Shimsha* (Dt 11:30) "the [place of the] setting of the sun," i.e., the West, whereas here the city is in the East.

66. A name often mentioned in early Arabic poetry, referring either to a snow-covered mountain in India or to a place in the vicinity of Mosul in northern Iraq or in eastern Anatolia. Yāqūt, *Muʿjam*, III, 6–8 argues that India is incorrect and that either of the other two is meant by these references. Here northern Iraq would seem more likely.

67. Hebrew *darōm* means "south."

68. Hebrew *ṣafōn* means "north."

69. On the Indian Ocean in southern Arabia. See Yāqūt, *Muʿjam*, III, 313–314.

70. Lit. "helper" when used with *ghayth*, as in *ghayth mughīth* meaning "a rain which brings help" or "general rain," hence—ironically here—the good omen. See Lane, VI, 2306, 2314.

flood came and swept them away, destroying them. For this reason the place was named "the sweeping place" (al-Juḥfah).

Thamūd entered al-Ḥijr and its environs and perished there. Ṭasm and Judays entered al-Yamāmah and perished, while Umaym entered the land of Abār[71] and perished there. It lies between al-Yamāmah and al-Shiḥr and no one goes there nowadays, for the jinns have taken possession of it. It was called Abār for Abār b. Umaym.

The descendants of Joktan b. Eber entered the Yemen. It was named the Yemen (south) as they moved southward into it. Some folk (*qawm*) descended from Canaan entered Syria, which was named al-Sha'm as they moved northward into it. Syria had been called the land of the Canaanites, but the children of Israel came and slew them there and drove them off. After that Syria belonged to the children of Israel until the Byzantines (Rūm) attacked and slew them, exiling all but a few of
[222] them to Iraq. Then the Arabs came and conquered Syria. It was Peleg—that is, Peleg b. Eber b. Arpachshad b. Shem b. Noah—who divided the land among the descendants of Noah, as we have described.

The accounts received from the Messenger of God and from the scholars before us concerning the genealogies of the nations who are on the earth today, according to Aḥmad b. Bashīr b. Abī ʿAbdallāh al-Warrāq—Yazīd b. Zurayʿ—Saʿīd —Qatādah—al-Ḥasan—Samurah: The Messenger of God said, "Shem was the father of the Arabs, Japheth was the father of the Byzantines, and Ham was the father of the Abyssinians."

According to al-Qāsim b. Bishr b. Maʿrūf—Rawḥ—Saʿīd b. Abī ʿArubah—Qatādah—al-Ḥasan—Samurah b. Jundub: The Prophet said, "Noah begat three: Shem, Ham, and Japheth. Shem was the father of the Arabs, Ham was the father of the Blacks, and Japheth was the father of the Byzantines."

According to Abū Kurayb—ʿUthmān b. Saʿīd—ʿAbbād b. al-ʿAwwām—Saʿīd—Qatādah—al-Ḥasan—Samurah: The Messenger of God said, "Shem was the father of the Arabs, and Ja-

71. Also Ubār or Wabar, a place in the Yemen, according to Yāqūt, *Muʿjam*, I, 71.

pheth was the father of the Byzantines, while Ham was the father of the Abyssinians."

According to ʿAbdallāh b. Abī Ziyād—Rawḥ—Saʿīd b. Abī ʿArūbah—Qatādah—al-Ḥasan—Samurah: The Prophet said, "Noah begat Shem, Ham, and Japheth [Yāfith]." ʿAbdallāh continues: Rawḥ said, "Go, keep in your memory [the name] Yāfith." But I once heard it pronounced Yāfit. This tradition has been related on the authority of ʿAbd al-Aʿlā b. ʿAbd al-Aʿlā—Saʿīd—Qatādah—al-Ḥasan—Samurah and ʿImrān b. Ḥaṣīn—the Prophet. [223]

According to ʿImrān b. Bakkār al-Kalaʿī—Abū al-Yamān-Ismāʿīl b. ʿAyyāsh—Yaḥyā b. Saʿīd: I heard Saʿīd b. al-Musayyīb saying, "Noah begat three, each one of whom begat three: Shem, Ham, and Japheth. Shem begat the Arabs, Persians, and Byzantines, in all of whom there is good. Japheth begat the Turks, Slavs, Gog, and Magog, in none of whom there is good. Ham begat the Copts, Sudanese, and Berbers."

It is related by Ḍamrah b. Rabīʿah—Ibn ʿAṭā'—his father: Ham begat all those who are black and curly-haired, while Japheth begat all those who are full-faced with small eyes, and Shem begat everyone who is handsome of face with beautiful hair. Noah prayed that the hair of Ham's descendants would not grow beyond their ears, and that wherever his descendants met the children of Shem, the latter would enslave them.

The people of the Torah claim that Shem was born to Noah when the latter was five hundred years old. Then Arpachshad was born to Shem when Shem was one hundred and two years old. According to what has been asserted, Shem lived for six hundred years altogether. Then Qaynān was born to Arpachshad, and Arpachshad lived four hundred and thirty-eight years. Qaynān was born to Arpachshad when he was past the age of thirty-five, and Shelah in turn was born to Qaynān after the latter was thirty-nine. The length of Qaynān's life is not [224]
given in the books with the others, because of the reason we have mentioned.[72] Then Eber was born to Shelah after Shelah

72. The biblical Kenan (Qaynān) was the son of Enosh son of Seth son of Adam. See Gen 5 and I Chron 1. No other occurrence of the name is found in the Bible, as Ṭabarī states.

was thirty. Shelah lived four hundred and thirty-three years in all. Then Peleg was born to Eber, as was Peleg's brother Joktan. Peleg was born forty years after the flood.

When the people had become more numerous they planned, in spite of their recent experience with the flood, to build a city so large it would contain them all so that they would not have to disperse, or a tall edifice which would save them from drowning if the flood came again. Mighty and powerful God desired to weaken and disappoint them in order to teach them that power and strength were His. So He dispersed them and scattered their company and separated their languages.

Eber lived four hundred and seventy-four years. Then Reu was born to Peleg, and Peleg lived two hundred and thirty-nine years. When Reu was born to Peleg the latter was past thirty. Then Serug was born to Reu. Reu lived two hundred and thirty-nine years, and Serug was born to him after he had passed the age of thirty-two. Then Nahor was born to Serug, whose life spanned two hundred and thirty years, Nahor being born to him when he was thirty. Following that, Terah, the father of Abraham, was born to Nahor. This name was the one Terah's father had given him, but when Terah became Nimrod's custodian of the treasury of his gods, he named him Āzar. It has been said that Āzar was not the name of Abraham's father, but was rather the name of an idol; this latter tradition is related on the authority of Mujāhid.[73] It has also been said that the word *āzar*
[225] means "crooked" and that he disgraced him with it. This was after twenty-seven years of Nahor's life had passed. Nahor lived two hundred and forty-eight years in all. Abraham was born to Terah. Between the Flood and Abraham's birth, one thousand and seventy-nine years elapsed. Some people of the book say that the period between the Flood and Abraham's birth was one thousand two hundred and sixty-three years, and that this was three thousand three hundred and thirty-seven years after the creation of Adam.

To Joktan the son of Eber was born Yaʿrub and Yaʿrub begat Yashjub b. Yaʿrub and Yashjub begat Saba' b. Yashjub and Saba'

73. See above, n. 55.

begat Ḥimyar b. Saba' and Kahlān b. Saba' and ʿAmr b. Saba' and al-Ashʿar b. Saba' and Anmār b. Saba' and Murr b. Saba' and ʿĀmilah b. Saba'. ʿAmr b. Saba' begat ʿAdī b. ʿAmr and ʿAdī begat Lakhm b. ʿAdī and Judhām b. ʿAdī.

Some Persian genealogists claim that Noah was the same person as Afarīdhūn who overcame al-Azdahāq and deprived him of his rule, while others claim that Afarīdhūn was Dhū al-Qarnayn, the companion of Abraham[74] who achieved at Beersheba what God mentioned in His book. Others say that he was Solomon b. David. I mention Afarīdhūn here only because of the statement which I previously quoted about him—the statement to the effect that he was Noah. His story was similar to Noah's in that he, too, had three sons, was a just man, comported himself well, and was reportedly responsible for destroying al-Ḍaḥḥāk. It is said that Noah killed al-Ḍaḥḥāk when he was sent (on his mission). This is according to the statement of the one whom I mentioned. It is also said that Noah was sent only to his own people, and that this was the people of [226]
al-Ḍaḥḥāk.

As for the Persians, they ascribe to him the genealogy I mention. That is to say, they claim that Afarīdhūn was a descendant of Jam Shādh, the king whom al-Azdahāq slew. We have already explained the story of Jam Shādh. Between Afarīdhūn and Jam were ten ancestors.[75]

According to Hishām b. Muḥammad b. al-Sā'ib: We received word that Afarīdhūn—who was of the stock of Jam, the king before al-Ḍaḥḥāk, and asserted that he was the ninth of Jam's sons and that his birthplace was in Danbawand—went forth until he came to the dwelling of al-Ḍaḥḥāk, and he seized the latter, and bound him up, and ruled for two hundred years. He

74. Generally identified with Alexander of Macedonia, but Muslim commentators also hold him to have been a contemporary of Abraham—thus distinguishing an earlier and a later figure by this name. Thus the Dhū al-Qarnayn mentioned here is the earlier figure bearing this name, who is considered by some commentators to have been a prophet, by others merely a devout, believing ruler. See *EI²*, s.v. al-Iskandar; *Shorter Encyc.*, 175–6, s.v. al-Iskandar; ibid., 76, s.v. *Dhū'l-Ḳarnain*; Friedlander, *Die Chadhirlegende*, 294 ff.

75. So in Anklesaria, 295, where the entire genealogy of ten generations is given. Each figure in the genealogy lived for one hundred years, thus equaling the one thousand years of the evil reign of al-Ḍaḥḥāk.

turned back injustices and commanded the people to worship God and (to act with) equity and benevolence. He directed his attention to the lands and other things which al-Ḍaḥḥāk had seized from the people by force, and he returned them all to their owners except when the owner could not be found. When that happened he endowed the property for the poor and the common people. It is said that he was the first to name the food-animals, and the first to concern himself with medicine and with the stars, and that he had three sons. The eldest was named Sarm, the second Ṭūj, and the third Īraj.[76] Afarīdhūn feared that his sons would not agree with one another and would wrong each other, so he divided his kingdom into three parts among them. He indicated the division by means of arrows on which the names of the regions were written.[77] He
[227] then ordered each one of them to choose an arrow. Byzantium and the region to the west fell to Sarm; the Turks and Chinese to Ṭūj; while the third son, Īraj, received Iraq and India. Afarīdhūn handed over the crown and the throne to him and then died, whereupon Īraj's two brothers fell upon him and killed him. Between them they ruled the world for three hundred years.

The Persians assert that Afarīdhūn had ten forefathers, all of whom were named Athfiyān.[78] They reportedly did that out of fear of what al-Ḍaḥḥāk might do to their descendants. This was because they possessed a narrative prophesying that one of them would snatch al-Ḍaḥḥāk's rule from him, thereby avenging Jam. They were known and distinguished by the nicknames which they were given. One of them was called Athfiyān owner of the red cattle. Another was Athfiyān owner of variegated cattle. There was Athfiyān owner of such-and-such cattle. He was Afarīdhūn son of Athfiyān Burkāw,[79] the meaning of which is "owner of much cattle," son of Athfiyān

---

76. In Iranian tradition the three sons are called Salm (see n. 91, below), Tūj (Tūr), and Airaj (Īraj). See *Dīnkart* 8, IX, 2 8.

77. This division by means of arrows does not occur in the *Shāhnāmeh*, where Afarīdhūn simply divides the realm among his three sons.

78. See Anklesaria, loc. cit. The name, given here and in other Arabic texts as Athfiyān, is there Āspyān.

79. An Arabic rendering of Persian *purgāw*, "possessor of many cows."

Naykkāw,[80] meaning "owner of excellent cattle," son of Athfiyān Sīrkāw,[81] meaning "owner of big, fat cattle," son of Athfiyān Būrkāw,[82] meaning "owner of cattle which are the color of wild asses," son of Athfiyān Akhshīn Kāw,[83] meaning "owner of yellow cattle," son of Athfiyān Siyāhkāw,[84] meaning "owner of black cattle," son of Athfiyan Asbīdh Kāw,[85] meaning "owner of white cattle," son of Athfiyān Kabarkāw,[86] meaning "owner of ash-grey cattle," son of Athfiyān [228] Ramīn,[87] meaning "every variety of color and of herds," son of Athfiyān Banfarūsan son of Jam al-Shādh.

It is said that Afarīdhūn was the first to be named with *kay*,[88] for he was called Kay Afarīdhūn. *Kay* may be explained as meaning "pure, free from blemish," just as when *rūḥānī* is said, they mean by it that its subject is virtuous, pure, infallible, and related to spiritual things. It is also said that the meaning of *kay* is "anything seeking defect." Some assert that *kay* has to do with "splendor" and that splendor covered Afarīdhūn when he slew al-Ḍaḥḥāk. The Persians mention that he was a large, handsome, splendid, experienced man, and that most of his fighting was done with an iron mace topped with the head of an ox. They say also that the reign of his son Īraj over Iraq and its vicinity was during his lifetime, and that Īraj's days are thus included in Afarīdhūn's reign. He was the ruler of all the climes and he wandered through the lands. When he sat upon his throne on the day he took power, he said, "We are those who are victorious, by God's help and assistance, over al-Ḍaḥḥāk; those who subdue Satan and his minions." Then he exhorted the people and ordered them to deal equitably and to

---

80. Persian *nēkgāw*, "good cow."
81. Persian *sīrgāw*, "full, well-fed cow."
82. Persian *bōrgāw*, "bay, reddish-brown cow *Bundahishn*, 295: *bōrgāw*.
83. Meaning unclear.
84. *Siyahgāw* or *Siyāhgāw* in Persian; *Bundahishn*, 295: *siyā-gāw*.
85. *Asfīdgāw* or *Sefīdgāw* in Persian; *Bundahishn*, loc. cit: *spēd-gāw*.
86. Meaning unclear. Perhaps *gabz/kabz*, "big or grand of body;" op. cit.: *gēpr-gāw*.
87. Persian *ramakīn/ramagīn*, "one whose cattle are in herds;" ibid.: *rama-gāw*.
88. *Kay*, New Persian, probably from Avestan *k avi*. A title used by the second dynasty of Persian kings, the Kayānids (Achaemenids). Afarīdhūn belonged to the first dynasty, the Pishwdādī kings or "primordial monarchs."

busy themselves with being just and spreading goodness
[229] among themselves. He urged them to be grateful and devoted to God. He appointed seven men to the rank of Qūhiyārī[89]—'meaning "those who transform the mountains." Each of them was given a region in Danbawand and elsewhere as a sort of conveyance of property.

They say that when Afarīdhūn captured al-Ḍaḥḥāk, the latter said to him, "Do not kill me, by your grandfather Jam!" Afarīdhūn, disapproving of his words, said to him, "Your ambition became lofty and great within you, and you let it lead you on and coveted it for itself." He informed al-Ḍaḥḥāk that his father was too great a man to be compared with him (al-Ḍaḥḥāk). He told al-Ḍaḥḥāk that he would kill him with an ox which was in his grandfather's house.[90]

It is said that Afarīdhūn was the first to tame elephants and ride them, and to produce mules, and to use geese and pigeons. He was also the first to treat with theriac, to fight enemies and to kill and banish them. It is further reported that he divided the earth among his three sons Ṭūj, Salm,[91] and Īraj. He gave Ṭūj sovereignty over the lands of the Turks, Khazars, and Chinese, and this region was called Sīn Bughā.[92] He also attached to Sīn Bughā the regions adjoining it. To his second son Salm he assigned rule over the Byzantines, the Slavs, the Bulgars, and whatever was within their borders.

He apportioned the middle of the earth and its cultivated land—that is, the clime of Babylon which they called Khunārath[93]—to Īraj, his youngest son and the one most beloved to him. He did that after he had attached to that clime the areas contiguous with it—Sind, Hind, the Ḥijāz, and the like. For that reason the clime of Babylon was named Īrānshahr. In it,

---

89. Persian *kūhyār* for *kūhzād* or *kūhdād*, one who is born or created in the mountain." Afarīdhūn was reared in the mountains as a child, where he was hidden from al-Ḍaḥḥāk.

90. That is, the ox-headed mace mentioned above.

91. As in the Persian sources. See n. 76, above.

92. The text reads Sīnbughaw. Probably Sīnbagh but written with an extra -āw, perhaps by analogy with the -gāw suffix of the names above.

93. Actually used as the name of Afarīdhūn's realm, it refers to Middle Persian Khwanirah (from Avestan, Khᵛaniratha), the "central, inhabited continent of the earth." See Nöldeke, *Nationalepos*.

too, enmity broke out between the descendants of Afarīdhūn [230]
and their children thereafter. The kings of Khunārath and the Turks and the Byzantines began to fight and to seek each other out over questions of spilled blood and inheritance.

It is said that when Ṭūj and Salm learned that their father had favored Īraj and given him precedence over them, they showed great hatred to him and grew more and more envious of him. Eventually they attacked their brother Īraj, and together they killed him. Ṭūj threw a lasso at him and strangled him. This is why the Turks have used the lasso ever since.[94]

Īraj had two sons, called Wandān and Isṭawanah, as well as a daughter named Khūzak, whose name some give as Khūshak.[95] Ṭūj and Salm slew Īraj's two sons with their father, but the daughter survived. It is said that the day Afarīdhūn overcame al-Ḍaḥḥāk was Rūz Mihr of Mihr-Māh, and the people adopted that day as a festival to celebrate the end of al-Ḍaḥḥāk's oppressive rule over them. They named it al-Mihrjān.[96]

It is said that Afarīdhūn was a just ruler, and also a giant; he was nine spear-lengths tall, each spear-length being three fathoms, his waist was three spear-lengths wide, and his chest was four spear-lengths wide. It is also said that he pursued the followers of Nimrod and the Nabateans who remained in the Sawād; he chased after them until he tracked their leaders down and wiped out the last trace of them. His rule lasted five hundred years.

---

94. A reference to the struggle between the Iranians, descendants of Īraj, and the Turanians, descendants of Tūr (Tūj), which occupies the whole of the mythical portion of the *Shāhnāmeh*. Afarīdhūn lives to see his grandson Manūchihr avenge Īraj's death by killing both of his uncles, Salm/Sarm and Tūr/Tūj. According to the *Shāhnāmeh* Tūr slew Īraj with a dagger, not a lasso.

95. The text reads Khūzak. In Persian, Vānīdar and Anastōb are the sons, and Gūza(g) is the daughter. Ṭabarī's rendering Khūzak is probably due to a misreading of *kh* for *j* = *g*.

96. See n. 21, above.

[231] # An Account of The Events Which Took Place between Noah and Abraham, the Friend of the Merciful

We have previously mentioned what happened to Noah and his children, and how they divided the earth among themselves after Noah died, as well as which areas each inhabited and where in the world they lay. Some peoples became tyrannical and insolent against God and Noah. God sent a messenger to them, but they did not believe him, and they persevered in their error, so God destroyed them. These were two tribes descended from Aram b. Shem b. Noah. One of them was ʿĀd b. Uz b. Aram b. Shem b. Noah, also called ʿĀd the First, and the second was Thamūd b. Gether b. Aram b. Shem b. Noah. They were the *ʿāribah* Arabs.

As for ʿĀd:

God sent them Hūd[97] b. ʿAbdallāh b. Ribāḥ b. al-Khalūd b. ʿĀd b. Uz b. Aram b. Shem b. Noah. Some genealogists claim that Hūd was Eber b. Shelah b. Arpachshad b. Shem b. Noah. The ʿĀd tribe had three idols which they worshipped, one of which

97. The prophet Hūd is the earliest of the five "Arab" prophets mentioned in the Qur'ān, where his story is repeated in several places. See *sūrahs* 7:65–72; 11:50–60; 26:123–40; 46:21; and *sūrah* 11 , which is named for him. For a discussion of his genealogy and current theories of identification, see EI^2, s.v. Hūd. His story occurs in Thaʿlabī, *Qiṣaṣ*, 53–57, and in Kisāʾī, 109–117.

they called Ṣadā, another Ṣamūd, and the third al-Habā'.[98] Hūd called upon them to recognize God's oneness and to worship only Him and none other, and to abandon the unjust treatment of people, but they did not believe him. They said, "Who is stronger than we?" And only a few of them believed in Hūd. When they persisted in their rebelliousness Hūd exhorted them, saying to them, "Do ye build on every high place a monument for vain delight? And do ye seek out strongholds, that haply ye may last for ever? And if ye seize by force, do ye seize as tyrants? Rather, do your duty to God and obey me. Keep your duty toward Him who has given you what you know, has given you cattle and sons and gardens and watersprings. I fear [232] for you when the retribution of an awful day comes."[99] Their answer to him was to say, "It is all one to us whether you preach or are not one of those who preach."[100] They said to him, "O Hūd! You have brought us no clear proof and we are not going to forsake our gods on your say-so. We do not believe in you. We believe only that one of our gods has possessed you in an evil way."[101]

As has been mentioned, God held back rain from them for three years, and they began to suffer because of this, and sent a delegation to pray for rain. Part of their story according to Abū Kurayb—Abū Bakr b. ʿAyyāsh—ʿĀṣim—Abū Wā'il—al-Ḥārith b. Ḥassān al-Bakrī: I was on my way to the Messenger of God when I passed by a woman in al-Rabdhah.[102] She said, "Will you carry me to the Messenger of God?" I said yes, and I carried her until I reached al-Madīnah. I entered the mosque and there was the Messenger of God on the platform. Bilāl[103] was there wearing a sword, and there were black banners. I said, "What is this?" They said, "ʿAmr b. al-ʿĀṣ has returned from his raid."

98. Both Thaʿlabī and Kisā'ī agree with Ṭabarī on two of these names, but have Hird instead of Ṣamūd.

99. Qur'ān, 16:124–135.

100. Ibid., 16:136.

101. Ibid., 11:53–54.

102. Or al-Rabadhah, a place in the vicinity of al-Madīnah on the way to Mecca. See Yāqūt, *Muʿjam*, II, 749.

103. Bilāl b. Rabāḥ, an early convert to Islam, of Abyssinian origin. He became a companion of the Prophet, serving as his "mace-bearer," steward, and personal servant, accompanying him on all military expeditions.

When the Messenger of God descended from the platform I went to him and asked his permission to speak. He granted it to me, and I said, "O Messenger of God! At the gate is a woman of the Banū Tamīm who asked me to carry her to you." He said, "O Bilāl! Give her leave." I entered and when I had sat down the Messenger of God said to me, "Was there any trouble between you [that is, your tribe] and Tamīm?" I said, "Yes, and luck turned against them. If you think that you should place the desert between us and them, then do so." The woman said, "And if someone harms you, who will avenge you, O Messenger of God?" I said, "I am like the scapegoat which carries wrongs. Did I carry you so that you should be an adversary to
[233] me? God forbid that I should be like the delegation of ʿĀd!" The Messenger of God said, "And what is the delegation of ʿĀd?" I said, "Because of the Omniscient One, you have forgotten that ʿĀd suffered drought and sent some people to pray for rain. In Mecca they passed by Bakr b. Muʿāwiyah, who gave them wine to drink, and whose two slave girls sang their praises for a month. then they sent a man from his place to the mountains of Mahrah,[104] where he prayed, and clouds appeared. And whenever the clouds appeared, he would say, "Go to so-and-so." Then one cloud appeared, and a voice proclaimed, "Take them [meaning the clouds] as fine and copious ashes; leave no one of ʿĀd alive." The man heard this but hid the news from them (that is, from ʿĀd) until the punishment befell them.

According to Abū Kurayb, Abū Bakr later said regarding the account of ʿĀd: The one who came to them set out, then he came to the mountains of Mahrah and ascended and said, "O God! I have not come to You for a captive whom I ask You to redeem, nor for a sick person whom I ask You to heal, but to ask You to give rain to ʿĀd as You used to." Then some clouds rose up before him from which a voice said, "Choose!" He said, "Go to Banū so-and-so." Then the last of them passed by, a black rain cloud, and the man said, "Go to ʿĀd." Then a voice proclaimed from it, "Take it as fine and copious ash, do not

104. An area of southern Arabia. See Yāqūt, *Muʿjam*, IV, 700.

leave anyone from ʿĀd!" He concealed what he had heard from ʿĀd while the people were drinking with Bakr b. Muʿāwiyah. Bakr b. Muʿāwiyah did not want to tell them (of their tribe's destruction) because they were with him, eating his food, so he began to sing and thereby made them aware.

According to Abū Kurayb—Zayd b. Ḥubāb Salāām Abū al-Mundhir al-Naḥawī—ʿĀṣim—Abū Wā'il—al-Ḥārith b. Yazīd al-Bakrī: I went forth to complain about al-ʿAlā' b. al-Ḥaḍramī to the Messenger of God. I passed by al-Rabdhah and there was an old woman of the Banū Tamīm abandoned there. She said, "O ʿAbdallāh! I need something from the Messenger of God. [234] Can you bring me to him?" So I carried her and we reached al-Madīnah. Abū Jaʿfar said, "I think that was I." I saw black banners, so I asked, "What is wrong with the people?" They replied, "They want him to send ʿAmr b. al-ʿĀṣ somewhere." So I sat until he finished. Then he entered his house (or, in another version, his dwelling). I asked permission to speak and he granted it. I entered and sat down and the Messenger of God said, "Was there any trouble between you and Banū Tamīm?" I responded, "Yes, and fortune was against them. I passed by al-Rabdhah and saw one of their old women abandoned there. She asked me to carry her to you, and she is at the gate now." The Messenger of God granted her permission to come in, and she did so. I said, "O Messenger of God! Place al-Dahnā' between us and Banū Tamīm as a barrier!"[105] The old woman became furious and excited, and she said, "Where will you force the one who harmed you, O Messenger of God?" I said, "I am like the one whom people call 'a scapegoat bearing sins.' I carried this one and did not dream that she would be an adversary to me. I pray to God and His Messenger that I not be like the emissary of ʿĀd!" He said, "And what is the emissary of ʿĀd?" I said, "Because of the Omniscient One it slipped your mind." But he was making me relish the tale, so I said, "'ʿĀd was suffering drought and sent Qayl as an emissary. He stopped with

105. An area west of al-Baḥrayn and north of al-Yamāmah. The Banū Tamīm were located to the west of this area, i.e., nearer to al-Madīnah. The wish expressed here is that they might be to the east of al-Dahnā'—a desert area. See Brice, *Atlas*, 19.

Bakr, who gave him wine to drink for a month, and two slave girls whom they called the 'two locusts' sang for him. Then he went out to the mountains of Mahrah and proclaimed, 'I did not come for a sick person, to cure him, nor for a captive, to redeem him, O God! Give rain to ʿĀd as You used to give it!' And black rain clouds passed by him, and from them a voice proclaimed, 'Take them as fine and copious ash, let no one of ʿĀd remain!' The woman was saying, 'Do not be like the emissary of ʿĀd,' for I have heard that no more wind was sent against them, O Messenger of God, than the amount that would blow in my ring." Abū Wā'il also reports this story.

[235] As for Ibn Isḥāq, he said what Ibn Ḥumayd told us: Salamah heard from him that when the drought befell ʿĀd, they prepared a delegation to Mecca from among themselves to ask for rain. So they sent Qayl b. ʿAnz and Luqaym b. Huzāl b. Huzayl b. ʿUtayl b. Ḍadd, the elder son of ʿĀd, and Marthid b. Saʿd b. ʿUfayr, who was a Muslim but hid his conversion, and Jalhamah[106] b. al-Khaybarī, the maternal uncle of his mother's brother Muʿāwiyah b. Bakr. Then they sent Luqmān b. ʿĀd b. so-and-so b. so-and-so b. Ḍadd b. ʿĀd the Elder. Each of these men went forth accompanied by a group of his relatives, so that the entire delegation numbered seventy men.

When they arrived at Mecca they alighted at the home of Muʿāwiyah b. Bakr in the outskirts of Mecca, he having come out of the sanctuary. He sheltered them and honored them, since they were his maternal uncles and in-laws. Huzaylah bt. Bakr was the sister of Muʿāwiyah b. Bakr by both his father and his mother, just as Lahdah bt. al-Khaybarī was to Luqaym. She had borne him four sons: ʿUbayd b. Luqaym b. Huzāl, ʿAmr b. Luqaym b. Huzāl, ʿĀmir b. Luqaym b. Huzāl, and ʿUmayr b. Luqaym b. Huzāl. They were with their maternal uncles in Mecca with the family of Muʿāwiyah b. Bakr—they were ultimately the only survivors from ʿĀd.

When the ʿĀd delegation alighted at the home of Muʿāwiyah
[236] b. Bakr they remained with him for a month, drinking wine while the "two locusts," two female singers of Muʿāwiyah b.

106. Kisā'ī, 113, has Jahlamah.

Bakr, sang to them. Their journey took a month, and their stay lasted a month. Muʿāwiyah saw how long they remained, while their people had sent them to seek aid against the tribulation which had befallen them. It distressed him, and he said, "My uncles and in-laws have perished while these are staying with me. But they are my guests, who have alighted at my home, and by God, I do not know what to do. I would be ashamed to order them to go away and do what they were sent to do, for then they would realize that they are exasperating me by staying with me while those of their people who stayed behind perish of trouble and thirst." He complained of this to his two female singers, the "locusts," and they said, "Compose a poem about this and we will sing it to them. They will not know who composed it, but it may make them leave." Muʿāwiyah b. Bakr accepted their suggestion and recited,

Woe unto you, O Qayl, woe! Arise and murmur softly
"perhaps God will water us with a light cloud

And He will water the land of ʿĀd." Indeed ʿĀd
have become unable to pronounce words

From the terrible thirst; both the old
and the young have lost hope

Their women were well off
but now their women are longing for milk

And wild beasts approach them openly
and fear no arrow from any member of ʿĀd

While you remain here with whatever you desire [237]
all day and all night long.

May God make ugly your delegation of a people
may they receive neither greeting nor peace!

When Muʿāwiyah had recited that song, the "two locusts" sang it to the delegation. When they heard it they said to each other, "Our people have sent us only to seek help through us against this tribulation which has descended upon them, but we have delayed. Let us enter the sanctuary and seek rain for our people!"

Marthid b. Saʿd b. ʿUfayr said, "By God! You will not be sent rain through your prayers, but if you obey your prophet and return to him, then you will be given rain." In saying this, he revealed to them the fact that he had converted to Islam. When Jalhamah b. al-Khaybarī, the maternal uncle of Muʿāwiyah b. Bakr, heard these words and realized that Marthid b. Saʿd was a follower of Hūd, he said:

O Abū Saʿd, you are of a noble tribe
and your mother is of Thamūd

Whereas we will never obey you as long as we live,
nor will we do what you desire.

Do you ask us to abandon the religion of Rafd
and Raml and the family of Ḍadd and the ʿUbūd?

To abandon the religion of noble forefathers
who possessed ideas, and to follow the religion of Hūd?

Rafd, Raml, and Ḍadd were clans of ʿĀd, as was al-ʿUbūd. Jalhamah b. al-Khaybarī said to Muʿāwiyah b. Bakr and his father Bakr, "Restrain Marthid b. Saʿd from [going with] us. We will not let him go to Mecca with us, since he is a follower of the religion of Hūd and has abandoned our religion." Then they set out for Mecca to ask for rain for ʿĀd there. After they had
[238] left, Marthid b. Saʿd went forth from the dwelling of Muʿāwiyah to follow them. He caught up with them in Mecca before they had prayed for anything. When he reached them he arose to pray to God while the delegation of ʿĀd was gathered together praying. He said, "O my God! Grant me my request alone, and do not include me in anything for which the delegation of ʿĀd asks."

Qayl b. ʿĀnz was the chief of the delegation of ʿĀd. The delegation of ʿĀd prayed, "O God! Grant unto Qayl b. ʿĀnz whatever he asks of you! And place our request together with his request."

Luqmān b. ʿĀd, the master of ʿĀd, remained apart from the

delegation. Then, when they had completed their prayer, he said, "O God! I have come to you with my own need, so grant me my request." Whereas when Qayl b. ʿĀnz prayed, he said, "O our God! If Hūd is telling the truth, give us rain, for we have acted wrongfully and we have perished." So God brought forth three clouds, one white, one red, and one black, and someone proclaimed to Qayl from the clouds, "O Qayl! Choose from among these clouds for yourself and your people." Qayl replied, "I choose the black cloud, for it is the cloud fullest of water." Thereupon a voice proclaimed to him:

> You have chosen fine, copious ash,
> which will not spare anyone of ʿĀd
>
> It will leave neither parent nor child,
> but it will make them all extinct
>
> Except for Banū al-Lawdhiyyah,
> the rightly-guided.

The Banū al-Lawdhiyyah were the children of Luqaym b. Huzāl b. Huzaylah, daughter of Bakr. They lived in Mecca together with their maternal uncles, and were not with the rest of the ʿĀd in their land, for they were the other ʿĀd. They were the only ʿĀd people who survived. God sent the black cloud, which Qayl b. ʿĀnz had chosen, with the vengeance it carried against ʿĀd. It came toward them from a valley of theirs called al-Mughīth.[107] When they saw it, they took it for a good omen [239]
and said, "Here is a cloud bringing us rain." God said, "Nay, but it is that which ye did seek to hasten, a wind bearing painful torment, destroying all things by commandment of its Lord"[108]—that is to say, destroying everything which it was commanded to destroy. The first one to realize what was in it and to know that it was an ill wind was a woman of ʿĀd called Muhaddid.[109] When she discerned what was in it, she screamed and lost consciousness. When she awoke they said,

---

107. See n. 70, above.
108. Qur'ān, 46:24–25.
109. The name means "menacing, threatening," from the basic root meaning "to break, crush, demolish."

"What did you see, O Muhaddid?" She replied, "I saw a wind which had something like fire in it. There were men in front of it, leading it."

God "employed it against them for seven long nights and eight long days,[110] as God has said; *al-ḥusūm* means "lasting." It left no one alive of ʿĀd, whereas Hūd and those believers who were with him hid themselves in an enclosure. None of it struck him or those with him except what would be gentle to the skin and pleasant to the soul. It passed from ʿĀd, piercing everything between heaven and earth, marking everything with stones. The delegation of ʿĀd left Mecca and traveled until they passed by Muʿāwiyah b. Bakr and his father, and they stopped there. While they were with him, a man approached on a camel on a moonlit night, the third evening after the smiting of ʿĀd. He told them what had happened, and they asked, "And where did you part from Hūd and his companions?" He said, "I parted from them at the seacoast." And while they were doubting what he had told them, Bakr's daughter Huyzaylah said, "He is telling the truth, by the Lord of Mecca! And Muthawwib b. Yaghfur, son of my brother Muʿāwiyah b. Bakr is with them."

It has been said—and God knows best—that when Marthid
[240] b. Saʿd, Luqmān b. ʿĀd, and Qayl b. ʿĀnz prayed in Mecca, they were told, "You were granted your desire, so choose for yourselves, except that there is no path to eternal life; death is inevitable." And Marthid b. Saʿd said, "O Lord! Grant me righteousness and truth." And he was granted that. Luqmān b. ʿĀd said, "Grant me life!" But he was told, "There is no way to eternal life, so choose for yourself the length of existence of sheep droppings, or a boar on a mountain, or a rugged place on which only a trickle flows, or of seven eagles."[111] So Luqmān chose for himself the eagles, and it is asserted that he did indeed live the lifespan of seven eagles. He would take the fledgling as it emerged from its egg, keeping the male for its

110. Qur'ān, 69:7. In Arabic: *Sabʿa layālin wa-thamāniyata ayyāmin ḥusūman.*

111. The eagle or vulture, *nasr,* was reputed to live one thousand years, and symbolizes long life in Arabic poetry. This story of Luqmān and the eagle occurs in Thaʿlabī, *Qiṣaṣ,* 56–57, but not in Kisāʾī.

strength until, when it died, he would take another. He continued doing this until he reached the seventh. It is said that each eagle lived eighty years. When only the seventh remained, a brother's son said to Luqmān, "O uncle! Only this eagle's life span remains of the span of your life." And Luqmān said to him, "O nephew! This is Labad!" *Labad* in their language meant "time" or "fate." When death overtook Luqmān's eagle and his life ended, the (other) eagles flew in the morning from the mountaintop, but Labad did not rise with them. Those eagles of Luqmān's were always with him, and never left him. When Luqmān did not see Labad fly up with the other eagles, he rose to go to the mountain to see what Labad was doing. Luqmān found in himself a weakness which he had never felt before, and when he reached the mountain he saw his eagle Labad fallen from among the other eagles. He called, "Rise up, O Labad!" Labad tried to rise up, but was unable to do so, for his forefeathers had fallen out, and so they died together. [241]

When Qayl b. ʿĀnz heard what was said to him in the rain cloud, he was told, "Choose for yourself as your companion chose." He said, "I choose that what befell my people should befall me." He was told that that was destruction, and he said, "I do not care. There is no purpose in my surviving them." So the punishment which befell ʿĀd also befell him, and he perished. When Marthid b. Saʿd b. ʿUfayr heard the words of the rider who informed them of the destruction of ʿĀd, he said:

ʿĀd rebelled against their prophet and so became
thirsty; the heavens did not wet them.

Their deputies were sent out for a month to seek rain
but heavy clouds followed on thirst.

For their open denial of their Lord,
destruction wiped them out.

Indeed, God deprived ʿĀd of discernment
for their hearts were a wasteland, air,

From the clear account, that they heed it,
and neither good counsel nor misfortune is enough.

May my soul, my two daughters and the mother of my children
be ransom for the soul of our prophet Hūd;

He came to us when hearts were intent
upon tyranny, and the light had departed.

We have an idol who is called Ṣamūd,
facing him are a corpse and dust.

Those who were delegated to him, saw him
while misfortune overtook those who disbelieved.

As for me, I shall reach the people of Hūd
and his brothers when night falls.

It is said that their chief and greatest man at the time was al-Khuljān.

According to al-ʿAbbās b. al-Walīd—his father—Ismāʿīl b.
[242] ʿAyyāsh—Muḥammad b. Isḥāq: When the wind went forth against ʿĀd from the wādī, seven of them, one of whom was al-Khuljān, said, "Come, let us stand at the rim of the wādī and turn it back." But the wind went beneath each one of them and lifted him up, then dropped him and broke his neck. It left them, as God has said, "lying overthrown, as though they were hollow trunks of palm trees,"[112] until only al-Khuljān remained. He turned toward the mountain and took hold of one side of it and shook it, and it trembled in his hand. Whereupon he composed the following:

Only al-Khuljān alone remained.
o what a day, after the day which has struck me

With firm tread, mighty in its destructiveness.
had it not come to me, I would have come to it to find out about it.

Hūd said to him, "Woe unto you, O Khuljān! Surrender [to God] and you will be safe!" Al-Khuljān asked, "And what will I

112. Qur'ān, 69:7.

have with your Lord if I surrender?" Hūd replied, "Paradise." Al-Khuljān said, "And what are those I see in the clouds, as though they were Bactrian camels?" Hūd responded, "They are angels of my Lord." Al-Khuljān said, "And if I surrendered, would your Lord protect me from them?" Hūd replied, "Woe unto you! Have you ever seen a king protect someone from his own troops?" Al-Khuljān said, "Would that He might do as I wish." Then the wind came and took him and joined him with his companions.

Abū Jaʿfar said: God destroyed al-Khuljān and put an end to ʿĀd, except for those few who remained. They perished, but God saved Hūd and those who believed in him. It is said that Hūd lived one hundred and fifty years.

According to Muḥammad b. al-Ḥusayn—Aḥmad b. al-Mufaḍḍal—Asbāṭ—al-Suddī: And unto ʿĀd (was sent) their brother [243] Hūd, who said, "O my people! Serve God! You have no other god save Him!"[113] This means that Hūd came to ʿĀd and admonished them, reminding them of what God had related in the Qurʾān, but they persisted in disbelieving him, and challenged him to punish them. So he said to them, "Knowledge is with God alone. I pass on to you that with which I have been sent."[114] When ʿĀd were unbelievers, they were smitten with a drought so terrible that they became extremely exhausted. For Hūd prayed for their misfortune and God sent them the barren wind, that is, the wind that does not pollinate trees. When they saw it, they thought it was just a passing incident of the rainy season. But when it came near to them they saw camels and men which it was blowing around between heaven and earth. When they saw that, they rushed into their houses. When they entered their houses it came upon them and destroyed them there. Then it forced them out of their houses and brought them "a day of constant calamity."[115]

"Constant calamity" (*naḥs*) is lasting misfortune. The wind went on punishing them for "seven long nights and eight gruel-

---

113. Ibid., 11:50.
114. Ibid., 46:23.
115. Ibid., 54:19.

ing days."[116] It wiped out everything in its path. When it took them out of their houses, God said, "Sweeping men away [from their houses] as though they were uprooted trunks of palm trees"[117] uprooted from their foundations and "hollow"[118] —they became hollow and fell down.

And after God had destroyed them, He sent black birds to
[244] them which picked them up and carried them out to sea, and cast them into it. It is as He said, "And morning found them so that naught could be seen of them save their dwellings."[119] The wind blew normally except for that day when it blew against the treasure-house and overcame them. They could see no limit to its power, for it was as He said, "They were destroyed by a fierce roaring wind."[120] *Ṣarṣar* means that which has a powerful sound.

According to Muḥammad b. Sahl b. ʿAskar—Ismāʿīl b. ʿAbd al-Karīm—ʿAbd al-Ṣamad—Wahb: When God punished ʿĀd with the wind which castigated them, it tore up huge trees by the roots, and smashed their houses down upon them. Whoever was not in a house was blown by the wind until it split the mountains with him, and thus all of them were destroyed.

As for Thamūd:

They were insolent toward their Lord, disbelieved in Him, and caused evil upon the earth. Because of this, God sent to them Ṣāliḥ[121] b. ʿUbayd b. Asif b. Māsikh b. ʿUbayd b. Khādir b. Thamūd b. Gether b. Aram b. Shem b. Noah as a messenger to call them to declare God's unity and to worship Him alone.

It is said that Ṣāliḥ was Ṣāliḥ b. Asif b. Kamāshij b. Iram b. Thamūd b. Gether b. Aram b. Shem b. Noah. One of their re-

---

116. Ibid., 69:7; see n. 110, above.

117. Ibid., 54:20.

118. Ibid., 69:7; lit. *munqaʿirīn.*

119. Ibid., 46:25.

120. Ibid., 69:6. In Arabic: *Fa-uhlikū bi-rīḥin ṣarṣarin ʿātiyatin.*

121. Another of the Arabian prophets mentioned in the Qur'ān, especially in *sūrahs*, 7, 11, 26, and 27. Unlike ʿĀd, Hūd's people, Thamūd is a historically well-attested tribe. See *Shorter Encyc.*, 499–500, s.v. Ṣāliḥ, and ibid., 591–92, s.v. Thamūd. The story of Ṣāliḥ is elaborated by Thaʿlabī, *Qiṣaṣ*, 58–63; Kisāʾī, 117–128.

sponses to him was to say, "O Ṣāliḥ! You have hitherto been the one in whom our hope was placed. Do you ask us not to worship what our fathers worshipped? Verily we are in grave [245] doubt about that to which you call us."[122] God had made their lives long, and they inhabited al-Ḥijr as far as Wādī al-Qurā between al-Ḥijāz and Syria. Sāliḥ went on urging them to worship God in spite of their rebelliousness and tyranny. His calling them to God only strengthened their determination not to respond. When this had gone on for some time—as had Ṣaliḥ's efforts—they said to him, "If you are truthful, then bring us a sign."

What happened then regarding them and Ṣāliḥ was told by al-Ḥasan b. Yaḥyā—ʿAbd al-Razzāq —Isrāʾīl—ʿAbd al-ʿAzīz b. Rufayʿ—Abū al-Ṭufayl: Thamūd said to Ṣāliḥ, "Bring us a sign if you are indeed truthful." Ṣāliḥ said to them, "Go to an elevation on the land," and it shook violently as a woman in labor shakes, and it opened up, and from its midst a camel came forth. Ṣāliḥ said, "This is God's camel, a token unto you. Let her feed in God's land, and do not hurt her, lest a painful torment seize you.[123] She has the right to drink, and you have the right to drink, each on an appointed day."[124] But when they wearied of her, they hamstrung her,[125] and Ṣāliḥ said to them, "Enjoy life in your dwelling place for three days! This is a promise that will not be belied,"[126] (that is, you have only three days left to live).

ʿAbd al-ʿAzīz said: Another man related to me that Ṣāliḥ told them, "As a sign of punishment, tomorrow morning you will be red, then yellow the day after that, and on the third day black." Punishment came to them in the morning, and when they saw that, they embalmed themselves and prepared themselves for death.

---

122. Qur'ān, 11:62.

123. Ibid., 7:73, also 11:64.

124. Ibid., 26:155.

125. *ʿAqarūhā*, i.e., they cut or hocked the leg tendons, an act which usually preceded the slaughtering of a camel. See Lane, V, 2107–08. This is the symbolic act for which Thamūd was punished. After having called upon Ṣāliḥ to provide a divine sign—the bringing forth of a pregnant camel from a rock—and being warned not to harm her, they carried out this act.

126. Qur'ān, 11:65.

According to al-Qāsim—al-Ḥusayn—Ḥajjāj— Abū Bakr b.
[246] ʿAbd al-Raḥmān—Shahr b. Ḥawshab—ʿAmr b. Khārijah: We said to him, "Tell us the tale of Thamūd." He said, "I shall relate to you what the Messenger of God said about Thamūd."

(ʿAmr b. Khārijah's account runs as follows:) Thamūd were the people of Ṣāliḥ to whom almighty God had granted long life in this world, and He made their lives invulnerable. So much so, that once when one of them began to build a house out of dried mud and it collapsed on him, that man still survived. When they saw that, they used their skills to make houses out of the mountains. They hewed the mountains out, cut through them, and hollowed them out, and they lived in comfort therein. Then they said, "O Ṣāliḥ! Ask your Lord for us to bring forth a sign to let us know that you are the Messenger of God." So Ṣāliḥ prayed to his Lord and He brought forth the she-camel for them. Her drinking right was fixed on one day, theirs on another. When it was her drinking day, they would leave her alone with the water and then milk her so that her milk filled every vessel, container, and waterskin. But once when her drinking day came they kept her away from the water and did not let her drink any of it; and yet they still filled every vessel, container, and waterskin. So God told Ṣāliḥ, "Your people are hamstringing your she-camel." He told them that, and they replied, "Verily we have not done that." He said, "If you are not hamstringing her, a son is about to be born to you who will hamstring her." They said, "What is the sign of that son? By God, as soon as we find him we will kill him!" He said, "He is a boy with fair skin, blue eyes, reddish-brown hair, and a ruddy complexion."

In that city there were two mighty and invincible shaykhs. One of them had a son whom he did not want to let marry, and the other had a daughter for whom he could not find an equal match. A meeting was arranged between them and one of them said to the other, "What prevents you from marrying your son off?" He answered, "I cannot find an equal match for him."
[247] The other responded, "Verily my daughter is an equal match for him, and I will arrange a marriage with you." So he married her to him and from them that son was born.

In the city there were eight unrepentant evildoers. When Ṣāliḥ said to them, "Only a child among you will hamstring her," they chose eight women who were midwives from the town and ordered them to circulate through the town. If they found a woman in labor, they were to observe what she bore. If it was a boy they were to slay it, but if it was a girl they were to refrain from harming her. When they found that child, the women shouted and said, "This is the one whom God's messenger Ṣāliḥ meant." Their orders required them to take him, but his two grandfathers intervened to stop them and said, "If Ṣāliḥ wants him, we will slay him!"

He was the most evil of children and each day he grew as much as others grew in a week, each week he grew as much as others grew in a month, and each month as much as others grew in a year. One day the eight evildoers who never did good gathered togeher with the two shaykhs and said, "Make this boy our leader because of his status and the nobility of his grandfathers." So they became nine. Now Ṣāliḥ refused to sleep in the city with them, spending his nights instead in a prayer-place called the Mosque of Ṣāliḥ. In the morning he would come to them and admonish them, and when it was evening he would go back to his mosque and spend the night there.

According to Ḥajjāj—Ibn Jurayj: When Ṣāliḥ told the eight evildoers that a boy would be born at whose hands they would be destroyed, they said, "What do you command us?" He said, "I command you to kill them" (that is, their male children). So they killed them except for one. When it reached the turn of [248]
that boy they said, "If we had not killed our sons, each one of us would have had one like this. This is the doing of Ṣāliḥ!" So they plotted among themselves to slay him, saying, "Let us pretend to go forth on a journey and let the people see us doing so. Then we will come back on a certain night of a certain month, and lie in wait for him at his praying place and kill him. People will think only that we had gone off on a journey [and will not suspect us]." They went to a large rock and lay in wait for him underneath it. God made that rock fall down on them, and it crushed them to death. Some men who had learned of their plan went out to them and found them crushed, and they went back to the city shouting, "O servants of God! It was not enough for Ṣāliḥ to order them to kill their

children, so he killed them themselves." The people of the city then gathered to hamstring the camel, but could not make themselves do it, except for that son of the tenth one.

According to Abū Jaʿfar—the Messenger of God: They wanted to trick Ṣāliḥ so they went to a hole in the path of Ṣāliḥ and eight of them hid in it, saying, "When he comes out toward us we will kill him. Then we will come to his family and attack them by night." But God gave a command to the soil and the hole caved in on them. Then others gathered and went to the she-camel while she was standing at her water-tank and the culprit said to one of them, "Bring her and I will hamstring her." So they brought her to him, but he found the job too hard and refused to do it. So they sent another, but he also found it too difficult. Whoever the culprit sent considered the matter
[249] too difficult until he himself went to her, stretched himself up, and struck her tendons, and she fell as she ran.

One of the people came to Ṣāliḥ and said, "Hurry, go to your camel, it has been hamstrung." At this he went to them, and they came forth to meet him and sought his forgiveness, saying, "O prophet of God, only so-and-so hamstrung her, so it is not a sin of ours." He said, "See if you can overtake her young. If you overtake him, perhaps God will remove the punishment from you." So they went forth seeking him. But when the young camel saw his mother upset, he went to a low mountain called al-Qārah and ascended it. They went to seize him, but God gave a command to the mountain and it grew so tall in the sky that not even the birds could reach it. Ṣāliḥ entered the city, and when the young camel saw him, he wept until his tears flowed. Then he approached Ṣāliḥ and grumbled once, then again, then again. Ṣāliḥ said, "Each grumble is the term of one day. Enjoy yourselves in your homes for these three days. This is no false promise. The sign of the punishment is that on the first day your faces will become yellow in the morning, on the second day they will become red, and on the third day black."

When they awoke in the morning, their faces were yellow as if daubed with saffron—young and old, male and female. When evening came they all shouted togehter, "Woe! One day of the term has passed and the punishment has come upon us." When the second day dawned, their faces were red as if dyed with blood. They shouted and clamored and wept, and knew that this was their punishment. When the evening came they all cried out together, "Two days of the term have passed and the punishment had befallen us." When they rose on the third morning, their faces were black as if painted with pitch. They all shouted, "Woe! The punishment has befallen us!" They [250] wrapped themselves in shrouds and embalmed themselves for the grave. Their embalming consisted of aloes and acid, while their shrouds were leather mats.[127] Then they threw themselves to the ground and began looking back and forth between heaven and earth, not knowing from whence their punishment would come to them—whether from above them in the heavens or from beneath their feet, from the ground, humbled and separated.

When they awoke on the fourth day, they heard a clamor from heaven which was as loud as every thunderbolt and the noise of everything on earth that makes a sound all together. Their hearts stopped in their breasts and they fell down prostrate in their homes.

According to al-Qāsim—al-Ḥusayn—Ḥajjāj —Ibn Jurayj: I have been told that when the great clamor overcame them, God destroyed all of them between sunrise and sunset. He spared only one man who was at the sanctuary of God, whom the sanctuary preserved from God's punishment. The question was asked, "Who was he, O Messenger of God?" He (Muḥammad) replied, "Abū Righāl." When he came to the city of Thamūd, the Messenger of God said to his companions, "Let none of you enter the city nor drink of their water." And he showed them the place where the young camel had gone up to al-Qārah.

According to Ibn Jurayj—Mūsā b. ʿUqbah—ʿAbdallāh b. Dīnār—Ibn ʿImrān: When the Prophet came to the city of

127. *Al-anṭāʿ*, used as dining cloths, game boards, and—more significantly—in executions. See Lane, VIII:3034.

Thamūd he said, "Verily do not visit these punished ones unless you are weeping. If you are not weeping then do not go to them, lest what happened to them happen to you."

According to Ibn Jurayj—Jābir b. ʿAbdallāh: When the Prophet came to al-Ḥijr he praised and lauded God. After prais-
[251] ing God, etc., he said, "Do not ask your Messenger for signs. These people of Ṣāliḥ asked their messenger for a sign, and God sent the she-camel to them. She would return from this pass and go forth from this pass, and she drank their water on the day of her share."

According to Ismāʿīl b. al-Mutawwakil al-Ashjaʿī—Muḥammad b. Kathīr—ʿAbdallāh b. Wāqid—ʿAbdallāh b. ʿUthmān b. Kuthaym—Abū al-Ṭufayl: When the Messenger of God went on the expedition to raid Tabuk he camped at al-Ḥijr and said, "O people! Do not ask your Prophet for signs! These folk of Ṣāliḥ asked their prophet to send them a sign and God sent them the she-camel as a sign. On the day of her turn to drink she entered among them from this pass and drank their water. On the day when it was their turn they would be supplied with it (water) and would take as much milk from her as they had taken water previously. Then she would go forth from the pass. But they became disobedient to their Lord's command and hamstrung her, so God promised them punishment after three days. It was a promise from God and was not false. So God destroyed all of them, in the East and the West, except for one man who was at God's sanctuary. God's sanctuary protected him from God's punishment. They said, "And who was that man, O Messenger of God?" He said, "Abū Righāl."

The people of the Torah claim that there is no mention of ʿĀd and Thamūd, nor of Hūd and Ṣāliḥ, in the Torah; but their repute among the Arabs of the Jāhiliyyah and of Islam was like the repute of Abraham and his people.

Were it not for (my) dislike of making the book too long and
[252] getting off the subject, I would quote poetry by poets of the Jāhiliyyah which mentions some of what I have said about ʿĀd and Thamūd and their affairs. From this, those who do not admit how well-known they were would learn the truth about their fame.

Some sages claim that Ṣāliḥ died in Mecca when he was fifty-eight years old, and that he had remained among his people for twenty years.

As Abū Jaʿfar said, now let us return to the discussion of Abraham, the Friend of God.

Discussion of Abraham, the Friend of the Merciful[128]

And of those Persian kings who were contemporary with him, for we have mentioned the line of descendants leading to him from Noah as well as the history of the era before that. He was Abraham b. Terah b. Nahor b. Serug b. Reu b. Peleg b. Eber b. Shelah b. Qaynān b. Arpachshad b. Shem b. Noah. There is disagreement about where he came from and where he was born. Some say his birthplace was al-Sūs[129] in the province of al-Ahwāz, while others say it was Babylon in the land of the Sawād, while still others say it was in the Sawād but in the region of Kūthā.[130] Others say that his birthplace was in al-

128. The patriarch Abraham, progenitor of both Jews and Arabs, is called "God's friend" in two passages of the Bible, Is 41:8 and II Chron 20:7. There are many parallels to these Muslim tales in Jewish aggadic literature, and considerable scholarly disagreement as to the direction of influence. See Ginzberg, *Legends*, V:209ff.; *Encyc. Judaica*, 2:111ff.

129. Biblical Shushan, for Susa, an ancient Elamite capital and later capital of the Achaemenid Empire. Known in Islam as the burial place of the prophet Daniel, in Judaism it is best known as the setting of the book of Esther. Located in the southwestern Iranian province of Khūzestān near the town of Ahwāz. See Yāqūt, *Muʿjam*, III, 188–90.

130. An area in southern Iraq between Kūfah and Baṣrah—or including Baṣrah. See Yāqūt, *Muʿjam*, IV, 274–75. A Talmudic passage uses this name for the birthplace of Abraham. See Ginzberg, *Legends*, V, 211, n. 20.

Warkā'[131] in the region of al-Zawābī[132] on the borders of Kaskar[133] and that after his birth his father took him to where Nimrod lived in the region of Kūthā. Others say that he was born in Ḥarrān but that his father took him to the land of Babylon.[134] Most of the earlier sages have said that Abraham was [253] born during the era of Nimrod b. Cush, while most historians say that Nimrod was an official of al-Azdahāq. Some have asserted that Noah was sent to this Nimrod against the land of Babylon and its environs. One group of ancient sages says that there was a king over him, whose name was Zarhā b. Ṭahmāsfān.[135]

According to Ibn Ḥumayd—Salamah—Muḥammad b. Isḥāq: According to what has been said to us—and God knows best—there was an inhabitant of Kūthā named Āzar from a town in the Sawād, in the environs of al-Kūfah.[136] At that time Nimrod the Sinner was the ruler of the East. He was called the Lion, and it is said that his rule encompassed the East and West of the earth, and that his capital was Babylon. His domain and that of his people was in the East before the rule of the Persians. It is said that there were only three kings (in all of history) who ruled over the entire earth and all its peo-

131. Biblical Erech, mentioned in Gen. 10:10 as a mainstay of the kingdom of Nimrod. Sumerian Unuq, Akkadian Uruk, it is in southern Iraq about 40 miles northwest of ancient Ur. See *Encyc. Judaica*, 6, 838 also Yāqūt, *Mu'jam*, IV, 922, where it is mentioned as the birthplace of Abraham.

132. According to Yāqūt, *Mu'jam*, II, 953, this term refers to the four rivers named Zāb in Iraq, two of which lie above Baghdād and two below. Here, then, the term refers to the southern rivers of that name.

133. A place in the area of Babylon, the exact location of which is the subject of dispute. See Yāqūt, *Mu'jam*, IV, 317– 18.

134. Thus reversing the biblical account in Gen 11 of Abraham's birth in Ur and his father's taking him to Ḥarrān.

135. An unknown figure. Although the latter name is a Persian clan or a gentilic, it does not occur in the *Shāhnāmeh*. In Persian epic literature, Cush was a relative of Zahhāk (al-Ḍaḥḥāk) and was sent by king Fereydoun (Afarīdhūn) to pacify the realm of Māzandarān. Hence the further connection of Nimrod to the al-Ḍaḥḥāk story.

136. Lit. Sawād al-Kūfah. Although the Sawād generally was used synonymously with al-'Irāq as a name for the alluvial plain of southern Mesopotamia, in a secondary sense it came to mean a "district" around a city; hence this refers to the environs of al-Kūfah. See LeStrange, *Lands*, 24, n. 1.

ple: Nimrod b. Arghu,[137] Dhū al-Qarnayn, and Solomon b. David.

One source claims that Nimrod was al-Ḍaḥḥāk himself.

Hishām b. Muḥammad said: We have been told—though God knows best—that al-Ḍaḥḥāk was Nimrod, that Abraham, the Friend of the Merciful, was born during his days, and that Nimrod was his master who wanted to burn him.

According to Mūsā b. Hārūn—ʿAmr b. Ḥammād—
[254] Asbāṭ—al-Suddī—Abū Ṣāliḥ and Abū Mālik—Ibn ʿAbbās and Murrah al-Hamdānī—Ibn Masʿūd and some of the companions of the Prophet: The first king who ruled over all the earth, east and west, was Nimrod b. Canaan b. Cush b. Shem b. Noah. There were four such kings who ruled all the earth: Nimrod, Solomon b. David, Dhū al-Qarnayn, and Nebuchadnezzar—two believers and two infidels.

According to Ibn Isḥāq—Ibn Ḥumayd—Salamah—Ibn Isḥāq: God desired to send Abraham, the Friend of the Merciful, as an argument against his people and as a messenger to His worshippers, since there had been no such messengers between Noah and Abraham except Hūd and Ṣāliḥ. As the time when God desired to do this drew near, the astrologers came to Nimrod and said to him, "Know that we have learned from our lore that a boy will be born in this city of yours who will be called Abraham. He will abandon your religion and break your idols in such and such a month of such and such a year." When the year which the astrologers described to Nimrod began, Nimrod had every pregnant woman in his city imprisoned except for Āzar's wife, the mother of Abraham, for he did not know she was pregnant. That was because she was a young maiden and her pregnancy was not very visible. During that month of the year, whenever a woman bore a boy, Nimrod commanded that he be killed. When the mother of Abraham found that she was in labor, she went out by night to a cave

137. Or biblical Reu, see n. 54, above. Nimrod is normally referred to as the son of Canaan b. Cush (see below), but note that he is also referred to as a son of Cush b. Ham (Ṭabarī, I, 217). In the version below, the number of kings is increased to four.

near her home and bore Abraham there. She took care of his [255]
needs as one does for a newborn, then shut the cave up on him and returned home. Later she went to look at him in the cave to see what he would do and found him alive, sucking his thumb. It is said—and God knows best—that God had placed Abraham's sustenance in it, and that is what came to him from his sucking.[138]

According to the story, Āzar asked Abraham's mother what had happened with her pregnancy and she said, "I gave birth to a boy and he died." He believed her and remained silent about it.

For Abraham, one day of growing up was like a month, and a month was like a year.[139] Abraham had been in the cave for only fifteen months when he said to his mother, "Take me out that I may look around." So she took him out one evening and he looked about and thought about the creation of the heavens and the earth and said, "Verily the One who created me and sustained me, who fed me and gave me drink, is my Lord—I have no god but Him." He looked out at the sky and saw a star, and said, "This is my Lord." Then he followed it with his eyes, watching it until it disappeared. When it had set he said, "I do not like things that set." Then he saw the moon rising and said, "This is my Lord." And he followed it with his eyes until it disappeared, and when it had set, he said, "If my Lord did not guide me, verily I would be one of those who go astray."[140]

When day came upon him and the sun rose, he saw the greatness of the sun and saw that here was something with more light than he had ever seen before. He said, "This is my Lord! This is greater!" And when it, too, set he exclaimed, "O my people! I am free from all the things which ye associate (with Him). I have turned my face toward Him that created the heav-

---

138. See the parallel aggadic tales in Ginzberg, *Legends*, I, 188–89. According to V, 210, n. 14, there were two spouts, one yielding honey and the other milk. In Thaʿlabī, *Qiṣaṣ*, 64, there were four, one yielding milk, another honey, another clarified butter, and the fourth water.

139. See the story of Ṣāliḥ for a similar account in Ṭabarī, I, 247, and again with Abraham, Ṭabarī, I, 257.

140. See Qur'ān, 6:77–78.

ens and the earth, as one upright by nature; I am not an idolator."[141]

[256] Then Abraham returned to his father Āzar, having seen the right course. He had recognized his Lord and he was free of the religion of his people, but he did not tell them that. He informed Āzar that he was his son, and the mother of Abraham agreed that it was true and told Āzar what she had done when Abraham was born. Āzar was happy about that and rejoiced greatly.

Āzar made his living by making the idols which his people worshipped, and he employed Abraham to sell them. It is said that Abraham would take them and would call out to people, "Who will buy what will harm him and be of no use to him?" So no one would buy them from him, and when they became unsellable, he would take them to the river and point their heads at it and say, "Drink!" mocking his people and their erroneous ways. At length his disrespect for them and his mocking of them spread about among his people and the inhabitants of his town, although Nimrod the king did not hear of it. Then, when the time seemed right to Abraham to reveal to his people the error of what they were doing, and to tell them of God's command and of how to pray to Him, he glanced up at the stars, and said, "I feel sick!"[142] God said, "And they turned their backs on him and left him."[143]

His saying "I am sick" meant he was attacked by illness. They fled from him when they heard it, but Abraham had only said it to make them go away so that he could do what he wanted with their idols. When they left him he went to the idols whom they worshipped instead of God, and he brought them food. He said, "Will you not eat? What is the matter? Why do you not speak?" reproaching their falsely elevated position and mocking them.

[257] On this same subject, scholars other than Ibn Isḥāq quoted

---

141. Ibid., 6:79–80. Although Kisāʾī lacks the tales of Abraham's miraculous growth and maturation, as well as of his finding God through the observation of nature, Thaʿlabi, *Qiṣaṣ*, 64–65, has similar accounts, as does the Jewish aggadic literature. See Ginzberg, *Legends*, V, 210, nn . 15–16.

142. This is based on Qur'ān, 37:83–89.

143. Ibid., 37:90.

Mūsā b. Hārūn—ʿAmr b. Ḥammād—Asbāṭ—al-Suddī—Abū Ṣāliḥ and Abū Mālik—Ibn ʿAbbās and Murrah al-Hamdānī—Ibn Masʿūd and some of the companions of the Prophet: Another story about Abraham is that a star arose over Nimrod so bright that it blotted out the light of the sun and the moon. He became very frightened about this and called upon the magicians and soothsayers, the prognosticators and physiognomists, to ask them about it. They said, "A man will arise in your domain whose destiny is to destroy you and your rule." At this time Nimrod lived in Babylon near al-Kūfah. He left his town and moved to another town, forcing all the men to leave with him but leaving the women. He ordered that any male child who was born should be slain, and he slew their children.[144]

Then, however, some task in Babylon came up for which he could trust only Āzar, the father of Abraham. He called Āzar and sent him to do the job, saying, "See that you do not have intercourse with your wife." Āzar said to him, "I am too tenacious in my religion for that." But when he entered Babylon he visited his wife and could not control himself; he had intercourse with her and fled with her to a town called Ur between al-Kūfah and al-Baṣrah. He placed her in a cavern there, promising to bring her food and drink and whatever else she needed.[145]

As for the king, after a long time went by and nothing happened he decided the astrologers had been wrong and told everyone, "It was the speech of lying magicians; return to your lands!" So they returned. Soon Abraham was born. He grew so fast that each day that passed was like a week, and each week like a month, and each month like a year. Meanwhile the king had forgotten the whole incident. Abraham grew up without ever seeing that there was anyone in creation besides him, his father, and his mother. Abraham's father said to his compan-

---

144. See Kisāʾī, 136–37; Tha ʿlabī, *Qiṣaṣ*, 63–64.

145. In Kisāʾī's account, the wife of Terah— foreshadowing the future fate of Abraham's wife Sarah—begins to menstruate after having ceased being fertile. The remainder of the account of the conception of Abraham is lacking there, however. Kisāʾī, 136. But see Thaʿlabī, *Qiṣaṣ*, 64, for an account parallel to this one.

[258] ions, "I have a son whom I have hidden. Do you fear the king on his account if I bring him out?" They said, "No, bring him!" So he went and brought him forth. When the boy came forth from the cavern, he looked at the beasts and cattle and creatures and began asking his father what they were. So his father told him that "this is a camel," "this is a cow," and "this is a horse," and "this is a sheep." Then Abraham said, "These creatures must have a master."

When he came out of the cavern it was after sundown. He raised his head toward the sky and saw a star—it was Jupiter—and he said, "This is my Lord!" But presently it disappeared, and he said, "I do not like things that set."[146] That is to say, "I do not like a lord who disappears."

According to Ibn ʿAbbās: He went forth from the cavern at the end of the month and for that reason he did not see the moon before he saw the stars. But when it was the end of the night he saw the moon rising and he said, "This is my Lord!" But when it set—he (Ibn ʿAbbās) says "disappeared"—he said, "If my Lord does not guide me, I shall indeed be one of those who go astray." When dawn came and he saw the sun rising, he said, "This is my Lord! This is greater!"[147] But when it too disappeared, God said, "Surrender yourself!" And Abraham replied, "I have already surrendered myself to the Lord of the Worlds!" He went to his people and called out to them, saying, "O my people! I am free of all the false partners which you associate with Him. I have turned my face toward Him Who created the heavens and the earth, as one upright by nature"[148]—he (Ibn ʿAbbās) says "one who is sincere." And he began to preach to his people and to warn them.

His father made his living by making idols, and he gave them to his sons to sell them. He would give them to Abraham, but when selling them Abraham would call out, "Who will buy that which will harm him and will not benefit him?" His brothers would come back having sold all their idols, while Abraham would come back with all of his still unsold. Then he

146. See Qur'ān, 6:77.
147. Ibid., 6:79.
148. Ibid., 6:79–80.

called upon his father, saying, "O my father! Why do you worship that which neither hears nor sees, nor can in any way help you?"[149] His father said, "Do you reject my gods, O Abraham? [259]
If you do not cease this, I shall surely stone you. Leave me for a long while"[150]—he (Ibn ʿAbbās) said, "forever".

His father told him, "Abraham, we have a festival. If you go to it with us, you would learn to like our religion." The day of the festival came, and they went to it. Abraham also went along with them, but on the way he threw himself down and said, "I am sick"[151]—he (Ibn ʿAbbās) says, "My foot is in pain." They sat down by his feet while he was lying down. When they went away he called at the last of them—for two of the people had remained—"By God, I shall deal with your idols after you have gone away and turned your backs."[152] They heard him say it. Then Abraham went back to the house of the gods, which was in a great hall. Opposite the entrance to the hall was a great idol, and at his side a smaller one, and next to him a smaller one, and so on down to the entrance to the hall. The people had prepared food and placed it before the gods, saying, "When we come back the gods will have blessed our food, and we will eat." When Abraham saw them with the food in front of them, he said, "Will you not eat?" And when they did not answer him, he said, "What ails you that you do not speak?" Then he attacked them, stiking them with his right hand.[153] He took a piece of iron and cut off each idol's extremities, then suspended the axe from the neck of the largest idol and went out. When the people came to get their food and saw their gods in this state, they said, "Who has done this to our gods? It must be some evildoer." Those who had overheard Abraham's earlier remark said, "We heard a youth make mention of them, one called Abraham."[154]

---

149. Ibid., 19:42.

150. Ibid., 19:46. This tale of Abraham selling idols for his father is paralleled in the aggadic accounts. See Ginzberg, *Legends*, I, 195.

151. Ibid., 37:89. See nn. 132, 133, above. Both Kisāʾī, 146, and Thaʿlabi, *Qiṣaṣ*, 66, have this story of the festival. The former account places it in the city of Cuthah-Rabba (transliteration of Thackston).

152. Qurʾān, 21:57.

153. Ibid., 37:91–93.

154. Ibid., 21:59–60. See Kisāʾī, 146; Thaʿlabī, *Qiṣaṣ*, 66.

[260] Abū Ja'far gives Ibn Isḥāq's version of the story as follows: Abraham approached them, "striking with his right hand," as God described it. Then he began breaking them up with an axe. When only the largest of the idols remained, he tied the axe to that idol's hand and left them. When his people returned they saw what he had done to their idols, and it frightened and distressed them. They said, "Who has done this to our gods? Surely it must be some evildoer."[155] Then they remembered and said, "We heard a youth make mention of them, one called Abraham."[156] They meant a youth who reviled, dishonored, and mocked them. "We have never heard anyone else say that, and we think he must be the one who did this to them."

Word of this reached Nimrod and the nobles of his people, and they said, "Then bring him before the people so that they may testify"[157]—that is, testify about what should be done to him.

Some interpreters of the text, among them Qatādah and al-Suddī, give this (phrase) as follows: That they may testify against him, for he was the one who had done it, and they (Nimrod and the nobles) said that they did not want to seize him without proof.

Returning to Ibn Isḥāq's account: When he was brought in with his people before their king Nimrod, they said, "Are you the one who did this to our gods, O Abraham?" He said, "But it was this one, their chief—that is, the biggest idol—who did it. So question them, if they can speak.[158] He became angry because you worshipped these little ones together with him while he is greater than they are, so he broke them." Then they left him alone and stopped telling each other that he had broken them. They said, "We have wronged him. We think it happened as he said." But then, knowing that the idols really could neither cause harm nor cause benefit nor commit physical violence, they demanded, "You know well that these do not speak"[159]—meaning, they do not utter sounds—"so tell us

---

155. Qur'ān, 21:59.
156. Ibid., 21:60.
157. Ibid., 21:61.
158. Ibid., 21:62–63.
159. Ibid., 21:65

who did this to them, for they do not strike with the hands. Then we will believe you."

Almighty God said, "Then they were utterly confounded [and they said], 'You know well that these do not speak.'"[160] [261] The fact is that they exposed the wrongness of their own belief in these idols when they said these words against Abraham. And when the proof appeared against them in the form of their statement that the idols could not speak, Abraham said, "Then why do you worship things which can bring you no profit at all, nor harm you, instead of worshipping God? Fie on you and on all that you worship instead of God! Have you no sense?"[161]

His people then argued with him about God, asking him to describe Him and telling him that their gods were better than what he worshipped. He said, "Do you dispute with me concerning God when He has guided me?"[162] He used in his argument God's own words, "Which of the two factions has more right to safety? If you have knowledge, answer the question."[163] He told them proverbs and provided examples to make them see that God had more right to be feared and worshipped than anything else that they worshipped besides Him.

According to Abū Jaʿfar: Then Nimrod said to Abraham, "Have you seen this God Whom you worship and to Whose worship you call others, and of Whose power you speak, and Whom you glorify above any other? Who is He?" Abraham replied to him, "My Lord, Who gives life and causes death." And Nimrod said, "I, too, give life and cause death." Abraham asked, "How do you give life and death?" He replied, "I shall take two men—two were condemned to death by my order—and I'll kill one of them, so I will have caused him to die, and I'll pardon the other and free him, so I will have made him live." But upon hearing that, Abraham said to him, "God causes the sun to rise in the East, so can you make it rise in the West?"[164] Knowing that it was as Abraham said, "Thus was

160. Id.
161. Ibid., 21:66–67.
162. Ibid., 6:81.
163. Ibid., 6:82.
164. Ibid., 2:258.

. . . [Nimrod] abashed,"[165] and he gave no answer; he knew
[262] that he was not able to do that. God said, "Thus was the unbeliever abashed"—that is to say, the proof was against him.[166] Then Nimrod and his people joined against Abraham, saying, "Burn him and stand by your gods, if you will be doing."[167]

According to Ibn Ḥumayd—Salamah—Muḥammad b. Isḥāq—al-Ḥasan b. Dīnār—Layth b. Abī Sulaym—Mujāhid: I recited this verse before ʿAbdallāh b. ʿUmar, and he said, "Do you know, O Mujāhid, who it was that advised burning Abraham in fire?" I answered, "No." He said, "One of the nomads of Persia." I said, "O ʿAbd al-Raḥmān, do the Persians have nomads?" He answered, "Yes, the Kurds are the nomads of Persia, and it was one of them who advised burning Abraham in fire."

According to Yaʿqūb—Ibn ʿUlayyah—Layth—Mujāhid: Regarding the order "Burn him and stand by your gods," it was a man from the nomads of Persia, meaning the Kurds, who gave it.

According to al-Qāsim—al-Ḥusayn—Ḥajjāj—Ibn Jurayj—Wahb b. Sulaymān—Shuʿayb al-Jabāʾī: The name of the man who said "burn him" was Hayzan, and God caused the earth to swallow him up. He will be tossed around therein until the Day of Resurrection.

Returning to Ibn Isḥāq's account: Then Nimrod gave orders, and wood was gathered for him. They gathered hard wood of various kinds of trees, and it is said that whenever a woman from Abraham's town was determined to get something done, she would vow that if she got her way she would help gather wood for the fire of Abraham in repayment of her debt. When
[263] they wanted to cast him into the fire, they brought him and lit every corner of the heap of wood which they had gathered for him, until the fire flared up. And they assembled to push him into it. Then heaven and earth and all the creatures therein except humans and jinns shouted to God, "Our Lord! Abraham,

165. Id.
166. This argument about Nimrod's divine powers is found in Kisāʾī, 142–43, and Thaʿlabī, *Qiṣaṣ*, 66.
167. Qurʾān, 21:68; that is, "if you want to act."

the only one on Your earth who worships you, is being burned in fire for Your sake. Permit us to help him!" It is said—and God knows best—that when they said that, God answered, "If he should ask for help from any of you, then you may help him, for I have given permission for that. But if he calls on no one but Me, I am his Friend; leave it between Me and him. I will protect him."[168] When they cast Abraham into the fire, God said, "O fire! Be coolness and peace for Abraham,"[169] and the fire did as God ordered.

According to Mūsā b. Hārūn—ʿAmr b. Ḥammād—Asbāṭ—al-Suddī: They said, "Imprison him in a building and cast him into Hell." They imprisoned him in a house and went to gather wood for him. The job became so all-important that if a woman became ill, she would say, "If God heals me, I will gather wood for Abraham." When they had gathered it for him, and had got so much that a bird passing over it would have been burned by the force of its heat, they brought Abraham and set him on top of the pyre. Then Abraham raised his head to heaven, and heaven and earth and the mountains and the angels all said, "Our Lord, Abraham is burning for Your sake." And He said, "I am most knowledgeable about him. If he calls on you, help him." When he raised his head to heaven, Abraham said, "O God! You are alone in heaven and I am alone on earth—there is no one besides me who worships You. God is sufficient for me, and how goodly is He in Whom I trust." [264]
When they pushed Abraham into the fire, God called out to it saying, "O fire! Be coolness and peace for Abraham,"[170] and it was Gabriel who called out.[171]

Ibn ʿAbbās said: "If its cold had not been followed by peace, Abraham would have died of the cold. Every fire on earth that

---

168. In Kisāʾī, 143–44, and the aggadic accounts. (See, Ginzberg, *Legends* , 198). Nimrod's order to burn Abraham is preceded by Abraham's imprisonment, during which the latter is sustained by angels.

169. Qur'ān, 21:69. This verse occurs in some Jewish accounts, undoubtedly translated from the Qur'ān. See Ginzberg, *Legends*, V, 212, n. 33.

170. Id.

171. Jabrāʾīl or Jibrīl, an angel and one of the divine messengers. It is his duty to bear God's orders to prophets and to reveal His mysteries to them. See *Shorter Encyc.*, 79–80.

day went out, thinking that it was the one that was meant."

When the fire was extinguished, they looked at Abraham and saw that there was another man with him, with Abraham's head in his lap. He was wiping the sweat from his face. It is mentioned that that man was the angel of shade.[172] God himself had sent down fire to mankind, which had benefitted from it (in general). They brought forth Abraham and took him to the king, though he had never previously come before him.

Returning to the story according to Ibn Isḥāq: God sent the angel of shade in the form of Abraham and he sat at his side in that form, comforting him.[173] For days Nimrod continued to believe that the fire had consumed Abraham and had finished him. Then one day he rode past it while it was burning all the wood that had been gathered for it, and he looked at it and saw Abraham sitting in it with a man resembling him at his side. Nimrod returned from that ride and said to his people, "I have seen Abraham alive in the fire, but perhaps it was only his image that appeared to me. Build me a tall structure from which I may look down upon the fire so that I can be sure." So they built him a tall structure from which he looked down into the fire. He saw Abraham sitting in it and saw the angel sitting by his side in a form similar to his. Nimrod called out to him, saying, "O Abraham! Great is your God Whose might and power
[265] even allow Him to prevent what I see from harming you. Will you be able to come out of it?" Abraham answered, "Yes!" Nimrod said, "Are you afraid that if you remain in it, it will harm you?" Abraham answered, "No." Then Nimrod said, "Arise, then, and come out of it!" So Abraham got up and walked through the fire until he had come out of it. When he came out to him, Nimrod said, "O Abraham! Who was the man whom I saw with you, like you in appearance, sitting at your side?" Abraham said, "That was the angel of shade whom my Lord sent to me to be with me in the fire, to comfort me. For me He made the fire coolness and peace." Then Nimrod

---

172. Lit. *ẓill*, shade, shadow, shelter, or protection.

173. Jewish accounts differ as to whether the angels Gabriel or Michael, or God alone, helped Abraham. See Ginzberg, *Legends*, loc. cit.

said, "O Abraham! I shall offer a sacrifice to your God because of His glory and power which I have seen, and because of what He did for you when you refused to worship or ascribe unity to any but Him. I shall offer up to Him four thousand cattle." Thereupon Abraham said to him, "God will not accept anything from you as long as you keep any vestige of this old religion of yours. You must leave it for my religion." Nimrod answered, "O Abraham! I cannot abandon my kingship, but I will slaughter the cattle for Him." And he slaughtered them. Then he left Abraham alone, and God held him back from him.

According to Ibn Ḥumayd—Jarīr—Mughīrah—al-Ḥārith—Abū Zurʿah—Abū Hurayrah: The best thing he said to Abraham was when he lifted up the cover from him when he was in the fire alone, his brow covered with sweat. And he said, "How excellent is the Lord, your Lord, O Abraham!"

According to al-Qāsim—al-Ḥusayn—Muʿtamir b. Sulaymān al-Taymī—some of his companions: Gabriel came to Abraham while he was being tied up and shackled to be thrown into the fire, and he said, "O Abraham! Do you need anything?" [266]
Abraham replied, "From you, no!"

According to Aḥmad b. al-Miqdām—al-Muʿtamir—his father—Qatādah—Abū Sulaymān: The fire burned nothing on Abraham except his fetters.

Abū Jaʿfar said the account returns to that of Ibn Isḥāq.

Some of Abraham's people became his followers when they saw what God did for him, though they were still afraid of Nimrod and of their community. Lot, the son of his brother, believed in him. He was Lot b. Haran b. Terah. Haran was Abraham's brother, and they had a third brother who was called Nahor b. Terah. Haran was the father of Lot, and Nahor was the father of Bethuel. Bethuel was the father of Laban. Rebecca, Bethuel's daughter, was the wife of Isaac b. Abraham and the mother of Jacob. Jacob's wives Leah and Rachel were both daughters of Laban. Sarah, the daughter of Abraham's paternal uncle, believed in him. Her father was Haran the Elder, Abraham's paternal uncle. She had a sister named Milcah, who was Nahor's wife.

Some claim that Sarah was the daughter of the king of Ḥarrān.

Discussion of Who Made That Claim

According to Mūsā b. Hārūn—ʿAmr b. Ḥammād—Asbāṭ—al-Suddī: Abraham and Lot set out for Syria. On the way Abraham met Sarah, who was the daughter of the king of Ḥarrān. She had criticized her people about their religion, so he married her, since he would thus be able to have a believing wife with-
[267] out having to convert her. Abraham called on his father Āzar to join his religion, saying to him, "O my father! Why do you worship that which cannot hear nor see, and which you do not need at all?" His father, however, refused to respond to his call, whereupon Abraham and his companions who followed his command decided to leave their people. They said, "We are free from you and from those things other than God which you worship. We disbelieve in you, O you [idols] who are worshipped beside God! And eternal enmity and hatred have arisen between us, O worshippers [of them], until you believe in God alone!"

Then Abraham went forth, a fugitive for the sake of his Lord, and Lot went with him.[174] Abraham married Sarah, the daughter of his paternal uncle, and took her out with him when he fled for the sake of being able to practice his religion and worship his Lord in safety. He settled in Ḥarrān and stayed as long as God willed him to stay. Then he left as a fugitive and traveled to Egypt, which was then under the rule of one of the earliest Pharaohs.

It is said that Sarah was one of the best human beings that ever existed. She would not disobey Abraham in any way, for which God honored her. When her goodness and beauty were described to Pharaoh, he sent a message to Abraham asking, "Who is this woman who is with you?" He replied, "She is my sister." He feared that if Pharaoh learned that Sarah was his wife, he would kill him to possess her. Pharaoh said to Abraham, "Adorn her and send her to me so that I may look at her." Abraham went back to Sarah and ordered her to prepare herself, then sent her to Pharaoh. She went in and approached him. When she sat next to him, he reached out to her with his

174. Qur'ān, 29:26.

hand, but his arm suddenly became stiff all the way up to his chest. When he saw that, he looked at her with awe and said, "Pray to God to release me! By God, I shall not cast suspicion on you. I shall indeed be good to you." So she said, "My God, if he is being truthful, release his hand." And God released his hand and he sent her back to Abraham. Pharaoh also gave her [268] Hagar, a Coptic slave-girl of his.[175]

According to Abū Kurayb—Abū Usāmah—Hishām—Muḥammad—Abū Hurayrah—the Messenger of God: Abraham told only three lies in his life. Two of them were about God—his saying "I feel sick"[176] and his saying "But this, their chief, is the one who did it."[177] While he was traveling through the land of a certain tyrant, he stopped at a place, and a man went to the tyrant, saying: "There is in your land"—or "There is here—a man with a wife who is one of the most beautiful of mankind." So the tyrant sent for Abraham, and when he came, he asked him, "What [relation] is this woman to you?" Abraham replied, "She is my sister." The tyrant said, "Go and send her to me." Abraham went back to Sarah and said, "This tyrant asked me about you, and I told him that you are my sister. So do not give me the lie when you see him. You are my sister in God, for in all this land there are no Muslims except ourselves."

Abraham took her to the tyrant and stood up to pray. When she came into the tyrant's presence, he bent forward to touch her, but was suddenly seized by a powerful paralysis. He said, "Pray to God and I will not harm you." So she prayed for him, and he was set free. Then he reached out for her again, and again, he was seized by the paralysis. And he said, "Pray to God and I will not harm you." So she prayed for him and he was released. Then he did the same thing yet again, and again he was seized. And he asked Sarah to pray for him and was released. He called the lowest of his chamberlains and said, "You did not

---

175. See Thaʿlabī *Qiṣaṣ*, 69–70, and Ginzberg, *Legends*, I, 222 –223. In Kisāʾī, 150–151, the king is called Zadok and rules over Jordan. In both Kisāʾī and the aggadic accounts, Hagar is the daughter of the king or Pharaoh, who gives her to Sarah as a servant.

176. Qurʾān, 37:89.

177. Ibid., 21:63.

bring me a human being, you brought me a devil. Take her away and give Hagar to her." She was taken out and given Hagar, and she went away with her. When Abraham saw her coming back, he interrupted his prayer and said, "What is the matter?" She answered, "God has protected me from the unbelieving libertine and has given me Hagar as a servant."

[269]

According to Muḥammad b. Sīrīn: When Abū Hurayrah related this account, he would say, "This is your mother, O Arabs!"[178]

According to Ibn Ḥumayd—Salamah—Muḥammad b. Isḥāq—ʿAbd al-Raḥman b. Abī al-Zinād—his father—ʿAbd al-Raḥmān al-Aʿraj—Abū Hurayrah—the Messenger of God: Abraham said only three things that were not true. He said, "I am sick," when there was no sickness in him; he said, "But this, their chief, is the one who did it, so question them if they can speak;" and when Pharaoh asked him about Sarah, "Who is this woman with you?" he answered, "My sister." Abraham never said anything untrue except these things.

According to Saʿīd b. Yaḥyā al-Umawī—his father—Muḥammad b. Isḥāq—Abū al-Zinād—ʿAbd al-Raḥmān al-Aʿraj—Abū Hurayrah: The Messenger of God said, "Abraham never lied except about three things." Then he mentioned the same.

According to Abū Kurayb—Abū Usāmah—Hishām—Muḥammad—Abū Hurayrah—the Messenger of God: Abraham lied only three times, twice about God—his saying, "I feel sick;" his saying, "But this, their chief, is the one who did it;" and his saying about Sarah, "She is my sister."

According to Ibn Ḥumayd—Jarīr—Mughīrah—al-Musayyib

[270]

b. Rāfiʿ—Abū Hurayrah: Abraham told only three lies—his saying, "I feel sick;" his saying, "But this, their chief, is the one who did it," but this second lie was only by way of admonition; and his saying, "She is my sister," when the king asked him about his wife Sarah.

According to Yaʿqūb—Ibn ʿUlayyah—Ayyūb—Muḥammad: Abraham told only three lies, two about God and one about himself. The first two were his saying, "I feel sick," and his

178. In Arabic, *yā banī mā' al-samā'* , "O sons of the water of heaven."

saying, "But this, their chief, is the one who did it;" the other was his tale about Sarah. And Muḥammad related the story of her and the king.

Abū Jaʿfar said: The account returns to that of Ibn Isḥāq. Hagar was a servant-woman of good appearance and Sarah gave her to Abraham, saying, "I consider her a clean woman, so take her. Perhaps God will grant you a son from her." For Sarah was barren and had grown old without bearing a son for Abraham. Abraham had prayed to God to grant him a pious son, but the prayer was not answered until he had become old and Sarah barren. So he had intercourse with Hagar, and she bore him Ishmael.[179]

According to Ibn Ḥumayd—Salamah—Ibn Isḥāq—al-Zuhrī—ʿAbd al-Raḥmān b. ʿAbdallāh b. Kaʿb b. Mālik al-Anṣārī—the Messenger of God: When you conquer Egypt, treat its people well, for they are kin (to you) and deserve protection.

According to Ibn Ḥumayd—Salamah—Ibn Isḥāq: I asked al-Zuhrī, "What is their kinship that the Messenger of God mentioned?" Al-Zuhrī answered, "Hagar, the mother of Ishmael, was one of them." [271]

It is said—though God knows best—that when this happened Sarah grieved greatly because her own years of childbearing were over. Abraham had left Egypt for Syria, for he was afraid of the Egyptian king and anxious about his evil ways. He settled in Beersheba in the land of Palestine, which is the desert land of Syria. Lot had settled in al-Mu'tafikah,[180] less than one day-and-night's journey from Beersheba.[181] God sent Abraham as a prophet, and it is said that he stayed in Beersheba, dug a well there, and set up a place of worship there. That well provided pure water which flowed copiously up over the ground, and his flocks came to drink there. Then the people

179. See the Jewish account in Ginzberg, *Legends*, op. cit., 237. See also Kisā'ī, 151, and Thaʿlabī, *Qiṣaṣ*, 70.

180. See Qur'ān, 53:53. The Arabic name for the "cities of the plain" overthrown and destroyed by God, from the root *'fk*, "to change a state or manner of being, to turn anything away or back." See Lane, I:69–70; LeStrange, *Palestine*, 510.

181. An obvious reference to the division of land between Abraham and Lot. See Gen 13, where Lot chose the Jordan plain, and Abram, as he was then known, chose the land of Canaan.

of Beersheba harmed him in some way, so he left there and went to another part of Palestine—a village called Qaṭṭ or Qiṭṭ[182] between al-Ramlah and Īliyā.[183] When he left Beersheba, the water sank back into the ground and vanished. So the people of Beersheba followed him until they overtook him, regretting what they had done. They said, "We have driven a pious man out of our community." They asked him to come back. He answered, "I will not come back to a place from which I was driven out." They said, "The water from which you used to drink, and we as well, has sunk back into the earth and disappeared." So he brought them seven goats from his flocks and said, "Take them with you. If you take them to drink from the well, the water will appear again as pure and flowing as it was before. Drink from it and do not let a menstruating woman dip water from it." They took the goats back with them; and when they stopped at the well the water reappeared for them, and they were able to drink from it. It re-
[272] mained thus until one day when a menstruating woman came to it and dipped water from it. Whereupon the water withdrew, and the well dried up again. It has remained dry to this day.[184]

Abraham used to give hospitality to whoever came to visit him, since God had made him prosperous and given him ample sustenance, wealth, and servants. When God wished to destroy the people of Lot, He sent His messengers to Abraham commanding him to leave their community. They had done vile deeds which no one in the two worlds had ever done before, disbelieving their prophets and rejecting the good counsel which Lot had brought them from their Lord. The messengers were ordered to visit Abraham and give him and Sarah tidings of the coming of Isaac and also of Jacob who was to come after

---

182. See Yāqūt, *Muʿjam*, IV, 137 ; LeStrange, *Palestine*, 483, reads Katt. No further identification or location is given. Thaʿlabī, *Qiṣaṣ*, 70, has Qaṭṭah.

183. That is, Jerusalem, from the Latin, Aelia Capitolina, the name given to the city by the Emperor Hadrian after the suppression of Jewish revolts in 117–18. See Baron, *Social*, II, 107; Yāqūt, *Muʿjam*, I, 423ff.

184. Probably a jumbled reference to the story of the covenant of Beersheba between Abraham and Abimelech regarding a well dug by Abraham. The covenant is marked by the symbolic present of seven ewe-lambs by Abraham. See Gen 21; Thaʿlabī, *Qiṣaṣ*, loc. cit.

him. When they came to Abraham he had had no guests for two weeks, and it was becoming unbearable to him to have no one visiting him or receiving hospitality from him. So when he saw the messengers he rejoiced.[185] He saw guests who had more goodness and beauty than any guests to whom he had given hospitality before, and he said, "No one but I myself will serve these people, with my own hands." So he went to his house servants and brought—as God says—a fatted calf[186] which he had roasted until it was well done. God says, "He brought forth a roasted calf."[187] He offered it to them, but they did not reach out to eat of it. When he saw this, Abraham mistrusted them and conceived a fear of them[188] since they did not eat his food. They said, "Do not be afraid! We are sent to the people of Lot."[189] Sarah was standing nearby, and when she heard of God's command she laughed, knowing what she knew of the people of Lot. Then they told her of the coming of Isaac and, after Isaac, of Jacob[190]—that is, they told her she [273]
would have a son and grandson. She struck her face[191] (in surprise) and said, "Woe is me! How can I have a child when I am a barren old woman?"[192] the quote continuing until: "He is the Owner of Praise, Owner of Glory!"[193]

According to what some scholars have told me, Sarah was ninety years old at the time and Abraham was one hundred and twenty.[194] When Abraham lost his fear and heard the news

185. Abraham's need for guests to share his food so that he could enjoy it is mentioned in Kisā'ī, 155–6; Tha'labī, *Qiṣaṣ*, 70–71. Ginzberg *Legends*, I, 241–2 relates that this visit took place almost immediately after Abraham's circumcision by God's command. In spite of his pain, Abraham himself went out on the road to find some stranger to whom he could give hospitality. For the biblical account see Gen 18.

186. See Qur'ān, 51:26.

187. Ibid., 11:69.

188. Ibid., 11:70.

189. Id.

190. Ibid., 11:71.

191. Qur'ān, :51:29.

192. Ibid., 11:72.

193. Ibid., 11:73.

194. Note the discrepancies in the various ages attributed to Abraham and Sarah at the time of Isaac's birth as well as that of his sacrifice in the paragraph below.

about Isaac and Jacob and the descendants he was to have through Isaac, his fear evaporated and he felt safe. He said, "Praise be to God Who has granted me, despite my age, Ishmael and Isaac. Verily my Lord is One Who hears prayer!"

According to al-Qāsim—al-Ḥusayn—Ḥajjāj—Ibn Jurayj—Wahb b. Sulaymān—Shuʿayb al-Jabāʾī: Abraham was sixteen when he was thrown into the fire, and Isaac was seven when he was sacrificed, while Sarah was ninety when she bore him. The place of his sacrifice was about two miles from Bayt Īliyā. When Sarah learned what God wanted with Isaac, she fell ill for two days and died on the third. It is said that Sarah was one hundred and twenty-seven years old when she died.

According to Mūsā b. Hārūn—ʿAmr b. Ḥammād——Asbāṭ—al-Suddī: God sent the angels to destroy the people of Lot. They approached in the form of young men and visited Abraham, seeking his hospitality. When Abraham saw them he honored them, went to his servants, and brought a fatted calf, which he slaughtered and then roasted on hot stones. This was roasted meat (*ḥanīdh*), and when he had roasted it he brought it to them. He sat with them while Sarah stood serving
[274] them. As God said, "And his wife, standing by"[195] while he was sitting—this according to Ibn Masʿūd's version. When he brought it to them, he said, "Will you not eat?"[196] They said, "Verily, Abraham, we eat food only for a price." He said, "This has a price." They said, "What is its cost?" He said, "That you mention God's name at the beginning and praise him at the end." Gabriel looked at Michael and said, "This one is worthy of the Lord's having taken him as a friend." When he saw that their hands did not reach out for the meat, he said to himself, "They do not eat," and grew afraid of them. When Sarah looked at him, she saw that he had honored them and that she stood to serve them. She laughed[197] and said, "How strange these

195. Qurʾān, 21:71.
196. Ibid., 51:27.
197. Note this second mention of Sarah's laughter; the first (Ṭabarī, 272), was when she heard of the punishment of Lot's people, and not—as in the Bible—on hearing the promise of a son, Gen. 18:12. Thaʿlabī, *Qiṣaṣ*, 71, inserts here the discussion of the scholars about what caused Sarah's laughter.

guests of ours are—we serve them by ourselves, honoring them, and they do not eat our food!"

Concerning the Command to Build the House[198]

After Ishmael and Isaac were born, God commanded Abraham to build a House for Him in which He would be worshipped and His name mentioned. Abraham did not know exactly where he was expected to build it, since God had not made this clear, and he felt uneasy about the matter. Some scholars say that God sent the Sakīnah[199] to him to show him where to build the House. The Sakīnah went with Abraham, who was also accompanied by his wife Hagar and his son Ishmael, who was a small baby.

Other scholars have said, rather, it was Gabriel whom God sent to him to show him where to build the House and what do do.

Concerning Those Who Said that God Sent the Sakīnah to Him for That [275]

According to Hannād b. al-Sirrī—Abū al-Aḥwaṣ—Simāk b. Ḥarb—Khālid b. ʿArʿarah: A man came to ʿAlī b. Abī Ṭālib and said, "Will you not tell me about the House? Was it the first House to be built on earth?" He replied, "No, but it was the first House built with the blessing of the standing-place of Abraham, and whoever enters it will be safe. If you wish, I will

198. That is, the Kaʿbah in Mecca. The roles of Abraham and Ishmael in building the House are central in Islamic belief and are thus placed here, interrupting the narrative of the fulfillment of the messengers' prophecies regarding the birth of Isaac and the destruction of the people of Lot. Kisāʾī, 154 deals with this account with great brevity. Thaʿlabī, *Qiṣaṣ*, 71–79 on the other hand, devotes much space to the stories of Zamzam and of the Kaʿbah. See also the biblical account of Sarah sending Hagar and Ishmael away, Gen 21, and Ginzberg *Legends*, I, 263f.

199. Mentioned in the Qurʾān, 2:248. Obviously based on the Hebrew Shekhinah, "the presence of God" in a spiritual sense. Muslim exegetes give a jinn-like description of Sakīnah, which is what is meant here; see below. See *Shorter Encyc.*, 489.

tell you how it was built". God said to Abraham, 'Build Me a House on earth!' Abraham felt uneasy, so He sent the Sakīnah. The Sakīnah is a gale-force wind with two heads, and one head followed the other until they reached Mecca and coiled up at the site of the House, the way a snake coils. Abraham was commanded to build where the Sakīnah had rested. When Abraham had finished it except for one stone, the boy went away to build something else. But Abraham said, 'No, I still need one more stone, as I will order you.' So the boy went looking for a stone, and when he found one he brought it to Abraham. But he found that Abraham had already set the Black Stone in place. He said, 'O my father, who brought you this stone?' Abraham answered, 'Someone who did not rely on your building brought it to me. It was Gabriel who brought it to me from heaven.' Then the two of them finished it."

According to Ibn Bashshār and Ibn al-Muthannā—Mu'ammal—Sufyān—Abū Isḥāq—Ḥārithah b. Muḍarrib—'Alī: When Abraham was commanded to build the House, Ishmael
[276] and Hagar went forth with him. When he approached Mecca he saw on his head, in the place of the House, the likeness of a muzzle which was the likeness of the head. Then God spoke to him, saying, "O Abraham! Build on My protection and My might, neither add nor subtract." When he had built, he went forth and left Hagar and Ishmael behind. Hagar said, "O Abraham! To whom are you entrusting us?" He replied, "To God." She said, "Then go! He will not lead us astray."

Ishmael became very thirsty. Hagar climbed al-Ṣafā to look (for water) but saw nothing. Then she went to al-Marwah, but the same thing happened. Then she returned to al-Ṣafā and looked around, but could not find Ishmael. After looking seven times[200] without success, she said, "O Ishmael! You have died where I cannot see you!" Then she found him, and he was scraping the ground with his foot from thirst. Gabriel called out to her saying, "Who are you?" She answered, "Hagar, mother of the son of Abraham." Gabriel said, "To whom did he entrust you?" She said, "He entrusted us to God." He an-

200. That is, prefiguring the rites of the Muslim pilgrimage.

swered, "He has entrusted you to One who is sufficient." The boy scraped the ground with his finger and the spring of Zamzam welled up. She began to dam up the water, but Gabriel said, "Leave it! It is sweet water."[201]

According to Mūsā b. Hārūn—ʿAmr b. Ḥammād—Asbāṭ—al-Suddī: God gave Abraham and Ishmael the order, "Cleanse My House for those who walk around it," Abraham set out for Mecca. He and Ishmael took pickaxes, without knowing where the House was. So God sent a wind, the gale-force wind, which had two wings and a head like that of a snake. It swept the area around the Kaʿbah clear for them to let them build the foundations of the original House. They followed it with pickaxes, digging until they had placed the foundations. That was when God said, "When We prepared for [277]
Abraham the place of the House."[202]

According to Ibn Ḥumayd—Salamah—Muḥammad b. Isḥāq—al-Ḥasan b. ʿUmārah—Simāk b. Ḥarb—Khālid b. ʿArʿarah—ʿAlī b. Abī Ṭālib: When God commanded Abraham to build the House and to call on humanity to perform the pilgrimage, he left Syria with his son Ishmael and Ishmael's mother Hagar. With him God sent the Sakīnah, a wind which had the power of speech. Abraham followed it wherever it led him until it had led him to Mecca. When it came to the place of the House, it spun round and round and said to Abraham, "Build on me! Build on me! Build on me!" Abraham laid the foundations and raised the House, working with Ishmael, until they came to the cornerstone. Abraham said to Ishmael, "O my little son! Find me a stone which I can put here as a sign to the people." He brought a stone, but Abraham did not like it and said, "Look for another one." Ishmael went to look, but when he came back a cornerstone had already been brought and Abraham had put it in place. He asked, "O my father! Who brought you this stone?" Abraham replied, "One who did not entrust me to you, O my son!"

---

201. In the Jewish aggadic sources Ishmael is saved because of his piety and his father's merits, while Hagar is portrayed as still praying to the idols of her youth. See Ginzberg, *Legends*, I, 264–66.

202. Qur'ān, 22:26.

Others have said that the one who left Syria with Abraham to guide him to the place of the House was Gabriel, and that the reason he took Hagar and Ishmael to Mecca with him was that Sarah was jealous of Hagar's having borne Ishmael by him.[203]

Concerning Those Who Said That

According to Mūsā b. Hārūn—ʿAmr b. Ḥammād—Asbāṭ—al-Suddī (with a chain of authorities which we have already men-
[278] tioned): Sarah said to Abraham, "You may take pleasure in Hagar, for I have permitted it." So he had intercourse with Hagar and she gave birth to Ishmael. Then he had intercourse with Sarah, and she gave birth to Isaac. When Isaac grew up, he and Ishmael fought. Sarah became angry and jealous toward Ishmael's mother and sent her away. Then she called her back and took her in. But later she became angry and sent her away again, and brought her back yet again. She swore to cut something off of her, and said to herself, "I shall cut off her nose, I shall cut off her ear—but no, that would deform her. I will circumcise her instead." So she did that, and Hagar took a piece of cloth to wipe the blood away. For that reason women have been circumcised and have taken pieces of cloth down to today.[204]

Sarah said, "She will not live in the same town with me." God told Abraham to go to Mecca, where there was no House at the time. He took Hagar and her son to Mecca and put them

---

203. Kisāʾī, 151, implies that Sarah had not yet given birth to Isaac when she made Abraham send Hagar away; here (Ṭabarī, I 274), both Ishmael and Isaac were born when God told Abraham to build a house and when Abraham took Hagar and Ishmael to Mecca with him. Thaʿlabī, *Qiṣaṣ*, 71ff., has differing accounts, but one, similar to Ṭabarī's account below, says that the expulsion of Hagar from the household was due to boyish conflicts between Ishmael and Isaac—which reflects the aggadic tales. See Ginzberg, *Legends* , I, 263–64.

204. This strange tradition probably reflects the antiquity of the practice of circumcision (both male and female) among the Arabs, which antedates Islam. See *Shorter Encyc.*, 254–55, s.v. *khitan*. Thaʿlabī, *Qiṣaṣ*, 71, mentions only that Sarah had Hagar's ears pierced, and gives that as the origin of this general practice.

there. Hagar said to him, "To whom have you left us here?" Then he told the story of her and her son.

According to Ibn Ḥumayd—Salamah—Ibn Isḥāq—ʿAbdallāh b. Abī Najīḥ—Mujāhid and other scholars: When God pointed out to Abraham the place of the House and told him how to build the Sanctuary, he set out to do the job and Gabriel went with him. It is said that whenever he passed a town he would ask, "Is this the town which God's command meant, O Gabriel?" And Gabriel would say, "Pass it by." At last they reached Mecca, which at that time was nothing but acacia trees, mimosa, and thorn trees, and there was a people called the Amalekites outside Mecca and its surroundings. The House at that time was but a hill of red clay. Abraham said to Gabriel, "Was it here that I was ordered to leave them?" Ga- [279]
briel said, "Yes." Abraham directed Hagar and Ishmael to go to al-Ḥijr, and settled them down there. He commanded Hagar, the mother of Ishmael, to find shelter there. Then he said, "My Lord! I have settled some of my posterity in an uncultivable valley near Your Holy House . . ." with the quote continuing until ". . . that they may be thankful."[205] Then he journeyed back to his family in Syria, leaving the two of them at the House.

Then Ishmael became very thirsty. His mother looked for water for him, but could not find any. She listened for sounds to help her find water for him. She heard a sound at al-Ṣafā and went there to look around, but found nothing. Then she heard a sound from the direction of al-Marwah. She went there and looked around, but found nothing.

Some also say that she stood on al-Ṣafā, praying to God for water for Ishmael, and then went to al-Marwah to do the same. Then she heard the sounds of beasts in the valley where she had left Ishmael. She ran to him and found him scraping the water from a spring which had burst forth beneath his hand, and drinking from it. Ishmael's mother came to it and made it swampy. Then she drew water from it into her waterskin to

205. Qur'ān, 14:37.

keep it for Ishmael. Had she not done that, the waters of Zamzam would have gone on flowing to the surface forever. According to Mujāhid's version, Gabriel dug out Zamzam with his heel for Ishmael when he was thirsty.

According to Yaʿqūb b. Ibrāhīm and al-Ḥasan b. Muḥammad
[280] —Ismāʿīl b. Ibrāhīm—Ayyūb—Saʿīd b. Jubayr—Ibn ʿAbbās: The first person to run between al-Ṣafā and al-Marwah was the mother of Ishmael. And the first Arab woman who voided ordure and dragged the edges of her garment over it was the mother of Ishmael. When she fled from Sarah, she let her garment trail behind her to wipe her footprints out. Abraham took her and Ishmael until he reached the place of the House with them, and he left them there. Then he set off to go back to Syria. She followed him and said, "To what have you entrusted us? What will we eat? What will we drink?" At first he did not answer, but then she said: "Did God order you to do this?" He replied, "Yes." She said, "Then He will not let us go astray." So she went back, and Abraham kept going. When he reached a mountain pass full of large rocks and came upon the valley, he said, "My Lord! I have settled some of my posterity in an uncultivable valley near Your Holy House, etc. . . ."[206]

Hagar had a worn-out waterskin which contained some water, but it gave out and she became thirsty. Then her milk ceased and Ishmael became thirsty. So she looked for the lowest mountain in the area—it was al-Ṣafā—and climbed it. Then she listened, hoping to hear a voice or to see a friendly person. But she did not hear anything, so she climbed down. When she reached the valley she ran even though she did not want to run, as is sometimes the case with exhausted people. Then she looked for another low mountain and climbed al-Marwah to have another look around. Then she heard a faint voice. Being unsure that she had really heard it, she said "Hush!" to herself, until she was sure of it. Then she said, "You have made me hear Your voice, so give me water, for I am
[281] dying and so is the one with me."

The angel took her to the place of Zamzam. Then he

206. Id.

stamped his foot, and a spring gushed forth. Hagar hurried to fill her waterskin. The Messenger of God said, "May God have mercy on the mother of Ishmael! If she had not been in such a hurry, Zamzam would still be a free-flowing spring." The angel said to her, "Do not fear that the people of this town will go thirsty, for this is a spring made for God's guests to drink. The father of this boy will come, and they will build a House on this site."

A group of people from the tribe of Jurhum[207] passed by on the way to Syria. Seeing birds over the mountain, they asked each other, "That kind of bird only circles over water—do you know of any water in this valley?" None of them did. Then they went to a high place and saw Hagar. They came to her and asked whether they might stop with her, and she allowed it.

At length death came to Hagar as it comes to all people, and after she died Ishmael married a woman from the Jurhumite group. Later Abraham came, asking after Ishmael's dwelling. It was pointed out to him and he went there to visit his son. But Ishmael was out, and instead of him Abraham met his wife, churlish and rude. He said to her, "When your husband comes home, tell him that an old man of such-and-such description has come here, and that he says to you (that is, to Ishmael), 'I am not pleased with the threshold of your door.'" Then he left her and went away. When Ishmael came she told him, as Abraham had ordered, and he said, "That was my father, and you are the threshold of my door." So he divorced her and married another Jurhumite woman. Later Abraham came to visit again, and, as before, it was not Ishmael but his wife—this one compliant and generous—who was there when he came. He said to her, "Where did your husband go?" She said, "He went hunting." He said, "What food do you have?" She said, "Meat and water." He said, "My God! Bless their meat and water threefold." And he said to her, "When your husband comes back, [282]

207. This tribe and the Amelekites were mentioned (Ṭabarī, I, 219) as *al-ʿArab al-ʿāribah* or "the authentic Arabs." Thus, when Ishmael marries a daughter of this tribe, it represents a blending of these "authentic" Arabs with the "Arabized" Arabs, that is, the descendants of Ishmael who settled among them; see Ṭabarī, I, 215.

tell him that an old man of such-and-such description has come here and says to you, 'I am satisfied with the threshold of your door, so hold firm to her.'" When Ishmael came home she told him this. Later Abraham came a third time and worked with Ishmael to raise the foundations of the House.[208]

According to al-Ḥasan b. Muḥammad—Yaḥyā b. ʿAbbād—Ḥammād b. Salamah—ʿAṭāʾ b. al-Sāʾib—Saʿīd b. Jubayr—Ibn ʿAbbās: Abraham, the Prophet of God, brought Ishmael and Hagar and set them down in Mecca at the place of Zamzam. As he was leaving, Hagar called out to him, "O Abraham, I ask you three times, who commanded you to set me down in a land without grain, without cows' udders, without people, without water, and without provisions?" He said, "My Lord commanded me." She said, "Verily, He will never lead us astray." As Abraham was retracing his path (back to Syria) he said, "O Lord! You know both the sadness we hide and the sadness we reveal. Nothing on earth or in heaven is hidden from God."[209]

When Ishmael grew thirsty, he began to scuff at the ground with his heel. Hagar climbed the mountain of al-Ṣafā. At that time the valley was *lākh*, that is to say, deep, so when she
[283] climbed al-Ṣafā and looked down to see whether she could see anything, she saw nothing. So she came down and ran along the valley until she came to al-Marwah. She climbed it but could not see anything from there either. She did that seven times and then came down from al-Marwah to Ishmael, and she found him scuffing the ground with his heel. The spring Zamzam had begun to flow, and she began scraping the ground away from the water with her hand. Wherever some water collected on the ground she scooped it up in her cup and poured it into her waterskin.

The Prophet said, "May God have mercy on her! Had she let

208. This tale occurs in Kisāʾī, 153–54, and Thaʿlabī, *Qiṣaṣ*, 72–73, the latter giving a more detailed account. A variation occurs in the Jewish aggada, with tent-pin instead of threshold as the key word; see Ginzberg, *Legends*, I, 267–69.

209. Qurʾān, 14:38.

it be, it would have remained a flowing spring until the Day of Resurrection."

At that time there were Jurhum people in a valley near Mecca. Some birds had stayed in the valley because they saw the water, and when the Jurhumites saw the birds they said, "They would not be there unless there was water there." So they came to Hagar and said, "If you wish, we will stay with you and keep you company for as long as the water belongs to you." She replied, "Yes." So they stayed with her while Ishmael grew up. When Hagar died, Ishmael married a Jurhumite woman.

Abraham asked Sarah's leave to go to visit Hagar and Sarah permitted it, laying down the condition that he not settle down there. Hagar had already died when Abraham came to Ishmael's house. He said to Ishmael's wife, "Where is your master?" She said, "He is not here. He went hunting." Ishmael often left [284]
the Sanctuary to go hunting. Abraham said, "Do you have any hospitality? Do you have any food or drink?" She said, "I have nothing, and there is no one with me." Abraham said, "When your husband comes, call out greeting to him and tell him that he should change the threshold of his door."

Abraham went, and when Ishmael came back he found the smell of his father. So he said to his wife, "Did anyone come to you?" She said, "An old man of such-and-such description came to me"—as though she were making light of him. Ishmael said, "What did he say to you?" She said, "He told me, 'Greet your husband with peace and tell him that he should change the threshold of his door.'" So he divorced her and married another.

Abraham stayed in Syria as long as God willed and then asked Sarah's leave to go to Mecca again to visit Ishmael. Once again she permitted him on the condition that he not settle down. Abraham came to Ishmael's door and said to his wife, "Where is your master?" She answered, "He has gone hunting, but he will soon come back, God willing, so stay, and may God be merciful to you!" He asked her, "Do you have any hospitality?" She said, "Yes." He said, "Do you have bread or wheat or barley or dates?" She brought milk and meat, and he prayed for

blessing for both of them. Had she brought bread or wheat or dates or barley, Mecca would have been the most plentifully supplied with those things of any place on God's earth. She said, "Stay so that I may wash your head." But he would not stay, so she brought him the standing-place[210] and put it at his right side. He set his foot on it and the trace of his foot remained on it. Then she washed the right side of his head, then turned the standing-place to his left and washed the left side. He said to her, "When your husband comes, greet him with peace and say to him, 'The threshold of your door has been put in order.'" When Ishmael came he sensed the smell of his fa-
[285] ther, so he said to his wife, "Did anyone come to you?" She answered, "Yes, an old man, the handsomest and best-smelling in the world. He said to me such-and-such and I answered such-and-such, and I washed his head, and this is the place of his feet on the standing-place." He said, "What did he say to you?" She replied, "He said to me, 'When your husband comes, greet him with peace and say to him: The threshold of your door has been put in order.'" Ishmael said, "That was Abraham."

Abraham stayed as long as God willed, and then God ordered him to build the House. So he and Ishmael built it. And when it was finished they were told, "And proclaim unto mankind the pilgrimage."[211] So Abraham began, whenever he passed people, to say, "O people! A House has been built for you, so go on pilgrimage to it." But everything that heard him—stones, trees, everything—said, "Here I am, my God, here I am."[212] Between the time when Abraham said, "Our Lord! I have settled some of my posterity in an uncultivable valley near Your Holy House,"[213] and the time when he said, "Praise be to God, who has given me Ishmael and Isaac in my old age,"[214] there passed a number of years which ʿAṭāʾ did not memorize.

---

210. *Maqām*, today usually, means "shrine" or "place of martyrdom." In the precincts of the Kaʿbah there is the *maqām* Ibrāhīm, which is the shrine of Abraham but harks back to the literal sense, as here, of his "standing place."

211. Qur'ān, 22:28.

212. Arabic *Labbayka allahumma labbayka*, the cry of the pilgrims as they perform the rites of the pilgrimage.

213. Qur'ān, 14:37.

214. Ibid., 14:39.

According to Muḥammad b. Sinān—ʿUbaydallāh b. ʿAbd al-Majīd Abū ʿAlī al-Ḥanafī ——— Ibrāhīm b. Nāfiʿ —Kathīr b. Kathīr—Saʿīd b. Jubayr—Ibn ʿAbbās: Abraham came and found Ishmael mending his arrows behind Zamzam and said to him, "O Ishmael! Your Lord has ordered me to build Him a House." [286]
Ishmael said to him, "Then obey your Lord and do what He ordered you to do." Then Abraham said, "He has commanded that you assist me." Ishmael answered, "Then I will do it." They began together, Abraham doing the building while Ishmael handed him the stones, and both of them saying, "O Lord! Accept this from us. You and You alone are the Hearer, the Knower."[215]

When the building had become tall and old Abraham was too weak to lift the stones that high, Ishmael came upon a stone which was the standing-place of Abraham. He started to hand it over, while both of them were saying, "Accept this from us. You and You alone are the Hearer, the Knower."[216] When Abraham had finished building the House as God had ordered, God ordered him to proclaim the pilgrimage among mankind, saying to him, "And proclaim unto mankind the pilgrimage. They will come to you on foot and on every lean camel; they will come from every deep ravine."[217]

According to Ibn Ḥumayd—Jarīr—Qābūs b. Abī Ẓabyān —his father—Ibn ʿAbbās: When Abraham completed the building of the House, he was ordered, "Proclaim to mankind the pilgrimage." He then said, "O Lord! What will my voice reach?"—(that is, Who will listen to me?). God answered, "Proclaim! The reaching is My responsibility." So Abraham proclaimed, "O people! Pilgrimage to the ancient House is prescribed for you." And everything between heaven and earth heard him—do you not see people coming from the ends of the earth, answering the call?

According to al-Ḥasan b. ʿArafah—Muḥammad b. Fuḍayl b. Ghazwān al-Ḍabbī—ʿAṭāʾ b. al-Sāʾib—Saʿīd b. Jubayr—Ibn ʿAbbās: When Abraham built the House, God inspired him to

215. Ibid., 2:127.
216. Id.
217. Ibid., 22:28.

"proclaim the pilgrimage to mankind." Abraham said, "Did
not your Lord adopt a House and command you to go on pil- [28
grimage to it?" And everything that heard him— stones, trees, hills, dust, or anything else—answered him with, "Here I am, my God, here I am."

According to Ibn Ḥumayd—Yaḥyā b. Wāḍiḥ—al-Ḥusayn b. Wāqid—Abū al-Zubayr—Mujāhid— Ibn ʿAbbās: God's words are, "So proclaim the pilgrimage to mankind." Abraham, the friend of God, stood up on the stone and proclaimed, "O people! The pilgrimage is prescribed for you!" And his voice reached even those yet unborn in the loins of men and the wombs of women. All who believed among those of past generations in God's knowledge that they would perform the pilgrimage between then and the Day of Resurrection answered Abraham, "Here I am, my God, here I am."

According to Ibn Bashshār—ʿAbd al-Raḥmān—Sufyān—Salamah—Mujāhid: Abraham was told, "Proclaim the pilgrimage to mankind." And he said: "O Lord, how shall I say it?" God replied, "Say, 'Here I am, my God, here I am.'" This was the first *Labbayka*.

According to Ibn Ḥumayd—Salamah—Muḥammad b. Isḥāq—ʿUmar b. ʿAbdallāh b. ʿUrwah: ʿAbdallāh b. al-Zubayr asked ʿUbayd b. ʿUmayr al-Laythī, "Have you heard how it was that Abraham called mankind to the pilgrimage?" And ʿUbayd b. ʿUmayr al-Laythī gave the following account:

When Abraham and Ishmael had raised the foundations of the House and had finished the work God wanted them to do on it, and the pilgrimage was at hand, Abraham faced to the south and called (mankind) to God and to pilgrimage to His House. And he was answered with "Here I am, my God, here I am." Then he faced to the east and called (mankind) to God and to pilgrimage to His House, and he was answered with
"Here I am, my God, here I am." Then to the west he called [28
(mankind) to God and to pilgrimage to His House, and he was answered with "Here I am, my God, here I am." Then to the north he called (mankind) to God and to pilgrimage to His House and was answered with "Here I am, my God, here I am." Then he took Ishmael out and went with him on the day of

Tarwiyah[218] and stayed at Minā with him and with the Muslims who were with him, and he prayed with them the prayers of midday, afternoon, sunset, and late evening. Then he spent the night with them until they arose, and he prayed the dawn prayer with them. In the morning he went out with them to ʿArafah, and he spoke to them there until sunset drew near. Then he joined the two prayers, midday and afternoon, and then he went and stood with them at the thorn-bush which is the standing-place of ʿArafah, where the prayer-leader stood teaching him and demonstrating to him. When the sun had set, he urged on the prayer-leader and those who were with him until they came to al-Muzdalifah. There he joined the two prayers of sunset and late evening. Then he spent the night with him and those with him until, when the dawn broke, he prayed the morning prayer with them. Then he stood with them at Quzaḥ of al-Muzdalifah. This is the standing-place where the prayer-leader stands. When day came, he demonstrated and explained to them what to do, including the throwing of the great stone. He showed them the sacrifice-ground of Minā, then performed the sacrifice and shaved his head. From Minā he went into the crowd to show them how to perform the march around the Kaʿbah. Then he took them back to Minā to show them how to throw the stones, until he had compelted the pilgrimage and proclaimed it to mankind.[219]

According to Abū Jaʿfar—the Messenger of God and some of his companions: Gabriel was the one who showed Abraham the ritual acts when he made the pilgrimage.

Discussion of That Account on the Authority of the Messenger of God [289]

According to Abū Kurayb—ʿUbaydallāh b. Mūsā and Muḥammad b. Ismāʿīl al-Aḥmasī—ʿUbaydallāh b. Mūsā —Ibn Abī

218. The eighth day of the pilgrimage. The name is interpreted as meaning either "satisfying thirst" (because camels are given drink) or, more likely, "paying attention," because Abraham gave attention (*rawwā*) to the vision which instructed him to sacrifice his son on this day.

219. All of the above are *manāsik al-ḥajj* or the ritual acts of the pilgrimage.

Laylā—Ibn Abī Mulaykah—ʿAbdallāh b. ʿAmr—the Prophet: Gabriel came to Abraham on the day of Tarwiyah and went with him to Minā, praying with him the midday, afternoon, sunset, late evening, and dawn prayers in Minā. Then in the morning he took Abraham to Arafat and set him down at the thorn bush where people stay, and prayed with him the midday and afternoon prayers together. He stood with Abraham until he had prayed the sunset prayer very quickly, then rushed him into a crowd and prayed with him the sunset and evening prayers together. Then they remained and together they prayed the dawn prayer very quickly, and then very slowly. After that he rushed Abraham to Minā, threw the stones, performed the sacrifice, shaved his head, and finally hurried to the House. Then God ordered Muḥammad to "follow the religion of Abraham, as one upright by nature. He was not an idolator."[220]

According to Abū Kurayb—ʿImrān b. Muḥammad b. Abī Laylā—his father—ʿAbdallāh b. Abī Mulaykah— ʿAbdallāh b. ʿAmr: The Messenger of God told a similar tale.

Then God Tested His Friend Abraham with the Sacrifice of His Son

[290] The earliest sages of our Prophet's nation disagree about which of Abraham's two sons it was that he was commanded to sacrifice. Some say it was Isaac, while others say it was Ishmael. Both views are supported by statements related on the authority of the Messenger of God. If both groups of statements were equally sound, then—since they both come from the Prophet—only the Qur'ān could serve as proof that the account naming Isaac is clearly the more truthful of the two.[221]

The account naming Isaac comes down to us through Abū Kurayb—Zayd b. al-Ḥubāb—al-Ḥasan b. Dīnār— ʿAlī b. Zayd b. Judʿān—al-Ḥasan—al-Aḥnaf b. Qays —al-ʿAbbās b. ʿAbd al-Muṭṭalib—the Prophet in a conversation in which he said,

---

220. Qur'ān, 16:123.

221. Kisā'ī, 160–62, also sees Isaac as the sacrificial victim, although he mentions differing opinions as well. Thaʿlabī, *Qiṣaṣ*, 80–82, presents the conflicting parties and the arguments on both sides, and then presents the story (82–83) in two versions with Isaac and Ishmael as victi ms.

"Then we ransomed him with a tremendous victim."[222] And he also said, "He is Isaac."

As for Who Said That:

According to Abū Kurayb—Ibn Yamān—Mubārak —al-Ḥasan—al-Aḥnaf b. Qays—al-Abbās b. ʿAbd al-Muṭṭalib: The quote, "We ransomed him with a tremendous victim," refers to Isaac.

The account naming Ishmael has come down to us through Muḥammad b. ʿAmmār al-Rāzī—Ismāʿīl b. ʿUbayd b. Abī Karī- [291] mah—ʿUmar b. ʿAbd al-Raḥīm al-Khaṭṭābī —ʿAbdallah b. Muḥammad al-ʿUtbī, a descendant of ʿUtbah b. Abī Sufyān—his father—ʿAbdallah b. Saʿīd—al-Ṣunābiḥī: We were with Muʿāwiyah b. Abī Sufyān and the subject of the victim, Ishmael or Isaac, came up. You have come to a person who knows the answer. We were with the Messenger of God when a man came to him and said, "O Messenger of God! Repeat to me the knowledge God has given you, O son of the two victims!" The Messenger of God laughed and they said to him, "Who are the two victims, O Messenger of God?" He said, "When ʿAbd al-Muṭṭalib was ordered to dig Zamzam, he vowed that if God would make it easy for him, he would sacrifice one of his sons. The choice fell upon ʿAbdāllah, but his maternal uncles prevented it, saying, 'Ransom your son with one hundred camels.' So he did that, and Ishmael was the other victim."

Now we will speak of those early authorities who said it was Isaac, and those who said it was Ishmael.

Concerning Those Who Said It Was Isaac:

According to Abū Kurayb—Ibn Yamān—Mubārak —al-Ḥasan—al-Aḥnaf b. Qays—al-ʿAbbās b. ʿAbd al-Muṭṭalib: The quote, "Then We ransomed him with a tremendous victim," refers to Isaac.

According to al-Ḥusayn b. Yazīd al-Ṭaḥḥān—Ibn

222. Qur'ān, 37:107.

[292] Idrīs—Dāwūd b. Abī Hind—ʿIkrimah—Ibn ʿAbbās: The one whom Abraham was ordered to sacrifice was Isaac.

According to Yaʿqūb—Ibn ʿUlayyah—Dāwūd—ʿIkrimah—Ibn ʿAbbās: The victim was Isaac.

According to Ibn al-Muthannā—Ibn Abī ʿAdī—Dāwūd—ʿIkrimah—Ibn ʿAbbās: The quote, "Then We ransomed him with a tremendous victim," refers to Isaac.

According to Ibn al-Muthannā—Muḥammad b. Jaʿfar—Shuʿbah—Abū Isḥāq—Abū al-Aḥwaṣ: A certain man boasted to Ibn Masʿūd, "I am so-and-so son of so-and-so, son of the noble elders." And ʿAbdallāh said, "This is Joseph b. Jacob, son of Isaac the victim of God, son of Abraham the Friend of God."

According to Ibn Ḥumayd—Ibrāhīm b. al-Mukhtār —Muḥammad b. Isḥāq—ʿAbd al-Raḥmān b. Abī Bakr—al-Zuhrī—al-ʿAlāʾ b. Jāriyah al-Thaqafī —Abū Hurayrah—Kaʿb: When God said, "Then We ransomed him with a tremendous victim," He was speaking of Abraham's son Isaac.

According to Ibn Ḥumayd—Salamah—Muḥammad b. Isḥāq—ʿAbdallāh b. Abī Bakr—Muḥammad b. Muslim al-Zuhrī—Abū Sufyān b. al-ʿAlāʾ b. Jāriyah al-Thaqafī, the confederate of Banū Zuhrah—Abū Hurayrah—Kaʿb al-Aḥbār: The son whom Abraham was commanded to sacrifice was Isaac.

According to Yūnus—Ibn Wahb—Yūnus—Ibn Shi-
[293] hāb—ʿAmr b. Abī Sufyān b. Usayd b. Jāriyah al-Thaqafī: Kaʿb said to Abū Hurayrah, "Should I tell you about Isaac, the son of the prophet Abraham?" Abū Hurayrah answered, "Certainly." So Kaʿb gave the following account:

When Abraham was told to sacrifice Isaac, Satan said, "By God! If I cannot deceive the people of Abraham with this, I shall never be able to do it." So when Abraham went out with Isaac to sacrifice him, Satan visited Abraham's wife, Sarah, in the shape of a man whom Abraham's people knew, and asked her, "Where is Abraham going so early with Isaac?" She said, "He went off early on some errand." Satan said, "No, by God! That is not the reason he left so early." Sarah asked, "Then what is the reason?" He said, "He took him out early to sacrifice him." Sarah said, "There is no truth to that, he would not

sacrifice his own son." Satan said, "By God, it is true." Sarah said, "And why would he sacrifice him?" He replied, "He claims that his Lord ordered him to do it." Sarah said, "If his Lord ordered him to do that, it is best that he obey." Then Satan left Sarah and went to Isaac, who was walking with his father, and said, "Where is your father taking you so early?" Isaac answered, "He is taking me on some errand of his." Satan said, "No, by God, he is not taking you out on an errand. He is taking you out early to sacrifice you." Isaac said, "My father would not sacrifice me." Satan told him, "Certainly he would." Isaac asked, "Why?" Satan told him, "He claims that his Lord ordered him to do it." Isaac answered, "By God! If the Lord told my father to do that, he should certainly obey Him."
So Satan left him and went on to Abraham, saying, "Why are [294]
you taking your son out early?" Abraham said, "I am taking him on an errand." Satan answered, "By God, you took him out early only to sacrifice him." Abraham asked, "Why would I do that?" Satan said, "You claim that your Lord ordered you to do it." Abraham said, "By God, If my Lord orders me to do that, I will surely do it." When Abraham took Isaac to sacrifice him, God stayed his hand and ransomed him with a "tremendous victim." Abraham said to Isaac, "Arise, my little son, for God has released you." And God said to Isaac, "I will grant you any prayer you choose to make now." Isaac said, "My God! I pray to You that I be granted this, that You grant entry into paradise to any worshipper, past or present, who encounters You and does not make anything a partner with You." (Here Kaʿb's account ends.)

According to ʿAmr b. ʿAlī—Abū ʿĀṣim—Sufyān—Zayd b. Aslam—ʿAbdallāh b. ʿUbayd b. ʿUmayr—his father: Moses said, "O Lord! Why are you addressed as 'O God of Abraham, Isaac, and Jacob?'" God answered, "Abraham never considered anything at all equal to Me, but put Me above all things; Isaac was generous to Me in the matter of the sacrifice and in other matters; and as for Jacob, the more tribulations I inflicted upon him the more good thoughts he thought about me."

According to Ibn Bashshār—Mu'ammal—Sufyān—Zayd b. Aslam—ʿAbdallāh b. ʿUbayd b. ʿUmayr—his father: Moses asked God, "O Lord! Why did you give Abraham, Isaac, and Jacob what you gave them?" And God's answer was the same (as that given above).

According to Abū Kūrayb—Ibn Yamān—Isrā'īl—Jābir—Ibn
[295] Sābiṭ: He was Isaac.

According to Abū Kurayb—Ibn Yamān—Sufyān—Abū Sinān al-Shaybānī—Ibn Abī al-Hudhayl: The victim was Isaac.

According to Abū Kurayb—Sufyān b. ʿUqbah—Ḥamzah al-Zayyāt—Abū Isḥāq—Abū Maysarah: Joseph told the king to his face, "You wish to eat with me when I, by God, am Joseph, son of Jacob the prophet of God, son of Isaac the victim of God, son of Abraham the friend of God."

According to Abū Kurayb—Wakīʿ—Sufyān—Abū Sinān—Ibn Abī al-Hudhayl: Joseph said to the king. . . . The (rest of the) account is roughly the same.

According to Mūsā b. Hārūn—ʿAmr b. Ḥammād—Asbāṭ—al-Suddī— Abū Mālik and Abū Ṣāliḥ —Ibn ʿAbbās and Murrah al-Hamdānī—Ibn Masʿūd and some of the companions of the Prophet: Abraham was instructed in a dream to "carry out your promise that if God granted you a son by Sarah you would sacrifice him."

According to Yaʿqūb—Hushaym—Zakariyā' and Shuʿbah—Abū Isḥāq—Masrūq: When God said, "Then we ransomed him with a tremendous victim," that was Isaac.

As for Those Who Said It Was Ishmael:

According to Abū Kurayb and Isḥāq b. Ibrāhīm b. Ḥabīb b. al-
[296] Shahīd—Yaḥyā b. Yamān—Isrā'īl—Thuwayr—Mujāhid—Ibn ʿAmr: The victim was Ishmael.

According to Ibn Bashshār—Yaḥyā—Sufyān—Bayān—al-Sha ʿbī—Ibn ʿAbbās: The quote, "Then We ransomed him with a tremendous victim," refers to Ishmael.

According to Ibn Ḥumayd—Yaḥyā b. Wāḍiḥ—Abū Ḥamzah Muḥammad b. Maymūn al-Sukkarī—ʿAṭā' b. al-Sā'ib—Saʿīd b. Jubayr—Ibn ʿAbbās: The one whom Abraham was commanded to sacrifice was Ishmael.

According to Yaʿqūb—Hushaym—ʿAlī b. Zayd—ʿAmmār, the client of the Banū Hāshim, and Yūsuf b. Mihrān—Ibn

ʿAbbās: Ishmael was the one meant by the statement, "Then We ransomed him with a tremendous victim."

According to Yaʿqūb—Ibn ʿUlayyah—Dāwūd —— al-Shaʿ bī—Ibn ʿAbbās: It was Ishmael.

On another occasion Yaʿqūb—Ibn ʿUlayyah said: Someone asked Dāwūd b. Abī Hind, "Which of his two sons was Abraham ordered to sacrifice?" And Dāwūd quoted al-Shaʿbī as having said, "Ibn ʿAbbās said that it was Ishmael."

According to Ibn al-Muthannā—Muḥammad b. Jaʿfar—Shuʿbah—Bayān—al-Shaʿbī—Ibn ʿAbbās: As for the one [297] whom God ransomed with a tremendous victim, it was Ishmael.

According to Yaʿqūb—Ibn ʿUlayyah—Layth— Mujāhid—Ibn ʿAbbās: God's words, "Then We ransomed him with a tremendous victim," refer to Ishmael.

According to Yūnus b. ʿAbd al-Aʿlā—Ibn Wahb —— ʿUmar b. Qays—ʿAṭāʾ b. Abī Rabāḥ—ʿAbdallāh b. ʿAbbās: The ransomed one was Ishmael, but the Jews claimed it was Isaac. The Jews, however, are untruthful.

According to Muḥammad b. Sinān al-Qazzāz—Abū ʿĀṣim —Mubārak— ʿAlī b. Zayd—Yūsuf b. Mihrān—Ibn ʿAbbās: The one whom God ransomed was Ishmael.

According to Muḥammad b. Sinān—Ḥajjāj—Ḥammād—Abū ʿĀṣim al-Ghanawī—Abū al-Ṭufayl —— Ibn ʿAbbās: A similar statement.

According to Isḥāq b. Shāhīn—Khālid b. ʿAbdallāh —— Dāwūd—ʿĀmir: The one whom Abraham wanted to sacrifice was Ishmael.

According to Ibn al-Muthannā—ʿAbd al-Aʿlā —— Dāwūd —ʿĀmir: This verse, "Then We ransomed him with a tremendous victim," refers to Ishmael, and the two horns of the ram are hanging in the Kaʿbah. [298]

According to Abū Kurayb—Ibn Yamān—Isrāʾīl—Jābir—al-Shaʿbī: The ransomed one was Ishmael.

According to Abū Kurayb—Ibn Yamān—Isrāʾīl—Jābir—al-Shaʿbī: I saw the ram's horns in the Kaʿbah.

According to Abū Kurayb—Ibn Yamān—Mubārak b. Faḍālah—ʿAbī b. Zayd b. Judʿān—Yūsuf b. Mihrān: It was Ishmael.

According to Abū Kurayb—Ibn Yamān—Sufyān—Ibn Abī Najīḥ—Mujāhid: It was Ishmael.

According to Ya'qūb—Hushaym—'Awf—al-Ḥasan: The quote, "Then We ransomed him with a tremendous victim," refers to Ishmael.

According to Ibn Ḥumayd—Salamah—Ibn Isḥāq: I heard Muḥammad b. Ka'b al-Quraẓī saying that the son whom God commanded Abraham to sacrifice was Ishmael. And if we look into the Book of God, in the story of Abraham and the sacrifice of his son, we find that it was indeed Ishmael. When God finished the story about the son of Abraham who was to be sacrificed, He said, "and We gave him tidings of the birth of Isaac, a prophet of the righteous."[223] And He said, "We gave her good tidings of Isaac, and after Isaac of Jacob."[224] He speaks here of a son and a grandson, which means that Isaac could not be the one whom God ordered Abraham to sacrifice, since he had a promise from God about his (Isaac's) future. Thus the one
[299] whom he was ordered to sacrifice was Ishmael.

According to Ibn Ḥumayd—Salamah—Muḥammad b. Isḥāq—Buraydah b. Sufyān b. Farwah al-Aslamī: Muḥammad b. Ka'b al-Quraẓī said that he asked the Caliph 'Umar b. 'Abd al-'Azīz about the matter when they were together in Syria, and 'Umar told him, "I have not looked into this matter, but I do not think it is as you say." Then he sent for a man whom he had with him in Syria, a former Jew who had converted to Islam and became a good Muslim. He was considered to be one of the great Jewish scholars, so 'Umar b. 'Abd al-'Azīz decided to get his view about the matter. He asked him, "Which of his two sons was Abraham commanded to sacrifice?" The man answered, "Ishmael, by God, O Prince of the Believers! The Jews know that, but they are envious of you, O Arabs, because it was your father who was named in God's command and to whom God ascribed such merit for his steadfastness in obeying God's command. They reject that and claim that it was Isaac because Isaac was their father."[225]

---

223. Ibid., 37:112.
224. Ibid., 11:71.
225. This account appears in the Tha'labī, *Qiṣaṣ*, 81.

According to Ibn Ḥumayd—Salamah—Ibn Isḥāq—al-Ḥasan b. Dīnār and ʿAmr b. ʿUbayd—al-Ḥasan b. Abī al-Ḥasan al-Baṣrī: There is no doubt that the son Abraham was ordered to sacrifice was Ishmael.

According to Ibn Ḥumayd—Salamah—Muḥammad b. Isḥāq: I heard Muḥammad b. Kaʿb al-Quraẓī say the same thing often.

As for the above-mentioned proof from the Qur'ān that it really was Isaac, it is God's word which informs us about the [300] prayer of His friend Abraham when he left his people to migrate to Syria with Sarah. Abraham prayed, "I am going to my Lord Who will guide me. My Lord! Grant me a righteous child."[226] This was before he knew Hagar, who was to be the mother of Ishmael. After mentioning this prayer, God goes on to describe His response to the prayer and mentions that He foretold to Abraham that he would have a gentle son. God also mentions Abraham's vision of himself sacrificing that son when he was old enough to walk with him. The Book does not mention any tidings of a male child being given to Abraham except in the instance where it refers to Isaac, in which God said, "And his wife, standing by, laughed when We gave her tidings of Isaac, and after Isaac, of Jacob,"[227] and, "Then he became fearful of them. They said, 'Fear not!' and gave him tidings of a wise son. Then his wife approached, moaning, and smote her face, and cried, 'A barren old woman.'"[228] Thus, wherever the Qur'ān mentions God giving tidings of the birth of a son to Abraham, it refers to Sarah (and thus to Isaac) and the same must be true of God's words "So We gave him tidings of a gentle son,"[229] as it is true of all such references in the Qur'ān.

Some say that God would not have ordered Isaac sacrificed because God foretold his birth before it happened and that of Jacob afterwards, but this claim does not necessarily prove their view correct. God only commanded Abraham to sacrifice Isaac when he was able to walk, and it is conceivable that Jacob [301]

226. Qur'ān, 37:99–100.
227. Ibid., 11:71.
228. Ibid., 51:28–29.
229. Ibid., 37:101.

could have been born to him before his father was commanded to sacrifice him. Some also say that the ram's horn was seen hanging in the Kaʿbah (which would suggest that the sacrifice took place near Mecca and must therefore have involved Ishmael, since Isaac was in Syria). This is not a sensible argument either, because the horn could possibly have been brought from Syria to the Kaʿbah and hung up there.

There follows a discussion of the account about the act of Abraham, the Friend of the Merciful, about his son whom he was commanded to sacrifice, and about the nature of the command and the reason behind it:

The reason God commanded Abraham to sacrifice his son was that, when Abraham fled from Iraq and from his people and went to Syria for the sake of his religion and his Lord, he prayed that God would grant him a righteous male child by Sarah, saying, "My Lord! Grant me a righteous child"[230] and "I am going to my Lord Who will guide me. My lord, grant me a righteous child."[231] And when the angels who were sent to al-Mu'tafikah, the people of Lot, visited Abraham, they gave him tidings of a gentle son as God had commanded them to do. And when they did this, Abraham said, "Then he is a sacrificial victim for God." When the boy was born and had become old enough to walk, Abraham was told, "Fulfill the promise which you made to God."

As for Those Who Said That:

[302] According to Mūsā b. Hārūn—ʿAmr b. Ḥammād—Asbāṭ—al-Suddī—Abū Mālik and Abū Ṣāliḥ—Ibn ʿAbbās and Murrah al-Hamdānī—ʿAbdallāh and some of the companions of the Prophet: Gabriel told Sarah, "Know that [you will have] a son named Isaac, and that after him will come Jacob." And she smote her cheek in wonder, as God said, "She smote her face."[232] She said, "Shall I bear a child when I am an old woman and my husband is an old man? This is indeed a strange

230. Ibid., 37:100.
231. Ibid., 37:99–100.
232. Ibid., 51:29.

thing." They said, "Do you wonder at the commandment of God? May the mercy and blessing of God be upon you, O people of this house! He is the Praiseworthy One, the Glorious One."[233] Sarah said to Gabriel, "What is the sign of this matter?" So he took a dry piece of wood in his hand and bent it between his fingers, and it quivered and turned green. Then Abraham said, "He is therefore a sacrifice to God."

When Isaac grew up, Abraham had a dream in which he saw him and was told, "Fulfill your promise that if God granted you a son by Sarah you would sacrifice him." Then Abraham said to Isaac, "Let us go out and offer a sacrifice to God!" So he took a knife and a rope and set out with Isaac. When they reached the mountains Isaac asked him, "O my father, where is your victim?" Abraham replied, "O my son! I saw in my dream that I should sacrifice you. But consider the matter. What do you think?" Isaac told him, "O my father! Do as you have been commanded. God willing, you will find me steadfast in belief. Fasten my bonds so that I do not move about, and tie back your garments so that none of my blood splashes them, lest Sarah see it and be saddened. And move the knife quickly on my throat so that death comes easily for me. And when you come back to Sarah, greet her with peace." Abraham approached him [303]
to kiss him after tying him up; both of them cried until the tears gathered in a pool beneath Isaac's side. Then he drew the knife across Isaac's throat, but the knife did not even scratch him, for God had placed a sheet of copper on Isaac's throat. When Abraham saw that, he turned him over and tried to cut him on the nape of his neck; as God has said, "Then, when they had both surrendered, and he had flung him down upon his face."[234] Then they turned the matter over to God, and God proclaimed, "O Abraham! You have carried out the dream in full. Turn around!" He turned around and saw a ram. He seized the ram and kissed his son, saying, "O my son! Today you have been given to me." This is the meaning of God's saying, "Then We ransomed him with a tremendous victim."[235]

---

233. Ibid., 11:72–73.
234. Ibid., 37:103.
235. Ibid., 37:107.

Then he went back to Sarah and told her the story, and Sarah became sad and said, "You wanted to sacrifice my son and did not tell me."

According to Ibn Ḥumayd—Salamah—Muḥammad b. Isḥāq: It is said that when Abraham visited Hagar he was carried on al-Burāq, setting out early from Syria. He rested at midday in Mecca, then left Mecca and spent the night with his family in Syria. This was before Isaac was able to walk and take care of himself, at which point Abraham expected him to do his duty by worshipping his Lord and glorifying His sanctity. Then Abraham was shown in a dream that he had to sacrifice Isaac.

Ishmael

According to Ibn Ḥumayd—Salamah—Ibn Isḥāq —— certain scholars: When Abraham was ordered to sacrifice his son, he said to him, "O my son! Take the ropes and the knife and let us
[304] go to this trail to gather firewood for your family there." He did not at this point mention anything about what he had been told to do. When he headed for the trail, Iblīs, the enemy of God, stood in his way in the form of a man in an attempt to dissuade him from carrying out God's command. He said, "Where are you going, old man?" Abraham answered, "I am heading for this trail for something I need in it." Iblīs said, "By God! I think that Satan has come to you in a dream and commanded you to sacrifice this little son of yours, so you are about to sacrifice him." But then Abraham recognized Iblīs and said to him, "Go away, O enemy of God! By God, I am obeying the command of my Lord in this matter."

Then Iblīs despaired of dissuading Abraham and appeared to Ishmael, who was walking behind Abraham carrying the ropes and the knife, and said to him, "O lad, do you know where your father is taking you?" Ishmael answered, "To get firewood for our family from this trail." Iblīs said, "By God! All he wants is to sacrifice you." Ishmael asked, "Why?" Iblīs said, "He claims that his Lord commanded him to do it." Ishmael said, "Then let him do what his Lord commanded; to hear is to obey."

When the boy refused to have anything to do with him, Iblīs

went to Ishmael's mother Hagar in her dwelling and said to her, "O mother of Ishmael! Do you know where Abraham has taken Ishmael?" She said, "He took him to gather wood for us on the trail." Iblīs said, "He took him only to sacrifice him." Hagar said, "Never! He is too merciful to him and loves him too much for that." Iblīs told her, "He claims that God commanded him to do it." She said, "If his Lord commanded him to do it, then one should surrender to the command of God."

So the enemy of God returned enraged, for he had not achieved anything with the family of Abraham. They had all refused to deal with him, by God's help, and they had agreed with God's command, saying, "To hear is to obey."

When Abraham was alone with his son on the trail—a trail on Mt. Thabīr,[236] it is said—he said to Ishmael, "O my son! I [305] saw in a dream that I was to sacrifice you. So consider, what do you think?" Ishmael told him, "O my father! Do as you were commanded. God willing, you will find me steadfast in faith."

According to Ibn Ḥumayd—Salamah—Muḥammad b. Isḥāq—certain scholars: Ishmael said to him, "O my father! If you want to sacrifice me, tighten my bonds so that nothing of me will strike you and lessen my reward, for death is mighty and I am not sure that I will not move with it when I become aware of its touch. Sharpen your knife-blade so that it will finish me off quickly and give me rest. When you lay me down to sacrifice me, turn me with my face down; do not lay me on my side, for I fear that if you look at my face pity will overcome you and hold you back from carrying out God's command. If you think that taking my shirt back to my mother may console her for my loss, then do it."

Abraham said, "How well you help me, my son, in carrying out God's command!" Then he bound Ishmael as he had said, and made him fast, and sharpened his blade. Then he laid him down on his front to guard his gaze from his face. Then he plunged the blade into Ishmael's throat, but God turned it on its backside in his hand. When he pulled it back and forth to complete the act the words were proclaimed, "O Abraham!

236. A name given to several mountains in the vicinity of Mecca; see Yāqūt, *Muʿjam*, I, 917ff.

You have carried out the dream. This victim is yours as a ransom for your son, so sacrifice it instead of him." God said, "Then when they had both surrendered, and he had flung him down on his face;"[237] however, victims are flung on their sides. One of the things which confirms that Ishmael did indeed say "Turn me on my face," as the account says, is God's
[306] saying, ". . . and flung him down on his face, We called unto him, 'O Abraham! You have already fulfilled the dream.' Thus do We reward the good. That was indeed a clear test. Then We ransomed him with a tremendous victim."[238]

According to Ibn Ḥumayd—Salamah—Ibn Isḥāq—al-Ḥasan b. Dīnār—Qatādah b. Diʿāmah —Jaʿfar b. Iyās—ʿAbdallāh b. ʿAbbās: A ram came forth to him from the Garden in which it had been grazing for forty autumns, so Abraham released his son. The ram followed him and he took it to the first stoning-place and threw seven pebbles at it, then set it free there. Then he took it to the middle stoning-place and threw seven pebbles at it, then released it. He caught up with it at the great stoning-place and again threw seven pebbles at it. Finally he took it to the slaughtering-place of Minā and sacrificed it. By Him in Whose hand is the soul of Ibn ʿAbbās! when Islam began, the ram's head and horns were hanging on the downspout of the Kaʿbah, thereafter it became debased, that is, dried up.

According to Muḥammad b. Sinān al-Qazzāz—Ḥajjāj—Ḥammād—Abū ʿĀṣim al-Ghanawī—Abū al-Ṭufayl—Ibn ʿAbbās: When Abraham was commanded to perform all the rituals, Satan appeared to him at the running-place and raced him, but Abraham outran him. Then when Gabriel took Abraham to the stoning-place of al-ʿAqabah, Satan appeared to him, but Abraham threw seven pebbles at him and he left. At the middle stoning-place he appeared to him again, and again Abraham threw seven pebbles at him and he left. Then he flung Ishmael on his face. Ishmael had on a white shirt, so he said to Abraham, "O my father! I have no garment in which you may
[307] bury me except this, so take it off me and then bury me in it."

---

237. Qur'ān, 37:103.
238. Ibid., 37:103–107.

Then Abraham turned and saw a horned, black-eyed, white ram, and he sacrificed it.

Ibn ʿAbbās said: You have seen us studying this species of ram.

According to Muḥammad b. ʿAmr—Abū ʿĀṣim—ʿĪsa and al-Ḥārith—al-Ḥasan—Warqāʾ, all of them—Ibn Abī Najīḥ—Mujāhid: God's words, "and he flung him down on his face,"[239] mean "he put his face toward the earth." Ishmael said, "Do not sacrifice me while looking at my face, lest you have pity on me and do not finish me off. Tie my hand to my neck, then place my face to the ground."

According to Abū Kurayb—Ibn Yamān—Sufyān —Jābir—Abū al-Ṭufayl—ʿAlī: The victim mentioned in the quote, "We ransomed him with a tremendous victim,"[240] was a black-eyed, horned, white ram fastened to an acacia tree in Thabīr.

According to Yūnus—Ibn Wahb Ibn Jurayj—ʿAṭāʾ b. Abī Rabāḥ—Ibn ʿAbbās: The quote, "We ransomed him with a tremendous victim," refers to a ram. ʿUbayd b. ʿUmayr said that it was slain on the spot, while Mujahid said that it was sacrificed at Minā at the sacrificing-place.

According to Ibn Bashshār—ʿAbd al-Raḥmān— Sufyān—Ibn Khuthaym—Saʿīd b. Jubayr— Ibn ʿAbbās: The ram which Abraham sacrificed was the ram which the son of Adam had offered up, and it was accepted from him.

According to Ibn Ḥumayd—Yaʿqūb—Jaʿfar —Saʿīd b. Jubayr: As for the quote, "We ransomed him with a tremendous victim," the ram which Abraham sacrificed had grazed in the Garden for forty years. Its wool was mixed white and black, like red-dyed wool.

According to Abū Kurayb—Muʿāwiyah b. Hishām— [308]
Sufyān—a man—Abū Ṣāliḥ———Ibn ʿAbbās: The quote, "We ransomed him with a tremendous victim," refers to a mountain goat.

According to Ibn Ḥumayd—Salamah—Ibn Isḥāq —ʿAmr b. ʿUbayd—al-Ḥasan: Ishmael was ransomed only by a mountain

239. Ibid., 37:103.
240. Ibid., 37:107.

goat, which was sent down to him from Thabīr. God's words, "We ransomed him with a tremendous victim," do not refer only to this sacrifice, but rather to the practice of slaughtering animals according to His religion, for that is the *sunnah* until the Day of Resurrection. Know that sacrifice wards off an evil death, so sacrifice, O servants of God![241]

In a poem about the reason for which Abraham was commanded to sacrifice his son, Umayyah b. Abī al-Ṣalt[242] verifies the account of al-Suddī to the effect that the sacrifice was required of Abraham to fulfill a vow which he had made:

Abraham, the one who carries out the vow
to satisfaction, and the bearer of easy-burning firewood

For his firstborn, could not desist from him
or see himself in a company of enemies.

"O my son! I have consecrated you to God
as a slaughtered kid, but be steadfast; a ransom for you is ready.

Bind the fetters; I shall not turn from the knife
the head of the manacled captive."

For he has a knife which is quick in the flesh
a cutting edge curved like a crescent moon.

[309] While he was taking his garments from him
his Lord ransomed him with the best of rams.

"So take this and release your son; verily I
do not dislike what you two have done."

---

241. Although nothing in the Qur'ān specifically connects the sacrifice performed on the tenth day of the pilgrimage to the sacrifice required of Abraham, later Muslim writers have made this connection.

242. Umayyah b. Abī al-Ṣalt, a poet of Thaqīf at the time of the Prophet; *GAL*, I, 27–28.

A God-fearing father and the other, his offspring;
they fled from him on hearing, "Do it!"

People often are unhappy about a thing
which brings relief, like the untying of bonds.

According to Ibn Ḥumayd—Yaḥyā b. Wāḍiḥ—al-Ḥusayn, meaning Ibn Wāqid—Zayd—ʿIkrimah: God's words, "when they had both surrendered,"[243] refer to their surrender to God's command. The boy was satisfied to be the sacrifice, and the father was content to sacrifice him. The son said, "O my father! Throw me down on my face, lest you look at me and have pity on me, or I look at the knife and become anxious. Thrust the knife from beneath me and obey God's command." For it is as God said, "Then, when they had both surrendered, he flung him down on his face." When he had done that, "then We called unto him, 'O Abraham! You have already fulfilled the dream.' Thus do We reward the good."[244]

After God had put Abraham to the test—when Nimrod b. Cush tried to burn him in the fire, and when He commanded him to sacrifice his son after he had become old enough to walk and Abraham hoped for his help in coming closer to his Lord, and when He made him raise the foundations of the House and devote himself to its rituals—after all this, He put Abraham to the test with still further commands which He has mentioned, for He said, "And when his Lord tried Abraham with commands and he fulfilled them."[245]

The earliest scholars of the Islamic community (*ummah*) disagreed about the nature of these commandments with which God tested Abraham and which Abraham obeyed. Some [310]
say that the commands were thirty portions, that is to say, the laws of Islam.[246]

---

243. Qur'ān, 37:103.
244. See ibid., 37:103–105.
245. Ibid., 2:124.
246. Abraham is here instructed in the fulfillment of the basic duties of Islam which are looked upon as the duties of "natural religion" (*fiṭrah*). In the aggadic accounts, Abraham is shown the course of the history of his descendants and is told that if they study the Torah and maintain the Temple service they will avoid hellfire and alien rule; see Ginzberg, *Legends*, I, 236.

Concerning Those Who Said That:

According to Muḥammad b. al-Muthannā—ʿAbd al-Aʿlā—Dāwūd—ʿIkrimah—Ibn ʿAbbās: Concerning God's words, "and when his Lord tried Abraham with commands," Abraham was the only man who was tried with this obligation and who fulfilled it correctly. God tested him with commands and he fulfilled them. God wrote his exemption for him when He said, "And Abraham who paid his debt."[247] Ten of the commands are in "al-Aḥzāb" (*sūrah* 33), ten in "Barā'ah" (*surah* 9), and ten in "al-Mu'minīn" (*surah* 23) and in "Sa'ala Sạ'il" (*sūrah* 70). Thus Islam has thirty portions.

According to Isḥāq b. Shāhīn al-Wāsiṭī—Khālid al-Ṭaḥḥān—Dāwud—ʿIkrimah—Ibn ʿAbbas: No one who was tested with this obligation stood up to it except for Abraham, who was tested with Islam (surrender) and fulfilled it all. Thereupon God wrote his immunity[248] for him, saying, "And Abraham who paid his debt." He mentioned ten (commands) in "Barā'ah": "Those who turn repentant; those who worship; those who praise;"[249] and ten in "al-Aḥzāb": "Men who surrender unto God, and women who surrender;"[250] ten in *sūrat* "al-Mu'minīn," up to where He says, "And who pay heed to their prayers;"[251] and ten in "Sa'ala Sā'il": "And those who are attentive at their worship."[252]

According to ʿAbdallāh b. Aḥmad al-Marwzaī—ʿAlī b. al-Ḥasan—Khārijah b. Muṣʿab—Dāwūd b. Abī Hind— [311]
ʿIkrimah—Ibn ʿAbbās: Islam consists of thirty parts, and no one ever tested with this obligation carried it out, except Abraham. God said, "And Abraham who paid his debt,"[253] granting him immunity from the fire.

Other scholars have said that the commands were ten practices of Islam, five being in the head and five in the body.

---

247. Qur'ān, 53:37.
248. That is, from hellfire. See below.
249. Ibid., 9:112.
250. Ibid., 33:35.
251. Ibid., 23:1–9.
252. Ibid., 70:34.
253. Ibid., 53:37.

Concerning Those Who Said That:

According to al-Ḥasan b. Yaḥyā—ʿAbd al-Razzāq—Maʿmar—Ibn Ṭāwūs—his father—Ibn ʿAbbās: This quote, "And when his Lord tried Abraham with commands," means that God tested him with the acts of ritual purification, five in the head and five in the body. Those in the head are: trimming the mustache, rinsing the mouth, cleansing the nostrils with water, using the toothstick, and parting the hair (with the fingers). Those in the body are: paring the nails, shaving the pubic hair, circumcision, plucking the armpit, and washing off the traces of feces and urine with water.

According to al-Muthannā—Isḥāq—ʿAbd al-Razzāq—Maʿmar—al-Ḥakam b. Abān—al-Qāsim b. Abī Bazzah—Ibn ʿAbbās: A similar list, except that he did not mention traces of urine.

According to Ibn Bashshār—Sulaymān b. Ḥarb— Abū Hilāl—Qatādah: God's words, "And when his Lord tried Abraham with commands,"[254] mean that he tested him with circumcision, shaving the pubic hair, washing the fore-part and rear, using the toothstick, trimming the mustache, paring the nails, and plucking the armpit. Abū Hilāl notes that he forgot one characteristic.

According to ʿAbdān al-Marwazī—ʿAmmār b. al-Ḥasan— [312]
ʿAbdallāh b. Abī Jaʿfar—his father—Maṭar—Abū Khālid: Abraham was tested with ten Islamic practices: rinsing the mouth, cleansing the nostrils with water, trimming the mustache, using the toothstick, plucking the armpit, paring the nails, washing the finger-joints, circumcision, shaving the pubic hair, and washing the rear and the vulva.

Others have said the same, except that they said that six of the ten commands were to do with the body and four of them were to do with the cultic stations.

Concerning Those Who Said That:

According to al-Muthannā—Isḥāq—Muḥammad b. Ḥarb—Ibn Luhayʿah—Ibn Hubayrah—Ḥanash—Ibn ʿAbbās: As for His

254. Ibid., 2:124.

saying, "And when his Lord tried Abraham with commands and he fulfilled them,"[255] six of the commands are in the person and four are in the cultic stations. Those which are in the person are shaving the pubic hair, circumcision, plucking the armpit, paring the nails, trimming the mustache, and bathing on Friday. The four which are in the cultic stations are walking around the Kaʿbah, running between al-Ṣafā and al-Marwah, stoning the pillars, and hurrying.

Others have said that the commands consisted of His saying, "I have appointed you a leader for mankind,"[256] and of the rituals of the pilgrimage.

Concerning Those Who Said That:

According to Abū Kurayb—Ibn Idrīs—Ismā'īl b. Abī Khālid—Abū Ṣāliḥ: When God said, "And when his Lord tried
[313] Abraham with commands and he fulfiled them," the commands He meant include the words, "I have appointed you a leader for mankind," and the verses of the rituals.

According to Abū al-Sā'ib—Ibn Idrīs—Ismāʿīl b. Abī Khālid—Abū Ṣāliḥ, the client of Umm Hāni': When God said, "And when his Lord tried Abraham with commands," those commands included the words, "I have appointed you a leader for mankind," the verses of the rituals, and the words, "And when Abraham was raising the foundations of the House."[257]

According to Muḥammad b. ʿAmr—Abū ʿĀṣim— ʿĪsa b. Abī Najīḥ—Mujāhid: Regarding His words, "And when his Lord tried Abraham with commands and he fulfilled them," God said to Abraham, "I am trying you with a command. What is it?" Abraham said, "You are appointing me a leader for mankind." God said, "Yes." Abraham asked, "And what of my offspring?" God said, "My covenant does not include wrongdoers."[258] Then Abraham said, "You will make this House a resort for mankind."[259] God said, "Yes." Abraham said, "And

255. Id.
256. Id.
257. Ibid., 2:127.
258. Ibid., 2:124.
259. Ibid., 2:125.

You will make this town a sanctuary." God said, "Yes." Abraham said, "You will make us submissive unto You, and will make of our offspring a nation submissive unto You." God said, "Yes." Abraham said, "You will show us our ways of worship, and You will relent toward us."[260] God said, "Yes." Abraham said, "And You will bestow fruits upon the people, upon those of them that believe."[261] God said, "Yes."

According to al-Qāsim—al-Ḥusayn—Ḥajjāj—Ibn Jurayj—Mujāhid: A similar story. Ibn Jurayj said: Both Mujāhid and ʿIkrimah agree on this.

According to Ibn Wakīʿ—his father—Sufyān—Ibn Abī Najīḥ—Mujāhid: The quote, "And when his Lord tried Abraham with commands and he fulfilled them," means that Abraham was tested with the commands in the verses which come after that one. God said, "Verily I am appointing you a leader for mankind." Abraham asked, "And my offspring?" God said, "My covenant does not include wrongdoers."

According to al-Muthannā b. Ibrāhīm—Abū Hudhayfah—Shibl—Ibn Abī Najīḥ: ʿIkrimah told me this, and when I re- [314]
peated it to Mujāhid he did not disapprove of it.

According to Mūsā b. Hārūn—ʿAmr b. Ḥammād—Asbāṭ—al-Suddī: Those commands with which Abraham was tested were: "Our Lord! Accept from us. You, only You, are the Hearer, the Knower. Our Lord! Make us submissive to You and make of our seed a nation submissive to You. And show us our ways of worship and relent toward us. You, only You, are the Relenting, the Merciful. Our Lord! Raise up in their midst a messenger."[262]

I relate the following according to ʿAmmār b. al-Ḥasan—ʿAbdallāh b. Abī Jaʿfar—his father—al-Rabīʿ: Regarding God's word "And when his Lord tried Abraham with commands," the commands were His word "I have appointed you a leader for mankind," and His Word "And when We made the House a resort for mankind and a sanctuary," and His word "Take as your place of worship where Abraham stood," and

260. Ibid., 2:128.
261. Ibid., 2:126.
262. Ibid., 2:127–129.

His word "We imposed a duty on Abraham and Ishmael, etc.," and His word "And when Abraham was raising the foundation of the House, etc." All of these were among the commands with which Abraham was tested.

According to Muḥammad b. Saʿd—his father—his paternal uncle—his father—his father—Ibn ʿAbbās: Regarding God's word, "And when his Lord tried Abraham with commands," those commands included, the words "I have appointed you a leader for mankind," and "And when Abraham was raising the foundations of the House." They also included the verses regarding the acts of worship and the standing-place which He appointed for Abraham, and the sustenance which He provided for the dweller of the House. Muḥammad was sent among the seed of the two of them.

There are also those who have said that the commands specifically referred to the acts of the pilgrimage.

[315] *Concerning Those Who Said That:*

According to Ibn Bashshār—Salm b. Qutaybah—ʿAmr b. Nabhān—Qatādah—Ibn ʿAbbās: Regarding God's word, "And when his Lord tried Abraham with commands," those commands were the acts of the pilgrimage.

According to Bishr b. Muʿādh—Yazīd—Saʿīd—Qatādah—Ibn ʿAbbās: Regarding His word, "And when his Lord tried Abraham with commands," those were the ritual acts.

I relate (the following according to)—ʿAmmar b. al-Ḥasan—Ibn Abī Jaʿfar—his father—Ibn ʿAbbās: The commands with which Abraham was tested were the ritual acts.

According to Aḥmad b. Isḥāq al-Ahwāzī—Abū Aḥmad al-Zubayrī—Isrāʾīl—Abū Isḥaq—al-Tamīmī—Ibn ʿAbbās: God's word, "And when his Lord tried Abraham with commands and he fulfilled them," refers to the acts of the pilgrimage.

According to Ibn al-Muthannā—al-Himmānī—Sharīk—Abū Isḥāq—al-Tamīmī—Ibn ʿAbbās: A similar version.

According to al-Ḥasan b. Yaḥyā—ʿAbd al-Razzāg—Maʿmar
[316] —Qatādah—Ibn ʿAbbās: God tested him with the ritual acts.

Others, however, have denied this, saying that He tested him with other things including circumcision.

Concerning Those Who Said That:

According to Ibn Bashshār—Salm b. Qutaybah—Yūnus b. Abī Isḥāq—al-Shaʿbī: In the quote, "And when his Lord tried Abraham with commands," those commands included circumcision.

According to Ibn Ḥumayd—Yaḥyā b. Wāḍiḥ—Yūnus b. Abī Isḥāq—al-Shaʿbī: Something similar.

According to Aḥmad b. Isḥāq—Abū Aḥmad: When Abū Isḥāq asked al-Shaʿbī about God's word, "And when his Lord tried Abraham with commands," al-Shaʿbī said, "One of them is circumcision, O Abū Isḥāq!"

Others have said that the commands were six tests: the star, the moon, the sun, the fire, emigration, and circumcision, and that Abraham was tested with all of them and remained steadfast in faith through all of them.

Concerning Those Who Said That:

According to Yaʿqūb b. Ibrāhīm—Ibn ʿUlayyah—Abū Rajāʾ: I asked al-Ḥasan about the quote, "And when his Lord tried Abraham with commands and he fulfilled them." Al-Ḥasan said, "He tested him with the star and was satisfied with him; He tested him with the moon and was satisfied with him; He tested him with the sun and was satisfied with him; He tested him with fire and was satisfied with him; He tested him with emigration; and He tested him with circumcision."

According to Bishr—Yazīd b. Zurayʿ—Saʿīd—Qatādah—al-Ḥasan: When God tested Abraham with a command, he was steadfast in obeying it. He tested him with the star, the sun, and the moon, and he did well with those and knew that his Lord is eternal and He will not cease. Then he turned his face to the One Who created the heavens and the earth, as one up- [317]
right by nature; he was not one of those who attributed partners to God. Then He tested him with emigration, and he left

his land and took his people to Syria, journeying to God. Before the emigration He tested him with fire and he was steadfast, and He tested him with the sacrifice of his son and with circumcision, and he was steadfast.

According to al-Ḥasan b. Yaḥyā—ʿAbd al-Razzāq—Maʿmar—someone—al-Ḥasan: His word, "And when his Lord tried Abraham with commmands," means He tested him with the star, the sun, and the moon.

According to Ibn Bashshār—Salm b. Qutaybah—Abū Hilāl—al-Ḥasan: The quote "And when his Lord tried Abraham with commands," means He tested him with the star, the sun, and the moon, and found him steadfast.

According to Aḥmad b. Isḥāq al-Mukhtār—Ghassān b. al-Rabīʿ—ʿAbdal-Raḥmān namely Ibn Thawbān—ʿAbdallāh b. al-Faḍl—ʿAbd al-Raḥmān al-Aʿraj—Abū Hurayrah—the Messenger of God: Abraham was circumcised after eighty years, in al-Qadūm.

Two accounts have come down to us from the Prophet on the subject of the commands with which Abraham was tested. One of them is according to Abū Kurayb—al-Ḥasan b. ʿAṭiy-
[318] yah—Isrāʾīl—Jaʿfar b. al-Zubayr—al-Qāsim—Abū Umāmah—the Messenger of God: Do you know what debt was meant by the quote, "And Abraham who paid his debt?"[263] They said, "God and His Messenger knows best." He said, "He paid the duty of each day, four prostrations during the day."

The other one is according to Abū Kurayb—Rishdīn b. Saʿd—Zabbān b. Fāʾid—Sahl b. Muʿādh b. Anas—his father: The Messenger of God used to say, "Should I not tell you why God named Abraham His friend who paid his debt? It was because, whenever it was morning and whenever night came, he used to say, 'So glory be to God when you enter the night and when you enter the morning . . .' and so on to the end of the verse."[264]

When God realized Abraham's steadfastness of faith through all the tests He gave him, his fulfilling of all the duties which He laid upon him, and his preferring obedience to Him in ev-

263. Ibid., 53:37.
264. Ibid., 30:17–18.

erything over anything else, He took him as His friend and appointed him a leader for all those of His creatures who were to come after him. He chose him as messenger to His creation and appointed for his descendants prophecy, scripture, and mission. He singled them out with revealed scriptures and profound wisdom. He appointed from among them authorities and leaders, chiefs and sovereigns. Whenever one noble passed from among them, He would replace him with a lofty lord and preserved for them mention among the last. All the nations take Abraham as a friend, and extol him, and speak of his excellence as an honor to him from God in this world. The esteem which God has stored up for Abraham in the hereafter is more splendid and tremendous than anyone can describe.

Let us now return to the account of the enemy of God and of
Abraham, who refused to believe in what Abraham had [319]
brought from God and who rejected Abraham's counsel out of ignorance and error about God's indulgence with him.

Nimrod b. Cush[265]

b. Canaan b. Ham b. Noah, and what happened to him in this world when he rebelled against his Lord, even though God was forbearing with him and did not make haste to punish him for his unbelief in Him and for his attempt to burn His friend Abraham for calling upon him (Nimrod) to believe only in God and to abandon his gods and idols. Nimrod's arrogance and rebelliousness against his Lord went on for a long time—some say for four hundred years—in spite of God's forbearance with him. The proofs of Himself which God advanced to Nimrod and the examples which He showed him only made Nimrod persist in his transgression. As some have mentioned, God punished him in this world. This punishment, which extended over a span of time as long as that during which God had been forbearing with him, was carried out by means of the weakest of His creatures—a gnat to which God gave dominion over Nimrod.

---

265. The story of the children of Cush and Nimrod is given by Kisā'ī, 128–136: Tha'labī, *Qiṣaṣ*, 84–85, is closer to the account given here.

Accounts Which Have Reached Us about Him

Concerning what I have mentioned about his ignorance and the vengeance which God set in motion against him, according to al-Ḥasan b. Yaḥyā—ʿAbd al-Razzāq—Maʿmar—Zayd b. Aslam: The first tyrant on earth was Nimrod. People used to go to him seeking provisions of food. When they came to him he would ask them, "Who is your lord?" They would say, "You." When Abraham came to him, he asked him, "Who is your lord?" Abraham answered, "My Lord is He Who gives life and
[320] causes death." Nimrod told him, "I give life and cause death." Abraham said, "God brings the sun from the East; so cause it to rise in the West." "Thus was the disbeliever abashed."[266] So he sent Abraham away without food.

Abraham went back to his family. On the way he passed a dust-colored sand dune and said to himself, "Let me take some of this and bring it to my family, to make them feel better when I come to them." So he took some of it to bring to his family. He put his baggage down and slept. His wife arose, went to his baggage and opened it, and found there the best food anyone had ever seen. So she prepared some of it and presented it to him. To his knowledge the family had no food, so he asked, "From where did this come?" She answered, "From the food which you brought." So he knew that God had supplied it to him, and he praised God.

Then God sent an angel to the tyrant, saying, "Believe in Me and I will leave you in your realm." Nimrod said, "Is there any lord besides me?" The angel came a second time and said the same, and again Nimrod refused. And he came a third time, and yet again Nimrod refused. So the angel said to him, "Gather your assembly in three days." The tyrant gathered his assembly, and God gave a command to the angel and he unleashed upon them a swarm of gnats. The sun was blotted out by their numbers. God sent the gnats against them, and they ate their flesh and drank their blood, and nothing but their bones was left.

---

266. Qurʾān, 2:258.

The king was as before, however; none of that befell him. But God sent to him a single gnat which entered his nostril and went on beating the inside of his head with hammers for four hundred years. The most merciful to him of his friends was he who bunched up his hands and beat Nimrod's head with them. He had been a tyrant for four hundred years and God punished him for four hundred years—just as long as he had reigned—and then He caused him to die. He was the one who built a tower to heaven, only to have God strike at its foundations—it was about this that God said, "So God struck at the foundations of their building."[267]

According to Mūsā b. Hārūn—ʿAmr b. Ḥammad—Asbāṭ—al-Suddī—Abū Mālik and Abū Ṣāliḥ—Ibn ʿAbbās and—Murrah—Ibn Masʿūd and—some of the companions of the Prophet: The one who argued with Abraham about his Lord gave orders that Abraham be sent out of the city, and he was sent out. He met Lot, the son of his brother, at the gate and called upon him, and he believed in him. Abraham said, "I am a fugitive unto my Lord."[268] [321]

Nimrod had vowed to seek out Abraham's God. He took four eagle fledgelings and nurtured them on meat and wine so that they grew up tough and strong. Then he tied them to a chest and sat in that chest. He suspended a piece of meat over them, and they flew up trying to reach it. When they had risen high in the sky, Nimrod looked down and beheld the earth. He saw the mountains crawling below like creeping ants. When they had risen still higher he looked down again and saw the earth with a sea surrounding it, as though it were a sphere in water. After climbing still higher for a long time, he came into a region of darkness and could not see what was above him, nor what was below him. He became frightened and threw the meat down, and the eagles followed it, darting downwards. When the mountains saw them coming near, darting down, and heard their noise, they became afraid and almost moved from their places, but did not do so. As God says, "Verily they have plot-

---

267. Ibid., 16:26. See the building of the tower by Nimrod in the aggadic account, Ginzberg, *Legends*, I, 178–181.

268. Qur'ān, 29:26.

ted their plot, and their plot is with God, even if their plot were one whereby the mountains should be moved."[269] The reading of Ibn Masʿūd has it, "though their plot were almost one."
[322] They took off from Jerusalem and they fell down in the Mountain of Smoke.

When Nimrod saw that this method would accomplish nothing, he began building the tower. He built it taller and taller until, when it reached heaven, he went up to the top to look, in his pride, at the God of Abraham. Then he voided excrement though he had not done so. God seized his building by its foundations and the roof fell down upon them, "and doom came upon them whence they knew not"[270]—from their place of safety. And He took them from the foundations of the building, and it was demolished. Then it fell, and on that day the languages of mankind became confused from fright, and mankind came to speak seventy-three languages. Before that the only language had been Syriac. It was thus called Babel.

According to Ibn Wakīʿ—Abū Dāwūd al-Ḥafarī—Yaʿqūb—Ḥafṣ b. Ḥumayd or Jaʿfar—Saʿīd b. Jubayr: "Even if their plot were one whereby the mountains should be moved."[271] Nimrod, master of the eagles, ordered a chest brought. He was placed in it, and placed another man in it with him. Then he commanded the eagles and they carried them aloft. When they had risen to a great height, Nimrod asked his companion, "What do you see?" He answered, "I see the water and the island"—meaning the world. After they had climbed higher, he again asked his companion, "What do you see?" He answered, "We are only growing farther from heaven." And Nimrod said, "Descend!"

Someone else has said: A voice proclaimed, "O tyrant, where do you want to go?" The mountains heard the rustling of the eagles and thought it was something from heaven, and would have moved, for that is His Word, "Even if their plot were one whereby the mountains should be moved."

According to al-Ḥasan b. Muḥammad—Muḥammad b. Abī

---

269. Ibid., 14:46.
270. Ibid., 16:26.
271. Ibid., 14:46. That is, it would still count for nothing against God.

ʿAdī—Shuʿbah—Abū Isḥāq—ʿAbd al-Raḥmān b. Dāniyal—ʿAlī: Regarding the verse "even if their plot were one whereby [323] the mountains should be moved," the one who argued with Abraham about his Lord took two small eagles and raised them until they became tough, strong, and mature. Then he tied a foot of each one of them to a chest by a string. He starved them, and sat in the chest with another man. Then he raised a staff in the chest, with meat at its top end, and the eagles ascended. Nimrod began saying to his companion, "Look! What do you see?" He described what he saw, finally saying, "I see the world as though it were insects." Then he said "Aim!" And he aimed it and they descended. And this is His word, "even if their plot were one whereby the mountains should be moved." Abū Isḥaq said: Thus in the reading of ʿAbdallāh, it is, "Though their plot were almost. . . ."

This is what is mentioned of the story of Nimrod b. Cush b. Canaan.

Some say that this Nimrod b. Cush b. Canaan was the king of the entire earth, east and west. This is a statement which scholars familiar with the biographies of kings and with the accounts of the past reject. This is because they accept the fact that Abraham was born during the era of al-Ḍaḥḥāk b. Andarmāsb, (concerning whom we have given some accounts above), and that at that time this al-Ḍaḥḥāk was the king of all the earth. One of those who knew about the era of al-Ḍaḥḥāk, who was uncertain about the extent of Nimrod's power, said that he did not know the truth of the matter even though certain accounts had been related to him on the subject. These accounts said that there were four kings who ruled the whole world, two unbelievers and two believers. The unbelievers were Nimrod and Nechuchadnezzar, while the believers were Solomon b. David and Alexander. Those chroniclers who speak of the matter say that it was al-Ḍaḥḥāk who was king of the [324] earth, east and west, during Abraham's time, and that Nimrod and al-Ḍaḥḥāk were the same person. Scholars expert in the accounts of the forebears and in knowledge of the affairs of the peoples of ancient times have a different view, because according to them it is well known that Nimrod was of Nabatean origin, whereas al-Ḍaḥḥāk was of Persian origin. On the other hand, scholars expert in the accounts of past generations and ancient nations have mentioned that al-Ḍaḥḥāk placed the Sawād and its surroundings to the right and the left under the rule of Nimrod, and made him and his descendants governors there. Al-Ḍaḥḥāk traveled around a great deal from country to country, but his homeland and that of his grandparents was Danbawand and the mountains of Ṭabaristān. It was there that Afarīdhūn shot at him when he overcame him and bound him in iron.

In the same way, Nebuchadnezzar was warlord of the lands[272] extending from al-Ahwāz to the land of the Byzantines lying west of the Tigris, before Luhrasb[273] ruled there. This was because Luhrasb was busied with fighting the Turks. He built Balkh[274] to keep them at bay, it is said, and he had to stay there for a long time to fight them.

Anyone who was not knowledgeable about the affairs of these people, or about how long they lived, and who was overconfident of his knowledge about the region— about, for example, who appointed whom—might very well think that they (Nimrod and Nebuchadnezzar) were kings in their own right. But no one who is learned in the history of mankind and of ancient kings—as far as we know—would claim that any Nabatean was king in his own right over so much as a foot of ground, much less king of all the world. Scholars of scripture and men learned in the accounts of past generations assert, and anyone who has troubled to look at historical books must agree, that Nimrod's rule over the region of Babylon on behalf of al-Azdahāq Bīwarasb lasted four hundred years, and that his
[325] authority was passed on to a man of Nimrod's stock after he died. This man was named Nabaṭ b. Qaʿūd, and he ruled for one

272. According to Yāqūt, *Muʿjam*, I, 298, Aṣbahbudhān was the generic title of the rulers of Ṭabaristān just as Kisrā was used for the rulers of Fārs and Qayṣar for those of Byzantium. It was also the name of a town in Daylam in which the ruler resided, two miles from the (Caspian) sea. Aṣbahbadh was a title meaning "lord of the army" (*sipāh* = army, *badh* = lord) or warlord.

273. Luhrasb/Luhrasp, the fourteenth king to rule over Iran in the *Shāhnāmeh*. He was the father of Gushtasp, during whose reign Zoroaster appeared; see Wolff, *Glossar*.

274. Balkh, a city in Khurāsān (today Afghanistan), built by Luhrasp, captured by the Arabs under the Caliph ʿUthmān; Yāqūt, *Muʿjam*, I, 713f.

hundred years. After him rule over the region of Babylon passed to Dāwaṣ b. Nabaṭ, who ruled for eighty years; after him to Bālish b. Dāwaṣ, who ruled for one hundred and twenty years; and finally to Nimrod b. Bālish, who ruled for a year and a few months.[275] That makes seven hundred and one years and a few months—all during the reign of al-Ḍaḥḥāk. After Afarīdhūn overthrew al-Azdahāq and became the supreme ruler, he slew Nimrod b. Bālish and drove the Nabateans away into exile. He killed a great number of Nabateans because of their support for Bīwarasb and for the deeds of Nimrod and his sons. Some scholars claim that even before Bīwarasb died he had already become alienated from Nimrod's line and no longer looked upon them (with favor) as he had.

We will now return to the story of the events which took place during Abraham's days, including the story of

Lot b. Haran

b. Terah, son of Abraham's brother, and his people—the people of Sodom.[276] It is said that Lot traveled from the land of Babylon with his paternal uncle Abraham, the Friend of the Merciful, believing in him and following his religion. They went to Syria as fugitives, and with them went Sarah bt. Nahor, who some say was Sarah bt. Hanāl bt. Nahor. It is said that Abra- [326]
ham's father Terah went with them, still opposing Abraham's religion and remaining an unbeliever. When they reached Ḥarrān Terah died, still an unbeliever. Abraham, Lot, and Sarah went on to Syria and then to Egypt, which was then ruled by a Pharaoh. It is mentioned that this Pharaoh was Sinān b. ʿAlwān b. ʿUbayd b. ʿUwayj b. ʿImlāq b. Lud b. Shem b. Noah. It is also said that he was a brother of al-Ḍaḥḥāk, who had appointed him governor of Egypt. I have already given some of

275. These names—not of Iranian origin—have not been identified.

276. The biblical story of Lot is found in Gen 18-19; see Kisāʾī, 155–59; Thaʿlabī, *Qiṣaṣ*, 90–94. See also Ginzberg, *Legends*, I, 245–57 for some aggadic accounts. In Islam, Lot is a prophet sent to the wicked people of Sodom, referred to in Muslim literature as "the folk of Lot."

the story of what happened between him and Abraham above.[277]

After this, Abraham, Lot, and Sarah went back to Syria. It is said that Abraham settled in Palestine and settled his nephew Lot in Jordan, and that God sent Lot to the people of Sodom. The people of Sodom were disbelievers in God, and were also immoral, as God has said, "You commit lewdness such as no creature has done before you. For do you not come into males, and do you not cut the roads, and do you not commit abominations in your assemblies?"[278] As has been said, "cutting the road" means that they committed lewdness with anyone who came into their town.

Concerning Those Who said That:

According to Yūnus b. ʿAbd al-Aʿlā—Ibn Wahb—Ibn Zayd: As for God's statement, "you cut the roads," the road is the way of the traveler. When the traveler, the son of the road, passed by them, they would block the road and perform with him that ugly deed.

As for what they did in their assemblies, scholars disagree about what it was. Some say that they used to shorten whoever
[327] passed by them. Others say that they used to break wind in their assemblies, while some said that they used to have intercourse with each other there.[279]

Concerning those who said that they used to shorten whoever passed by them, Ibn Ḥumayd heard the following from—Yaḥyā b. Wāḍiḥ—ʿUmar b. Abī Zā'idah—ʿIkrimah: Concerning His statement, "You commit abominations in

277. See Ṭabarī, I, 268–269.

278. Qur'ān, 29:28–29.

279. Kisā'ī gives only the Qur'ānic statement above while Thaʿlabī *Qiṣaṣ*, and Ṭabarī repeat different views as to what these sins of Lot's folk really were. The account in Ginzberg, *Legends*, loc. cit., lists "revolting orgies" and robbing wayfarers in a variety of ways, most of which involved some form of torture, including a procrustean bed which was either too short or too long. The hapless wayfarer was made to fit the bed by force, which often resulted in his death. It is this latter practice which is probably meant here by "they used to shorten whoever passed by them."

your assemblies," it means that they used to molest wayfarers, shortening those who passed by them.

According to Ibn Wakīʿ—his father—ʿImrān b. Zayd—ʿIkrimah: (It means) cutting (the road) off.

According to Mūsā b. Hārūn—ʿAmr b. Ḥammād—Asbāṭ—al-Suddī—Abū Mālik and Abū Ṣāliḥ—Ibn ʿAbbās and Murrah al-Hamdānī—Ibn Masʿūd and some of the companions of the Messenger of God: The quote, "And you commit abominations in your assemblies," means they would shorten everyone who passed by them, and that was the abomination.

As for those who said they used to break wind in their assemblies, ʿAbd al-Raḥmān b. al-Aswad al-Ẓifārī heard the following from Muḥammad b. Rabīʿah—Rawḥ b. Ghuṭayf al-Thaqafī—ʿAmr b. al-Muṣʿab—ʿUrwah b. al-Zubayr—ʿĀʾishah: About His statement, " And you commit abominations in your assemblies," the abomination was breaking wind.

As for those who said they had intercourse with each other [328]
in their assemblies,[280] Ibn Wakīʿ and Ibn Ḥumayd heard from Jarīr—Manṣūr—Mujāhid: Regarding His statement, "And you commit abominations in your assemblies," they used to have intercourse with each other in their assemblies.

According to Sulaymān b. ʿAbd al-Jabbār—Thābit b. Muḥammad al-Laythī—Fuḍayl b. ʿIyāḍ—Manṣūr b. al-Muʿtamir—Mujāhid: Concerning His statement, "And you commit abominations in your assemblies," they used to have sexual intercourse with one another in the assembly.

According to Ibn Ḥumayd—Ḥakkām—ʿAmr—Manṣūr—Mujāhid: The same.

According to Ibn Wakīʿ—his father—Sufyān—Manṣūr—Mujāhid: They used to have intercourse with men in their assemblies.

According to Muḥammad b. ʿAmr—Abū ʿĀṣim—ʿĪsā and al-Ḥārith—al-Ḥasan—Warqāʾ, together—Ibn Abī Najīḥ—Mujāhid: In the quote, "And you commit abominations in

---

280. Thus giving rise to the use of the term *lūṭī* to mean sodomite, pederast, and *liwāṭ* for sodomy, pederasty. See Lane, VII, 2082; Wehr, 883.

your assemblies," the assemblies and the abominations were their intercourse with men.

According to Bishr—Yazīd—Saʿīd—Qatādah: God's statement, "And you commit abominations in your assemblies," means they used to commit lewdness in their meetings.

According to Yūnus—Ibn Wahb—Ibn Zayd: Concerning God's statement, "And you commit abominations in your meetings," their meetings were the assemblies, and the abomination was their disgusting act which they would per-
[329] form. They would accost a rider and seize him and mount him. Ibn Zayd quoted, "Will you commit lewdness while you are in misfortune?" and "Such as no one has done before you in both worlds."[281]

According to Ibn Wakīʿ—Ismāʿīl b. ʿUlayyah—Ibn Abī Najīḥ—ʿAmr b. Dīnār: God's statement, "Such as no one did before you in both worlds," refers to the fact that no male jumped upon a male before the people of Lot.

Abū Jaʿfar spoke correctly about this matter, relaying the statement: By the abomination which they would commit in their meetings, God meant that in their assemblies they used to cut off anyone who passed them and mock him. The account of this comes from the Messenger of God, related by Abū Kurayb and Ibn Wakīʿ—Abū Usāmah—Ḥātim b. Abī Ṣaghīrah—Simāk b. Ḥarb—Abū Ṣāliḥ, the client of Umm Hāni'—Umm Hāni'—the Messenger of God: Regarding the statement, "And you commit abominations in your assemblies," they would cut off wayfarers and mock them, and that was the abomination they committed.

According to Aḥmad b. ʿAbdah al-Dabbī— Sulaymān b. Ḥayyān—Abū Yūnus al-Qushayrī—Simāk b. Ḥarb—Abū
[330] Ṣāliḥ—Umm Hāni': I asked the Prophet about God's statement, "And you commit abominations in your assemblies." And he said, "They used to cut off wayfarers and mock them."

According to al-Rabīʿ b. Sulaymān—Asad b. Mūsā—Saʿīd b. Zayd—Ḥātim b. Abī Ṣaghīrah—Simāk b. Ḥarb—Bādhām Abī Ṣāliḥ., the client of Umm Hāni'—Umm Hāni': I

281. Qur'ān, 29:28.

asked the Prophet about this verse, "And they commit abominations in their assemblies." And he said, "They would sit on the road and cut off wayfarers and mock them."

Lot called on them to worship God. By God's command he tried to prohibit them from doing those things which God disliked such as brigandage, committing lewd acts, and entering males in the posteriors. Because they persisted in doing those things and refused to repent of them, he threatened them with painful doom. But his threats did not restrain them, and his admonitions only increased their perseverence, insolence, and provocation of punishment from God. They rejected his admonitions, saying to him, "Bring God's doom upon us, if you are telling the truth!"[282] At length Lot asked his Lord for help against them, since the matter was dragging on and on, as was their persistence in sinfulness. Then God—when he wanted to disgrace them and destroy them and help His messenger Lot against against them—sent Gabriel and two other angels. It has been said that the two other angels were Michael and Isrāfīl, and that they came in the form of young men.[283]

Concerning Those Who Said That: [331]

According to Mūsā b. Hārūn—ʿAmr b. Ḥammād—Asbāṭ—al-Suddī—Abū Mālik and Abū Ṣāliḥ—Ibn ʿAbbās and Murrah al-Hamdānī—Ibn Masʿūd and some of the companions of the Prophet: God sent the angels to destroy the people of Lot. They arrived, walking, in the shape of young men, and they alighted with Abraham and sought hospitality from him. We have already mentioned what happened between them and Abraham in the account of Abraham and Sarah. When his awe left Abraham and he heard the news (of Isaac's birth), the messengers told him why they had come to him, and told him that God had sent them to destroy the people of Lot. Abraham argued and disputed with them, as God has said, "And when the

282. Ibid., 29:29.

283. The Jewish accounts say that each angel had a task: Michael to bring the tidings of Isaac's birth, Gabriel to destroy the sinful cities, and Raphael (here, Isrāfīl) to save Lot. See Ginzberg, *Legends*, V:237, n.154.

awe departed from Abraham, and the glad news reached him, he pleaded with Us on behalf of the folk of Lot."[284]

About his arguing with them about that, we have heard from Ibn Ḥumayd—Yaʿqūb al-Qummī—Jaʿfar— Saʿīd: He pleaded with Us on behalf of the folk of Lot.

When Gabriel and those with him came to Abraham, they said to him, "We are about to destroy the people of that township, for its people are wrongdoers."[285] Abraham said to them, "Will you destroy a town in which there are four hundred believers?" They said, "No." He said, "Will you then destroy a town in which there are three hundred believers?" They said, "No." He said, "Then will you destroy a town in which there are two hundred believers?" They said, "No." He said, "Then will you destroy a town in which there are one hundred believers?" They said, "No." He said, "Then will you destroy a town in which there are forty believers?" They said, "No." He said,
[332] "Then will you destroy a town in which there are fourteen believers?" They said, "No." Abraham had counted fourteen believers in Sodom, including Lot's wife, so he left off the argument and felt reassured.[286]

According to Abū Kurayb—al-Ḥimmānī—al-Aʿmash—al-Minhāl—Saʿīd b. Jubayr—Ibn ʿAbbās: The angel said to Abraham that if there were five in the city who prayed, he would remove the punishment from them.

According to Muḥammad b. ʿAbd al-Aʿlā—Muḥammad b. Thawr—Maʿmar—Qatādah: Concerning the statement, "He pleaded with us for the folk of Lot," it has reached us that he said to them on that day, "Do you think that there are fifty Muslims among the people of Sodom?" They said, "If there are fifty among them, we will not punish them." He said, "And forty?" They said, "Nor if there are forty." He said, "And thirty?" They said, "Nor if there are thirty." Until he reached ten, and they said, "And even if there are ten." He said, "There is no nation that does not have ten good people in it." When

---

284. Qur'ān, 11:74.
285. Ibid., 29:31.
286. For the aggadic rendering of Abraham's bargaining with God and the numbers agreed upon, see Ginzberg, *Legends*, I, 251–52; V, 239, n. 164.

the messengers told Abraham about the condition of the people of Lot, he said to them, "Lot is there." (Ṭabarī: He said this out of concern for Lot's safety in case Sodom were destroyed.) And the messengers said, "We are best aware of who is there. We are to deliver him and his household, all but his wife, who is one of those who is to stay behind."[287] Then the messengers of God moved on toward Sodom, the town of the people of Lot. It is mentioned that when they reached it, they met Lot at a plot of his land where he was working, and that at the stream they met Lot's daughter who was drawing water.

Concerning Those Who Say They Met Lot

According to Bishr b. Muʿādh—Yazīd—Saʿīd—Qatādah—Ḥudhayfah: When the messengers came to Lot, they reached him while he was working on a plot of his land. They had been [333] told—but God knows best—"Do not destroy them until Lot bears witness against them." They went to Lot and said, "We seek hospitality from you tonight." So he took them with him. Presently, after they had been walking for an hour, he turned to them and said, "Do you not know what the people of this town do? By God! I do not know of any people on the face of the earth more wicked than they are." He went on with them, and later said the same thing to them once again. When an evil old woman, Lot's wife, saw the approaching messengers, she went off to give notice to the people of Sodom.

According to Ibn Ḥumayd—al-Ḥakam b. Bashīr—ʿAmr b. Qays al-Mulāʾī —Saʿīd b. Bashīr— Qatādah: The angels came to Lot while he was in one of his fields, and God said to the angels, "If Lot bears witness against the people of Sodom four times, I give you leave to destroy them." So they said, "O Lot! We want your hospitality tonight." He said, "Have you not heard about them?" (That is, about the people of Sodom.) They asked, "What about them?" He said, "I bear witness by God, this is the worst town on earth in its deeds." He said that four times, thus bearing witness against them four times. Then the angels entered his dwelling with him.

287. Qur'ān, 29:32.

Concerning Those Who Said that the Messengers Met only Lot's Daughter

The first one they met when they neared Sodom was Lot's daughter, and Lot was not there.

According to Mūsā b. Hārūn—ʿAmr b. Ḥammād—Asbāṭ—al-Suddī—Abū Mālik and Abū Ṣāliḥ—Ibn ʿAbbās and Mur-
[334] rah al-Hamdānī—Ibn Masʿūd and some of the companions of the Prophet: After the angels left Abraham and headed for the town of Lot, they traveled for half a day. When they reached the river of Sodom, they met Lot's daughter drawing water for her family. Lot had two daughters, of which the elder was named Rīthā and the younger was named Raʿrabā. They said to her, "O girl! Is there a dwelling place near here?" She said, "Yes, but stay where you are, and do not come into the town until I come back to you." She was afraid of what her people might do to them, so she went to her father and said, "O my father! Some young men want you at the gate of the city. Never have I seen more handsome faces than theirs. Let your people not seize them and violate them." His people had forbidden Lot to show hospitality to anyone; they had said to him, "Leave them to us. We will give hospitality to the men." So he brought them to his house in secret, and no one but his family knew they were there. But Lot's wife went out to tell her people, saying, "In Lot's house there are men the likes of whom I have never seen, nor have I ever seen such handsome faces."[288] So the people came rushing to Lot's house.

When they came to him, Lot said, "O people! Fear God and do not humiliate my guests. Is there not an upright man among you? Here are my daughters. They are more chaste for you"[289]—that is, less immoral than what they wanted. They said, "Did we not forbid you to give men hospitality? You know well that we have no right to your daughters, and you

---

288. See Ginzberg, *Legends*, I, 254, where Lot's wife borrows salt from a neighbor, saying, "We had enough salt, until guests came to us . . ." thus inadvertently betraying the secret. Salt being the cause of her sin, she is turned into salt. But ibid., V, 241, n. 176, exonerates her .

289. Qur'ān, 11:78.

certainly know what we want."[290] When they would not accept anything he offered them, he said, "If only I had strength [to resist] you, or had some strong support."[291] He meant he wished he had someone who would help him against them or a clan that would intervene between them and him, to keep them from having what they sought from his guests. [335]

According to al-Muthannā—Isḥāq b. al-Ḥajjāj—Ismāʿīl b. ʿAbd al-Karīm—ʿAbd al-Ṣamad b. Maʿqil—Wahb: Lot said to them, "Would that I had strength against you or had some strong support." He found the messengers beside him, saying, "Verily your support is powerful!" When Lot had lost all hope that the townspeople would do anything he told them to do and could not bear the situation any longer, the angels said, "O Lot! We are messengers from your Lord; they shall not reach you. So leave with your family during the night, and let no one turn around to look back, save your wife. That which smites the townspeople will smite her too."[292]

When Lot realized that his guests were messengers of God and had been sent to destroy his people, he said, "Destroy them immediately!"

Concerning Those Scholars Who Claimed That Lot Said That:

According to Ibn Ḥumayd —Yaʿqūb—Jaʿfar—Saʿīd: The messengers went from Abraham to Lot, and when they reached Lot and the things that God has mentioned had happened to them, Gabriel said to Lot, "O Lot! We are going to destroy the people of this town, for truly its people are wrongdoers." Lot said to them, "Destroy them immediately!" And Gabriel said, "The time is fixed for the morning. Is not the morning near?"[293] And God commanded that Lot leave with his family during the night, and that not one of them should turn around and look back, except Lot's wife. So he left. And when the appointed [336]

290. Ibid., 11:79.
291. Ibid., 11:80.
292. Ibid., 11:81.
293. Id.

hour of destruction came, Gabriel picked up their land with his wing and turned it over. He lifted it so high that the inhabitants of heaven heard the crowing of the roosters and the barking of the dogs. "He turned them upside down and rained upon them stones of clay."[294] Lot's wife heard the crash and said, "O my people!" and a stone fell on her and killed her.

According to Ibn Ḥumayd—Yaʿqūb—Ḥafṣ b. Ḥumayd—Shimr b. ʿAṭiyyah: Lot had made his wife promise not to tell anyone about his secret guests. When Gabriel and those with him came into the house, and she saw men of such an appearance as she had never seen before, she went hurrying to her folk and came to the meeting to tell them that so-and-so was in her possession. They came hurrying, walking between a quick pace and a trot. When they reached Lot, he said to them what God has said in His book. Gabriel said, "O Lot, we are messengers of your Lord; they shall not reach you."[295] Lot said, "I am in His hands." So God obliterated their eyes, and they began feeling around the walls because they could not see.

According to Bishr b. Muʿādh—Yazīd—Saʿīd—Qatādah—Ḥudhayfah: When she saw the messengers, the evil old woman, Lot's wife, went to the people of Sodom and said, "Lot is giving hospitality to some people who are the handsomest I have ever seen, and the fairest-skinned and best-smelling." They came hurrying to Lot's house, as God has said, and Lot
[337] slammed the door. They began trying to persuade him to let them in. Gabriel asked his Lord for permission to punish them, and He granted it. So Gabriel slapped them with his wing and left them blind, wandering to and fro; it was the worst night that had ever befallen them. Then the angels told Lot, "We are messengers of your Lord, so leave with your family for part of the night." It has been mentioned that Lot's wife was with them when they left the town, but when she heard the sound of its destruction she turned around, and God dropped a stone on her and destroyed her.

According to Ibn Ḥumayd—al-Ḥakam b. Bashīr—ʿAmr b. Qays al-Mulāʾī—Saʿīd b. Bashīr—Qatādah: Lot's wife went out

---

294. See Qurʾān, 15:74.
295. Ibid., 11:81.

when she saw them—that is, when she saw the messengers—and went to her folk and said, "He is giving hospitality to some people tonight, and I have never seen people with handsomer faces or better smell." So they came hurrying, but Lot surprised them and blocked them off at the door. He said, "Here are my daughters, if you must do [something]."[296] They said, "Have we not forbidden you to [entertain] anyone?"[297] Then they went in to where the angels were, and the angels received them and slapped their eyes. Then they said, "O Lot! You have brought us sorcerers who have bewitched us as well as you until we awake in the morning." Then Gabriel lifted up the four towns of Lot, each of which held one hundred thousand people. He carried them up on his wing between heaven and earth until the inhabitants of the lowest heaven heard the sounds of their roosters. Then he turned them over and God set [338]
them upside down.

According to Muḥammad b. ʿAbd al-Aʿlā—Muḥammad b. Thawr and al-Ḥasan b. Yaḥyā—ʿAbd al-Razzāq, all of them —Maʿmar—Qatādah—Ḥudhayfah: When the messengers came to Lot, his wife, the evil old woman, went out to her people and said, "Lot is giving hospitality to some people with the handsomest faces I have ever seen." Then they went hurrying to him. An angel arose and bolted the door. He blocked it, and then Gabriel asked permission to punish them and God granted it. So Gabriel slapped them and smote them with his wing, leaving them blind, and they spent the worst night they had ever spent. Then the angels said, "We are messengers of your Lord; they shall not reach you. Leave with your family during the night and let none of you turn around—save your wife."[298] She heard a noise and turned around, whereupon a rock struck her while she was apart from her people, her place being known.

According to Mūsā b. Hārūn—ʿAmr b. Ḥammād—Asbāṭ —al-Suddī—Abū Mālik and Abū Ṣāliḥ—Ibn ʿAbbās and Murrah al-Hamdānī—Ibn Masʿūd and some of the companions of the

---

296. Ibid., 15:71.
297. Ibid., 15:70.
298. Ibid., 11:81.

Prophet: When Lot said, "Would that I had strength (to resist) you, or some strong support,"[299] Gabriel spread his wings and gouged their eyes out. They left treading on each other's heels, blind, saying, "Help! Help! In Lot's house there are the best sorcerers in the world!" And that is God's word,
[339] "They asked him for his guests for an ill purpose. Then We blinded their eyes."[300] They said to Lot, "We are messengers of your Lord; they shall not reach you. So leave with your family during the night, and follow behind to make sure that none of you turns around"[301]—that is, travel with them and go where you are commanded. Then God took them out to Syria, and Lot said, "Destroy them immediately!" But they said, "We were commanded [to do it] only in the morning. Is not the morning near?" When dawn came Lot left, taking his family with him except for his wife, for that is God's statement, "Except the family of Lot, whom We rescued at dawn."[302]

According to al-Muthannā—Isḥāq—Ismāʿīl b. ʿAbd al-Karīm—ʿAbd al-Ṣamad—Wahb b. Munabbih: The people of Sodom, among whom Lot lived, were an evil nation who dispensed with women by means of men. When God saw this, He sent His angels to punish them. They came to Abraham, and there took place between him and them that which God has mentioned in His book. When they had given Sarah tidings of a son, they arose and Abraham arose to walk with them. Then he said, "Tell me why you were sent and what your mission is." They answered, "We were sent to the people of Sodom to destroy them, for they are an evil nation who dispense with women by means of men." Abraham said, "Do you think there might be fifty righteous men among them?" They said, "If so, we would not punish them." He went on until he said, "A family?" They said, "If there is one righteous household among them"—that is, then they would not punish them. Abraham said, "Lot and his family." They said, "As for Lot's wife, her inclination is with that of her people." Abraham despaired, and

299. Id.
300. Ibid., 54:37.
301. Ibid., 11:81.
302. Ibid., 54:34.

they left him and went to Lot. When his wife saw them, their [340]
beauty and handsomeness pleased her and she sent word to the townspeople, "Some people have alighted with us, the handsomest and most beautiful folk we have ever seen." Word of this got around among them and they came to Lot's house from all directions, and they set up fences about it against them. Lot met them and said, "O people! Do not disgrace me with my guests. I will marry you with my daughters; they are purer for you." They said, "If we wanted your daughters, we already know where they are." He said, "If only I had strength to resist you, or had some strong support."[303] The angels became angry with him and said, "Verily your Support is powerful. A doom is coming to them which cannot be repelled."[304] One of them rubbed their eyes with his wing and wiped out their sight, and they said, "We have been bewitched! Let us go until we can return to him." Then that which God has already related in the Qur'an happened to them. Michael, the master of doom, thrust his wing into the earth under Sodom until he reached the lowest layer, and overturned it. Then stones descended from heaven and caught all those who were not in the town, wherever they were, and God destroyed them. But Lot and his family were saved, except his wife.

According to Abū Kurayb—Jābir b. Nūḥ—al-Aʿmash—Mujāhid: Gabriel seized the people of Lot from their flocks and houses, and lifted them up with their cattle and belongings until the inhabitants of heaven heard the barking of their dogs, then he turned them over.

According to Abū Kurayb—Mujāhid: Gabriel inserted his [341]
wing under the lowest earth of the folk of Lot, and then seized them with his right wing and took them from their flocks and cattle, then raised them up.

According to al-Muthannā—Abū Ḥudhayfah—Shibl—Ibn Abī Najīḥ—Mujāhid: God has said, "So when Our commandment came to pass, We overthrew it."[305] When they arose in the morning, Gabriel had come to their town and had ripped it

303. Ibid., 11:80.
304. Ibid., 11:76.
305. Ibid., 11:82.

from its foundations, then he inserted his wing and carried it on the underside of his wing.

According to al-Muthannā—Abū Ḥudhayfah—Shibl—Ibn Abī Najīḥ—Ibrāhīm b. Abī Bakr: Ibn Abī Najīḥ did not hear this from Mujāhid. He carried it on the underside of his wing with all that was in it, then he rose into the sky with it until the inhabitants of heaven heard the barking of their dogs. Then he overturned it, and the first to fall from it were its most noble people, for that is God's statement, "We have turned them upside down and We rained upon them stones of clay."[306]

According to Muḥammad b. ʿAbd al-Aʿlā—Muḥammad b. Thawr—Maʿmar—Qatādah: It has reached us that Gabriel seized the middle point of the town, then snatched it up so near to heaven that the inhabitants of heaven could hear the
[342] sound of their dogs. Then he turned them upside down, and then the stones rained upon them. According to Qatādah, there were four million of them.

According to Bishr b. Muʿādh—Yazīd—Saʿīd—Qatādah: It has been mentioned to us that Gabriel seized its girdle, then snatched it up so high into the sky that the angels could hear the noise of their dogs. Then he destroyed one after another, and threw rocks at the laggards one after another. There were three towns called Sodom. They lay between al-Madīnah and Syria. It has been mentioned to us that there were four million people in the town. And it was mentioned to us that Abraham looked down and said, "One day Sodom will perish."

According to Mūsā b. Hārūn—ʿAmr b. Ḥammād—Asbāṭ—al-Suddī, through a chain of transmitters which we have already mentioned: When the people of Lot rose in the morning, Gabriel came down and uprooted the earth from the seven earths, then bore it aloft until he brought it to the lowest heaven so that the inhabitants thereof heard the barking of their dogs and the noise of their roosters. Then he turned them over and killed them, as God said, "And al-Mu'tafikah He destroyed"[307]—al-Mu'tafikah being that which was overturned

306. Ibid., 15:74.
307. Ibid., 53:53.

when Gabriel rushed down to the earth and uprooted it with his wing. And as for those who did not die when the earth fell, God rained stones down upon them while they were under the earth, and upon those who were scattered around on the earth, as God says, "He turned them upside down and rained upon them stones of clay."[308] Then he overtook them in their towns. A man might be speaking and a stone would hit him and kill him, for that is God's word, "We rained upon them stones of clay."

According to Ibn Ḥumayd—Salamah—Ibn Isḥāq—Muḥammad b. Kaʿb al-Quraẓī: It was related to me that God sent Gabriel to al-Muʾtafikah, the city of Lot's people, and he carried it upward on his wing until the inhabitants of the lowest heaven heard the barking of its dogs and the noise of its hens. Then he turned it over on its face, whereupon God pursued it with stones. God says, "We overturned it and rained upon it stones of clay."[309] And God destroyed it along with the surrounding Muʾtafikahs, which were five cities: Ṣabʿah, Ṣaʿrah, ʿAmarah, Dumā, and Sodom,[310] the latter being the largest city. And God saved Lot and those of his family who were with him, except his wife who perished with the rest. [343]

On the Death of Sarah bt. Haran and of Hagar, the Mother of Ishmael; and on Abraham's Wives and Children

We have already mentioned the life span of Sarah, the mother of Isaac. As for the place of her death, both Arab and Persian scholars agree that it was in Syria. It is said that she died in the city of the giants in the land of Canaan, in Hebron, and that she was buried in the field which Abraham bought.[311] It is said

308. Ibid., 15:74.

309. Ibid., 11:82.

310. In the Bible (Gen 18–19) the names are Ẓeboiim, Ẓoar, Gomorrah (Heb., ʿAmorah), Admah, and Sodom.

311. The aggadic accounts vary, but some have Satan visit Sarah in the guise of an old man to tell her that Isaac is dead, whereupon she dies; see Ginzberg, *Legends*, I, 286, and ibid., V, 255 –56, nn. 256–259.

that Hagar lived for a while after Sarah died. Differing accounts have also come down to us.

According to Mūsā b. Hārūn—ʿAmr b. Ḥammād—Asbāṭ—al-Suddī, with a chain of transmitters which we have
[344] previously mentioned: Then Abraham longed for Ishmael and said to Sarah, "Permit me to go to my son so that I may look at him." She made him swear that when he went he would not stay, but would come back to her. He mounted al-Burāq and sent to see Ishmael. Ishmael's mother had died, and Ishmael had married a woman of the Jurhum tribe.[312]

Abraham had come to own more and more property and cattle, for the reasons which were related to us by way of Mūsā b. Hārūn—ʿAmr b. Ḥammād—Asbāṭ—al-Suddī, with a chain of transmitters which we have previously mentioned: Abraham was in need. He had a friend who sometimes gave things to him, so Sarah said to Abraham, "If you went to your friend, you could get food for us from him." But when Abraham reached his friend's home, the friend was away, and Abraham was ashamed to go back home empty-handed. So when he passed by a dry stream-bed, he filled his saddlebag from it. Then he sent the donkey to his family. When the donkey arrived, the saddlebag was full of excellent wheat. Abraham slept, and when he awoke he went to his family. Sarah had already prepared food for him, and she said to him, "Won't you eat?" He said, "Is there anything?" She said, "Yes, some of the wheat which you brought from your friend." He said, "You are right. I brought it from my Friend"—meaning God. Abraham planted it, and it sprouted for him and the plants grew while the plants of the people around him died. That wheat was the source of his wealth, for people would come and ask him for it and he would say, "Whoever says, 'There is no god but God,' may come in and take." Some of them said it and came in to take wheat, while others refused and left empty-handed. That is God's word, "And among them were those who believed therein and those who disbelieved therein. Hell is enough to burn them."[313]

312. See Ṭabarī, I, 283.
313. Qur'ān, 4:55.

As Abraham grew richer in wealth and cattle, he needed more room for dwelling and pasture. It is said that his dwelling place covered the land that lay between the desert of Midian [345]
and the Ḥijāz, as far as the land of Syria. His nephew Lot was staying with him, so he divided his wealth and gave Lot half of it, or so they say. He let him choose another place in which to live and stay. Lot chose the region of Jordan and went there, while Abraham stayed in his place. It is said that this was why Abraham gave preference to Mecca and settled Ishmael there, though he often entered the cities of Syria.

According to the account of Ibn Ḥumayd—Salamah—Ibn Isḥāq: When Abraham's wife Sarah bt. Haran died, Abraham married a Canaanite woman, Qaṭūrah bt. Yaqṭān. She bore his six children: Yaqsān b. Abraham, Zamrān b. Abraham, Madyān b. Abraham, Yasbaq b. Abraham, Sūḥ b. Abraham, and Basar b. Abraham.[314] Abraham had eight sons altogether, including Ishmael and Isaac. Ishmael was his firstborn, the eldest of all his offspring.

Yaqsān b. Abraham married Raʿwah bt. Zamar b. Yaqṭān b. Lūdhān b. Jurhum b. Yaqṭān b. Eber, and she bore him the Berbers and their mixed groups. Zamrān b. Abraham gave birth to the pipers, who are not known. To Madyān were born the people of Midian, who were the folk of the prophet Shuʿayb b. Mīkā'īl—all of them were descended from Madyān, and God [346]
sent Shuʿayb to them as a prophet.

According to al-Ḥārith b. Muḥammad— Muḥammad b. Saʿd—Hishām b. Muḥammad b. al-Sā'ib—his father: Abraham's father was a native of Ḥarrān, but a bad year befell him when he came to Hurmuzjird[315] in al-Ahwāz with his wife. This wife of his was Abraham's mother, and her name was Nūbā bt. Karītā b. Kūthā, of the sons of Arpachshad b. Shem b. Noah.

According to al-Ḥārith—Muḥammad b. Saʿd—Muḥammad

314. For the biblical names see Gen. 25:1–4; see also Kisā'ī, 162, and Thaʿlabī, *Qiṣaṣ*, 85. See also Ginzberg, *Legends*, V, 264–265.

315. Yāqūt, *Muʿjam*, IV, 968, says only, "A region which was on the borders [*aṭrāf*] of Iraq, which the Muslims raided during the wars of the conquests."

b. ʿUmar al-Aslamī—a number of scholars: Her name (Abraham's mother's name) was Anmūtā, one of the offspring of Afrāham b. Reu b. Peleg b. Eber b. Shelach b. Arpachshad b. Shem b. Noah, while some say that her name was Anmatalā bt. Yakfūr.[316]

According to al-Ḥārith—Muḥammad b. Saʿd—Hishām b. Muḥammad—his father: The river of Kūthā was dug by Karītā, Abraham's grandfather on his mother's side. His father was in charge of King Nimrod's idols. Abraham was born in Hurmuzjird, then moved to Kūthā in the land of Babylon. When Abraham grew up he rejected his people's beliefs and called upon them to worship God. This reached King Nimrod,
[347] who imprisoned him for seven years. Then he built for Abraham an enclosure of plaster, and kindled thick firewood therein, and threw Abraham into it. Abraham said, "God suffices me; how excellent is He in Whom I trust." And he left the fire safe and unhurt.

According to al-Ḥārith—Muḥammad b. Saʿd—Hishām b. Muḥammad—his father—Abū Ṣāliḥ—Ibn ʿAbbās: When Abraham fled from Kūthā and came out of the fire, his language was Syriac. But when he crossed the Euphrates from Ḥarrān, God changed his language and it was called Hebrew (*ʿIbrānī*) because he had crossed (*ʿabara*) the Euphrates. Nimrod sent men to look for him, telling them, "If you find anyone who speaks Syriac, do not leave him, but bring him to me." They met Abraham, but left him because he spoke Hebrew and they did not understand his language.

According to al-Ḥārith—Ibn Saʿd—Hishām—his father: Abraham migrated from Babylon to Syria, and Sarah came to him and offered herself to him, so he married her and took her with him. At that time he was thirty-seven years old, and he came to Ḥarrān and stayed there for a while. Then he came to Jordan and stayed there for a while. Then he went to Egypt and stayed there for a while; then went back to Syria and settled in the land of Beersheba between Īliyā and Palestine. He dug a well and built a house of prayer, but then some of the people of

316. Her name is not mentioned in the Bible, but Ginzberg, *Legends*, I, 286, gives it as Emtelai daughter of Karnabo. See also ibid., V, 208, n. b.

the land harmed him, so he left them and went to live between al-Ramlah and Īliyā. He dug a well there and stayed there, his wealth and servants already having become abundant. He was the first to show hospitality to guests, the first to crumble bread and soak it in broth, and the first to see white hair. The children born to Abraham were Ishmael, his eldest, whose mother was a Copt named Hagar; and Isaac, who was blind and whose mother was Sarah bt. Bethuel b. Nahor b. Serug b. Reu [348]
b. Peleg b. Eber b. Shelach b. Arpachshad b. Shem b. Noah. His other children were Madan, Madyan, Yaqsān, Zamrān, Asbaq, and Sūḥ, whose mother was Qanṭūrā bt. Mafṭūr of the *ʿāribah* Arabs. Yaqsān's sons reached Mecca, while Madan and Madyan remained in the land of Midian, which was named for the latter. The rest of them wandered from land to land, saying to Abraham, "O our father! You settled Ishmael and Isaac with you, but you ordered us to inhabit remote and wild lands." He answered, "I was thus commanded." Then he taught them one of the names of God, and they used to use it to ask for water and for help. Some of them settled in Khurāsān. Then the Khazars came, and they said, "The one who taught you must be the best of all the people of the earth, or the king of the earth." So they called their kings *khāqān*.[317]

Abū Jaʿfar said: Some pronounce Yasbaq as Yasbāq, and Sawaḥ/Sūḥ as Sāḥ. Some say that after Sarah's death Abraham married two Arab women. One of these was Qanṭūrā bt. Yaqṭān, who bore him six sons—(the ones we have mentioned) —while the other was Ḥajūr b. Arhīr, who bore him five sons—Kaysān, Shawarukh, Amīm, Lūṭān, and Nāfis.

Concerning the Death of Abraham, the Friend of God

When God wanted to take Abraham's soul, He sent the angel of [349]
death to him in the form of a decrepit old man.[318]

---

317. A possible reflex of the conversion of the Khazars to Judaism, ca. 740.

318. See Kisāʾī, 163; Thaʿlabī, *Qiṣaṣ*, 86, for essentially the same story. Jewish aggadic sources have the angel Michael sent by God as a reluctant messenger to announce his death to Abraham. See Ginzberg, *Legends* , I, 299ff.

According to Mūsā b. Hārūn—ʿAmr b. Ḥammād—Asbāṭ—al-Suddī, with a chain of transmitters which I have already mentioned: Abraham had much food, and would feed people and offer them hospitality. One day while he was feeding the people, he saw an old man walking in the heat. So he sent a donkey to him to bring him back so that he could feed him. Whenever the old man picked up a morsel of food and tried to put it in his mouth, he would put it in his eye or his ear, and then in his mouth. When it entered his belly, it came out from his posterior. Abraham had asked his Lord not to take his soul until he himself asked Him for death. When he saw the old man's condition, he asked him, "What is the matter with you, O old man, that you do this?" He said, "O Abraham, it is old age." Abraham asked, "How old are you?" He was two years older than Abraham, so Abraham said, "There are only two years between you and me. When I reach that age, will I become like you?" He answered, "Yes." Abraham said, "My God! Take me to You before that." Then the old man arose and took his soul, for he was the angel of death. After Abraham died—at the age of two hundred, or some say one hundred and seventy-five—he was buried at Sarah's tomb in the field of Hebron.

It is said that the leaves which God revealed to Abraham were ten in number. I heard this from Aḥmad b. ʿAbd al-Raḥ-
[350] mān b. Wahb—his paternal uncle ʿAbdallāh b. Wahb—al-Māḍī b. Muḥammad—Abū Sulaymān —al-Qāsim b. Muḥammad—Abū Idrīs al-Khawlānī—Abū Dharr al-Ghifārī: I asked, "O Messenger of God! How many books did God reveal?" He said, "One hundred and four books.[319] To Adam He revealed ten leaves, to Seth fifty leaves, and to Enoch thirty leaves. To Abraham he revealed ten leaves and also the Torah, the Injīl, the Zabūr, and the Furqān." I said, "O Messenger of God! What were the leaves of Abraham?" He answered, "They were all proverbs, such as, 'O dominated, afflicted, and deceived king! I did not send you to collect all the world, one part to another;

319. Thaʿlabī, *Qiṣas*., 88, has "one hundred leaves [*ṣaḥāʾif*] and four books." This section is preceded by a long recitation of acts which Abraham was the first to perform, and of his special merit. See Ṭabarī, I, 347 for Ṭabarī's scant mention of these attributes.

rather I sent you [to act justly] so that I would not have to hear the cry of the oppressed, for I will not reject that cry even from an unbeliever.' And they included parables, 'The intelligent man, who is not overcome about his reason, must keep various hours—an hour in which he confides to his Lord, an hour in which he contemplates God's works, an hour in which he takes stock of his soul and of all the acts it has committed, an hour in which he is alone with the permitted food and drink which he needs. He must not depart from three things—providing for himself in the hereafter, seeing to his subsistence, and taking pleasure in what is not forbidden. The intelligent man must be careful with his time, attentive to his affairs, and careful of his tongue. When a man values his words as part of his deeds, his words are few except about what concerns him.'"

It is mentioned that Abraham had two brothers. One of them was called Haran, who was the father of Lot, and it is said that
Haran was the one who built the city of Ḥarrān and that it was [351]
named after him. The other brother was Nahor, the father of Bethuel, and Bethuel was the father of Laban and of Rebecca bt. Bethuel. This Rebecca, the wife of Isaac b. Abraham and the mother of Jacob, was the daughter of Bethuel while Leah and Rachel, Jacob's wives, were both daughters of Laban.

The Account of the Descendants of Ishmael b. Abraham, Friend of the Merciful

We have already mentioned the reasons for Abraham's journey to Mecca with his son Ishmael and Ishmael's mother Hagar, and why he settled them there. When Ishmael grew up he married a woman of the Jurhum tribe and later, as we have described, divorced her because his father Abraham ordered him to do so. Then he married another, who was named al-Sayyidah bt. Maḍāḍ b. ʿAmr al-Jurhumī. She was the wife of Ishmael about whom Abraham, when he came to Mecca, said, "Tell your husband when he comes, 'I am pleased with the threshhold of your door.'"[320]

According to Ibn Ḥumayd—Salamah—Ibn Isḥāq: Ishmael had twelve sons by al-Sayyidah bt. Maḍāḍ b. ʿAmr al-Jurhumī. They were Nābit b. Ishmael, Qaydar b. Ishmael, Adabīl b. Ishmael, Mabashā b. Ishmael, Masmaʿ b. Ishmael, Dumā b. Ishmael, Mās b. Ishmael, Adad b. Ishmael, Waṭūr b. Ishmael,
[352] Nafīs b. Ishmael, Ṭumā b. Ishmael, and Qaydamān b. Ishmael. It is claimed that Ishmael lived one hundred and thirty years.[321] From Nābit and Qaydar God dispersed the Arabs. God made Ishmael a prophet and sent him to the Amalekites, so it is said, and to the tribes of the Yemen.

The names of Ishmael's sons are sometimes pronounced differently than the way I have given them according to Ibn Is-

320. See Ṭabarī, I, 283–285.
321. See Gen 25:12–18.

ḥāq. Some pronounce Qaydar as Qaydār, Adabīl as Adbāl, Mabashā as Mabashām, and Dumā as Dhūmā; the other names are sometimes given as Masā, Ḥaddād, Taym, Yaṭūr, Nāfis, and Qādaman. It is said that when death came to Ishmael, he made his brother Isaac his heir, and married his daughter to Isaac's son Esau. It is said that Ishmael lived one hundred and thirty-seven years, and that he was buried in al-Ḥijr near the tomb of his mother Hagar.

According to ʿAbadah b. ʿAbdallāh al-Ṣaffār—Khālid b. ʿAbd al-Raḥmān al-Makhzūmī—Mubārak b. Ḥassān, the master of the saddle-cloths—ʿUmar b. ʿAbd al-ʿAzīz: Ishmael complained to his Lord about the heat of Mecca, and God told him, "I am opening for you one of the Garden's gates, so that its breath will move over you until the Day of Resurrection, and in that place you will be buried."

We will now return to the discussion of Isaac b. Abraham [353] and of his wives and descendants, since after the Persians no nation except for them has a continuous, unbroken history. This is because the Persian kings continued in unbroken succession from the days of Jayumart, about whom I have already spoken, until they vanished with the coming of the best nation brought forth from humanity, the nation of our prophet Muḥammad. Prophecy and kingship continued in an unbroken succession in Syria and its environs among the children of Israel b. Isaac, until those things vanished from among them with the coming of the Persians and Byzantines after John b. Zacharias and after Jesus b. Mary. When we reach the story of John and Jesus, God willing, we will mention the reason for the vanishing of prophecy from among them. As for the rest of the nations, except for the Persians, it is impossible to attain knowledge of their history since they did not have continuous rule in ancient or modern times, and even when they did we cannot determine the sequence of events in their history, or the sequence of their rulers—save what we have mentioned about the descendants of Jacob until the time I have mentioned. Yet there—even though its span was interrupted during the time when it vanished from among them—we know the exact amount of time which passed between when it disappeared and the present. Yemen, on the other hand, had kings

who ruled, but there is no unbroken sequence; long intervals stretch between one king and the next, and scholars have not been able to work out the length of these intervals because they have not been meticulous about it, nor have they carefully worked out the life-spans of the kings, since they were
[354] not historically important. Whatever any of them did which was worth remembering, he only did because he was a governor over his territory for some higher ruler, rather than being a ruler in his own right. An example is the importance of the family of Naṣr b. Rabīʿah b. al-Ḥārith b. Mālik b. ʿAmam b. Nimārah b. Lakhm.[322] They occupied a gap in the Arab-Persian frontier extending from al-Ḥīrah to the Yemeni border and as far as the border of Syria. They continued to occupy this position from the era of Ardashīr Bābakān until Kisrā Barwīz b. Hurmuz b. Anūshirwān killed al-Nuʿmān b. al-Mundhir.[323] Then he transferred their authority over the Arab-Persian frontier to Iyās b. Qabīḍah al-Ṭāʾī.[324]

According to Ibn Ḥumayd—Salamah—Ibn Isḥāq: Isaac b. Abraham married Rebecca bt. Bethuel b. Ilyās, and she bore him Esau b. Isaac and Jacob b. Isaac. It is said that they were twins and that Esau was the elder of the two. Then Esau b. Isaac married the daughter of his paternal uncle, Basmah bt. Ishmael b. Abraham, and she bore him al-Rūm b. Esau. All the yellow people are from him.[325]

Some people claim that the Ashbān are among his descendants, but I do not know whether they are from the daughter of Ishmael or not. Jacob b. Isaac—who was Israel—married the daughter of his maternal uncle, Leah bt. Laban b. Bethuel b. Il-
[355] yās, and she bore him Reuben b. Jacob, who was the eldest of his descendants, and Simeon b. Jacob, Levi b. Jacob, Judah b. Jacob, Zebulon b. Jacob, Issachar b. Jacob, and a daughter named Dinah bt. Jacob. Some say that Issachar's name was Yashḥar.

Then Leah bt. Laban died, and Jacob replaced her with her

---

322. See Wüstenfeld, *Tabellen*, 5.

323. Al-Nuʿmān III (ca. 580–602), son of al-Mundhir IV, the last of the Lakhmids.

324. Ruled 602–611, but with a Persian resident in actual control of the government.

325. The biblical account is in Gen 36.

sister Rachel bt. Laban b. Bethuel b. Ilyās. She bore him Joseph b. Jacob and Benjamin b. Jacob, who is called Shaddād in Arabic. He also had two concubines named Zilfah and Bilhah, and he had four sons from them: Dan b. Jacob, Naphtali b. Jacob, Gad b. Jacob, and Asher b. Jacob. Jacob had twelve sons in all.

Some of the people of the Torah have said that Isaac's wife Rebecca was the daughter of Nahor b. Āzar, Isaac's paternal uncle, and that she bore Esau and Jacob in one womb (that is, as twins). They also say that Isaac ordered his son Jacob not to marry a Canaanite woman, but instead to marry one of his maternal uncle Laban b. Nahor's daughters. They also say that when Jacob wanted to marry, he went to his maternal uncle Laban b. Nahor as a suitor. Night fell while he was still on the road, and he slept leaning on a stone. He had a dream in which he saw a ladder raised up from his head to one of the gates of heaven, with angels climbing up and down on it.[326] Later he went to his maternal uncle and asked for the hand of his
daughter Rachel. Laban had two daughters, of whom Leah was [356]
the elder and Rachel the younger. He asked Jacob, "Do you have any money for which I should marry her to you?" He answered, "No, but I will serve you as a hired laborer until your daughter's dowry is paid in full." Laban said, "Her dowry is that you serve me for the period of seven pilgrimages"—that is, for seven years. Jacob said, "Then betroth me to Rachel, for I specify her as what I want in the exchange, and for her I will serve you." And his maternal uncle agreed to that bargain.

So Jacob worked for him as a herder for seven years, and when he had completed his side of the bargain, Laban gave him his elder daughter Leah. He brought her to Jacob in the night, and when Jacob awoke he found that he had not been given the daughter he had specified. So he went to Laban while he was in his people's meeting-place, and said to him, "You have deceived and cheated me. You have unlawfully made use of my labor of seven years, and fraudulently imposed on me one who is not my wife," Laban said to him, "O my nephew! You wanted to impose disgrace and infamy on me, your maternal

326. See Gen 28:10ff. for Jacob's dream. For the following story of Jacob and his sons see Kisā'ī, 163–67; Tha'labī, *Qiṣaṣ*, 88–90.

uncle, and on your father. When have you ever seen anyone marry off the younger daughter before the older one? Serve me another seven years and I will betroth her sister to you." In those days people used to marry two sisters to the same husband, until Moses came and the Torah was revealed to him.

So Jacob served Laban another seven years, and Laban handed Rachel over to him. Leah bore him the four tribes of Reuben, Judah, Simeon, and Levi, while Rachel bore him Joseph and Benjamin and their sisters. When Laban gave his daughters to Jacob he had given each of them a maidservant, and they presented these maidservants to Jacob. Each of them bore him three groups of tribes. Jacob left his maternal uncle and went back to live with his brother Esau.

Some have said that Dan and Naphtali were born to Jacob
[357] from Rachel's maidservant Zilfah. Rachel had asked him to seek children from Zilfah, since Rachel herself had not yet had any. Then Leah, competing with Rachel, presented her maidservant Bilhah to Jacob and asked him to seek children from her. Bilhah bore him Gad and Asher. Then, after he had given up hope of having any children by Rachel, she bore him Joseph and Benjamin. Jacob set out with these two children of his and with his two wives to go to his father's dwelling-place in Palestine, because he was afraid of his brother Esau, though the latter had never done anything but good to him. It has been mentioned that Esau attached himself to his paternal uncle Ishmael and married Ishmael's daughter Basmah, whom he took to Syria and who bore him a number of children. They multiplied until they overcame the Canaanites in Syria. Then they journeyed to the sea and the area of Alexandria, and from there to Byzantium. It is said that Esau was called Edom[327] because of his ruddiness, and that his descendants were thus called the children of the yellow one.

Rebecca bt. Bethuel bore Isaac twin sons, Esau and Jacob, when Isaac was sixty years old. Esau was the first to emerge from his mother's womb. It is said that Isaac favored Esau while their mother Rebecca tended toward Jacob. They claim

327. The text reads Adum. See Gen 36:1.

that Jacob tricked Esau with a sacrifice which they both offered at Isaac's command when he was old and his sight had grown dim. Most of Isaac's prayers were for Jacob, and blessing turned toward him through his father Isaac's prayers for him. This infuriated Esau and he threatened to kill Jacob, so Jacob fled from him to his maternal uncle Laban in Babylon. Laban established a relationship with him and married his two daughters Leah [358]
and Rachel to him. Jacob later left with Leah and Rachel, their two maidservants, his sons (the twelve tribes), and their sister Dinah, and went to Syria, the dwelling-place of his forefathers. He became united with his brother Esau, but later left Syria to him and moved to the coast. Then he went to Anatolia and took that as his homeland. According to the one who gives this account, the rulers of Anatolia—the Greeks—were of Jacob's descendants.

According to al-Ḥusayn b. Muḥammad b. ʿAmr al-ʿAbqarī—his father—Asbāṭ—al-Suddī: Isaac married a woman and she became pregnant with twins. When she was about to give birth to them, the two boys struggled in her womb, Jacob wishing to emerge before Esau. Esau said, "By God! If you go forth before me, I will obstruct my mother's womb, and I will kill her." So Jacob delayed and Esau emerged before him, but Jacob seized Esau's heel. Esau was given that name because he refused, or resisted (*ʿaṣā*), and he emerged before his brother who was named Jacob because he emerged grasping the heel (*ʿaqb*) of Esau. Jacob was the larger of the two in the womb, but Esau emerged before him.

As the two boys grew up, Esau was more loved by his father while Jacob was more loved by his mother. Esau was a hunter, and when Isaac grew old and blind, he said to Esau, "O my son! Feed me some game, and draw near me so that I may invoke a prayer over you which my father did for me." Esau was a hairy man while Jacob was a hairless man. Esau went forth seeking game, and his mother, who had overheard the conversation, said to Jacob, "O my son! Go to the flocks and slaughter a sheep therefrom, then roast it and dress yourself in its skin. [359]
Then go and present it to your father, and say you are Esau." Jacob did that, and when he came he said, "O my father, eat!" His father asked, "Who are you?" He said, "I am your son,

Esau." Isaac felt him and said, "The touch is that of Esau, but the smell is that of Jacob."[328] His mother said, "He is your son Esau, so pray for him." Isaac said, "Present your food." Jacob presented it and Isaac ate of it, then said, "Come closer." Jacob drew near him, and Isaac prayed that prophets and kings should be appointed from among his offspring. After Jacob left, Esau came and said, "I have brought the game as you ordered me to do." Isaac said, "O my son! Your brother Jacob has preceded you." Esau became angry and said, "By God! I shall surely kill him." Isaac said, "O my son, a prayer is left for you. Come here and I will invoke it for you." Then he prayed for Esau, saying, "May your offspring be as numerous as the dust and may no one rule them but themselves."

Jacob's mother told him, "Go to your maternal uncle and stay with him," because she was afraid Esau would kill him. So he went to his maternal uncle, traveling by night and hiding by day. For that reason he was called Israel, for he was high-ranking (*sariyy*) in the eyes of God.[329] He arrived at his maternal uncle, while Esau said, "You may have outdone me in the matter of the prayer, but you will not outdo me regarding the tomb; it is I who will be buried with my fathers Abraham and Isaac." He said, "If you do that, you will indeed be buried with him."

Jacob fell in love with the younger of his maternal uncle's two daughters. He asked her father for her hand in marriage, and her father betrothed her to him on condition that he tend his flocks for a specified period. When that period was finished, he gave her sister Leah to Jacob. Jacob said, "I wanted only Rachel." But his maternal uncle said, "Among our people we do not marry the younger one off before the elder one. Work for us as a herder again, and you can have Rachel."

So he did that, and when the period was complete he married
[360] Rachel as well. Jacob had both of them together, for that is

328. Compare with Gen 27:22, "The voice is the voice of Jacob, but the hands are the hands of Esau."

329. Compare the biblical etymology, Gen 32:29. See also the etymological discussions in Ginzberg, *Legends*, V, 307, n. 253.

God's statement, "And [it is forbidden to you] that you should have two sisters together, except for what has already happened in the past."[330] Jacob had both Leah and Rachel. Leah became pregnant and bore Judah, Reuben, and Simeon, while Rachel bore Joseph and Benjamin. It is said that Rachel died in childbirth while delivering Benjamin. Jacob's maternal uncle set part of his flock aside for Jacob, because he wanted to return to Bayt al-Maqdis.[331] They had no source of support on the trip, so Jacob's wife said to Joseph, "Take one of my father's idols; perhaps we may seek money from him." So he took it while he and Benjamin were in Jacob's chambers.[332] Jacob loved them and felt sorry for them because they had lost their mother. The most beloved creature to him was Joseph. When they approached the land of Syria, Jacob said to one of the shepherds, "If someone comes to you and asks who you are, say, 'We belong to Jacob, the servant of Esau.'" Esau met them and asked, "Who are you?" They said, "We belong to Jacob, the servant of Esau." So Esau held back from harming Jacob, and Jacob settled in Syria. His greatest concern was for Joseph and Benjamin, so Joseph's brothers envied him because they saw how their father loved him. Joseph had a dream in which he saw eleven stars, the sun, and the moon all bowing down to him. He told his father about it, and his father said, "O my son, do not tell your brothers about this dream, lest they begin plotting against you. Satan is an open enemy of man."[333]

330. Qur'ān, 4:23.

331. An Arabic name for Jerusalem. Probably Palestine is meant here.

332. Possibly a reference to the story of Rachel's taking her father's teraphim. Here Joseph is the culprit in order to justify the statement later made about Benjamin based on Qur'ān 12:77, "If he steals, a brother of his [i.e., Joseph] stole before."

333. Qur'ān, 12:5. This abrupt transition to the story of Joseph is not immediately followed up, but is interrupted by the stories of Job and Shu'ayb. In Kisā'ī, these lengthy accounts follow the story of Joseph (Job, pp. 192–204; Shu'ayb, pp. 204–208). Tha'labī interposes several other accounts between Joseph and the stories of Job and Shu'ayb. For the Islamic Job see *EI*^{2}, s.v. Ayyūb.

Job

[361] It has been said that one of Isaac's descendants was Job, the prophet of God.[334] Ibn Ḥumayd—Salamah—Ibn Isḥāq —someone who is not to be doubted—Wahb b. Munabbih: Job was a man of the Byzantines,[335] and his full name was Job b. Mawṣ b. Rāziḥ b. Esau b. Isaac b. Abraham. On the other hand, someone other than Ibn Isḥāq says that he was Job b. Mawṣ b. Raghwīl b. Esau b. Isaac, and someone also said that he was Job b. Mawaṣ b. Raghwīl. He says that his father was one of those who believed in Abraham on the day when Nimrod burned him. His wife, whom he was ordered to beat with a branch,[336] was a daughter of Jacob b. Isaac named Liyyā,[337] whom Jacob married to him.

According to al-Ḥusayn b. ʿAmr b. Muḥammad—his father—Ghiyāth b. Ibrāhīm: It is said—but God knows best —that God's enemy, Iblīs, met Job's wife and reminded her that she was Liyyā, the daughter of Jacob. He addressed her as "O Liyyā, daughter of the truthful one and sister of the truthful one!" For Job's mother was the daughter of Lot b. Haran.

It is said that his wife whom he was ordered to beat with the branch was Raḥmah bt. Ephraim b. Joseph b. Jacob. She owned
[362] all of al-Bathaniyyah[338] in Syria and all that it contained.

According to Muḥammad b. Sahl b. ʿAskar al-Najjārī—Ismāʿīl b. ʿAbd al-Karīm Abū Hishām—ʿAbd al-Ṣamad b. Maʿqil—Wahb b. Munabbih: Iblīs, may God curse him, heard

---

334. Jewish tradition differs as to Job's background, place of residence, and time. Most, but not all, traditions make him a pious Gentile—probably an Edomite—who lived at the time of Abraham or else in the days of the sons of Jacob, marrying the latter's daughter Dinah. The Talmudic tractate Baba Batra says that in the view of most scholars he was a Jew and endowed with prophecy. For the great range of views see Ginzberg *Legends*, X, 381, n. 3; *Encyc. Judaica*, 10:124–125. For a discussion of the book of Job see idem., 111–124.

335. That is, Rūm, which, as we have seen, was connected with Edom, the usual attribution of Job.

336. See Qur'ān, 38:45.

337. For Leah, mis-identified as a daughter of Jacob. As mentioned in n. 334, above, Jewish tradition has Job marry Dinah, the daughter of Jacob. *Encyc. Judaica*, 10:125; Ginzberg, *Legends*, II, 226.

338. A fertile area of Syria near Damascus; see Yāqūt, *Muʿjam*, I, 493–4.

the angels respond by blessing Job when God mentioned and praised him. Desire and envy overcame him, and he asked God to give him power over Job in order to seduce him away from his religion. God gave Iblīs mastery over Job's possessions, though not over his body or mind, and Iblīs assembled the most cunning and powerful devils. Job possessed all of al-Bathiniyyah in Syria and everything in it, east and west. He had a thousand sheep with their herdsmen, five hundred *feddans* tended by five hundred servants, each of whom had a wife and children and possessions. There was a she-ass to carry the tools of each *feddan*, and each she-ass had offspring—two, three, four, five, or more. When Iblīs had gathered all the demons together he asked them, "What power and knowledge do you have? For I have been given mastery over the possessions of Job"—meaning the right to inflict disaster, and seduction which no man can withstand. And each demon who possessed some power of destruction told Iblīs what it was, and Iblīs sent them off and they destroyed all of Job's possessions. Job, meanwhile, was praising God, and nothing that happened to his possessions deterred him from his diligence in worshipping God [363]
and thanking him for what he had given him, nor from the steadfastness for which God was testing him.

When the accursed Iblīs saw that, he asked God to give him mastery over Job's children. God gave him mastery over them, but still did not give him mastery over Job's body, heart, or mind. Iblīs then destroyed all of Job's children, and then came to Job pretending to be their teacher who was instructing them in wisdom. He played the role of being wounded and shattered, so that Job was moved and had pity for him and wept, and took a handful of dust and placed it on his head. Iblīs rejoiced at having gained that much from Job. But then Job repented and asked forgiveness, and his companions among the angels went up to God with his repentance, reaching God before Iblīs did. When the calamity which had befallen Job in the loss of his property and children did not deter him from worshipping his Lord, nor from diligence in obeying him, nor from patience toward what had happened to him, Iblīs asked God to give him mastery over Job's body. So God gave him mastery over Job's body except for his tongue, his heart, and his mind, over which he did not appoint him ruler. Iblīs came to Job while he was bowing down, and blew into his nostrils a breath which set fire to his body and moved all over him until his body stank. The people of the town removed him from the town to a dung-heap outside the town, and no one but his wife would come near him—(I have already mentioned the differences of opinion on her name and genealogy.)

Returning to the account of Wahb b. Munabbih: His wife visited him frequently, bringing whatever he needed. There were three people who followed his religion; when they saw the misfortunes which had descended upon him, they abandoned him and doubted him, but without actually leaving his religion. One of them was called Bildad, another Alīfaz, and the
[364] third Ṣāfir.[339] They went to Job when he was in the depths of his sufferings and verbally attacked him. When Job heard their words he turned to his Lord, imploring Him for His help. So God had pity on him and removed his misfortunes, giving back to him his family and possessions and the like, and saying to him, "Strike the ground with your foot. There is a cool bath and refreshing drink."[340] Then Job bathed in it and regained the beauty and handsomeness which had been his before his tribulations.

According to Yaḥyā b. Ṭalḥah al-Yarbūʿī—Fuḍayl b. ʿIyāḍ—Hishām—al-Ḥasan: Job was left out on a dung-heap of the children of Israel for seven years and some months, without asking God to do anything about his situation. There was no one on the face of the earth more honorable to God than Job. It is said that some people observed, "If this man's Lord had any use for him, he would not have done this to him." On hearing that, Job prayed.

According to Yaʿqūb b. Ibrāhīm—Ibn ʿUlayyah— Yūnus—al-Ḥasan: Job remained out on a dung-heap of the children of Israel for seven years and some months—the narrators differ about how many months it was.

This is all of the story of Job. The only reason we have told

339. Eliphaz the Temanite, Bildad the Shuhite, and Zophar the Naamathite; see Job 2:11.

340. Qur'ān, 38:43.

his story before telling that of Joseph is the reason mentioned above, that is, that he was said to be a prophet at the time of Joseph's father Jacob. It is said that Job lived ninety-three years, and that when he died he appointed his son Ḥawmal his heir , and that after him God sent his son Bishr b. Job as a prophet, calling him Dhū al-Kifl.[341] He commanded Bishr to call mankind to the recognition of His oneness. Bishr stayed in Syria all his life, until he died at the age of seventy-five. Then he appointed his son ʿAbdān his heir. After him God sent Shuʿayb b. [365] Ṣayfūn b. ʿAnqā b. Thābit b. Madyan b. Abraham to the people of Midian.[342] There is disagreement about Shuʿayb's genealogy. The people of the Torah give him the genealogy I have mentioned, while Ibn Isḥāq says, "He was Shuʿayb b. Mīkā'īl, one of the offspring of Madyan." This report was related by Ibn Ḥumayd—Salamah—Ibn Isḥāq.

Some people say that Shuʿayb was not a descendant of Abraham, but rather of someone who believed in Abraham, followed his religion, and emigrated to Syria with him. It is even said that he was a son of Lot's daughter, or that Shuʿayb's grandmother was Lot's daughter.

The Story of Shuʿayb

It is said that Shuʿayb's name was Jethro. I have mentioned his genealogy and the disagreements of the genealogists about it. It has been mentioned that he was shortsighted.

According to ʿAbd al-Aʿlā b. Wāṣil al-Asadī—Usayd b. Zayd

341. The Bible says that Job's second family consisted of seven sons—none of them named in the text—and three daughters, whose names are given (Job 42:13–14). The son called Dhū al-Kifl in Islamic tradition bears a name mentioned once in the Qur'ān, 21:85, as one like Ishmael and Idrīs who were steadfast. As a prophet he is mentioned only in passing, both here and in Kisā'ī, 204, but a fuller story of his life and mission is found in Thaʿlabī, *Qiṣaṣ*, 145.

342. Identified by later commentators (without Qur'ānic basis) as the biblical Jethro of Midian, father-in-law of Moses. Mentioned in the Qur' ān, 9:89, as coming later than Hūd, Ṣāliḥ, and Lot, he was sent to the "people of the thicket [*al-aykah*]," see ibid., 26:276ff., and to the people of Midian in Qur'ān 7:85ff.; 11:84–95; 29:36–37. For aggadic material about Jethro see Ginzberg, *Legends*, II, 289–96. See also *Encyc. Judaica*, 10:18–20, s.v. Jethro.

al-Jaṣṣāṣ—Sharīk—Sālim—Saʿīd b. Jubayr: God's statement, "We do behold you weak among us,"[343] means that he was blind.

According to Aḥmad b. al-Walīd al-Ramlī—Ibrāhīm b. Ziyād
[366] and Isḥāq b. al-Mundhir and ʿAbd al-Mālik b. Yazīd—Sharīk—Sālim—Saʿīd: The same.

According to Aḥmad b. al-Walīd—ʿAmr b. ʿAwn and Muḥammad b. al-Ṣabbāḥ—Sharīk: When God said, "We see you weak among us," He meant that he was blind.

According to Aḥmad b. al-Walīd—Saʿdawayh —ʿAbbād—Sharīk—Sālim—Saʿīd b. Jubayr: The same.

According to al-Muthannā—al-Himmānī—ʿAbbād—Sharīk—Sālim—Saʿīd: The quote "We see you weak among us" means he was blind and could not see.

According to al-ʿAbbās b. Abī Ṭālib—Ibrāhīm b. Mahdī al-Miṣṣīṣī—Khalaf b. Khalīfah—Sufyān—Sālim—Saʿīd b. Jubayr: The quote, "We see you weak among us," means that he was weak-sighted.

According to al-Muthannā—Abū Nuʿaym—Sufyān: God 's statement, "We see you weak among us," means that he was weak-sighted.

Sufyān said: He was called the preacher of the prophets. God sent him as a prophet to the people of Midian, who were the masters of the thorn-bush, the thorn-bush being a twisted tree.[344] They were a people who disbelieved in God, and who used dishonest weights and measures to despoil people of their wealth. God had given them ever more sustenance and had made their lives easy as an attempt to persuade them to be righteous, despite their disbelief in Him. Shuʿayb said to them, "O my people! Serve God. You have no other god but Him. Do not use short measures and short weights. I see you well-to-do, and I fear for you when the day of all-encompassing doom
[367] comes."[345] Some of what Shuʿayb said to his people and the people's response to him is recorded in God's book.

According to Ibn Ḥumayd—Salamah—Ibn Isḥāq—Yaʿqūb b.

343. Qur'ān, 11:91.
344. Or "thicket"; see n. 342, above.
345. Qur'ān 11:84.

Abī Salamah: Whenever the Messenger of God mentioned Shu'ayb, he used to say: "That one was the preacher of the prophets!" He said this because of the beauty of the way Shu'ayb kept repeating to his people the disputed matter. As their perseverence in sin and error dragged on, and Shu'ayb's exhortations and warnings of God's punishment failed to turn them back, God decided to destroy them, and He gave mastery over them.

According to al-Ḥārith—al-Ḥasan b. Mūsā al-Ashīb—Sa'īd b. Zayd, the brother of Ḥammād b. Zayd—Ḥātim b. Abī Ṣaghīrah—Yazīd al-Bāhilī: I asked 'Abdallāh b. 'Abbās about this verse, "So there came upon them the retribution of the day of gloom [or shade]. Lo! It was retribution of an awful day."[346] 'Abdallāh b. 'Abbās said, "God sent fire and great heat, which took away their breath. They ran into their houses, and it followed them there and took away their breath. They left their houses and fled out to the desert. God sent a cloud which shaded them from the sun, and made it cool and pleasant for them. So they called to each other until they had all gathered beneath it, whereupon God sent fire against them." 'Abdallāh b. 'Abbās said that that was the retribution of the day of shade. Lo! It was the retribution of an awful day.

According to Yūnus b. 'Abd al-A'lā—Ibn Wahb—Jarīr b. [368]
Ḥāzim—Qatādah: Shu'ayb was sent to two peoples; to his own nation, the Midianites, and to the masters of the thorn-bush. The thorn-bush was a sort of twining tree. When God wanted to punish them he sent powerful heat against them. Then he lifted the punishment from them as though it were a cloud. When it neared them they went out to it, seeking its coolness, but when they were beneath it, it rained fire upon them, for that is His word, "There came on them the retribution of the day of gloom."

According to al-Qāsim—al-Ḥusayn—Abū Sufyān—Ma'mar b. Rāshid—a man from among their companions—certain sages: The people of Shu'ayb had neglected a divine statute, and God expanded their sustenance. They neglected another

346. Ibid., 26:189.

divine statute, and God again expanded their sustenance. Every time they stopped obeying another part of the divine law, God would expand their sustenance, until the day came when He desired to destroy them. He imposed on them heat from which they were unable to become cool, and neither shade nor water benefitted them. Then one of them found shelter under some shade, and found a breeze, and called to his companions, "Come here to this breeze!" They hurried to him, and when
[369] they had all gathered there God sent fire against them, and that was the retribution of a day of shade.

According to Ibn Bashshār—ʿAbd al-Raḥmān—Sufyān—Abū Isḥāq—Zayd b. Muʿāwiyah: As for God's statement, "There came upon them the retribution of a day of gloom," it means that heat struck them within their houses, and a cloud was created which looked like shade. They rushed to it, and while they were sleeping under it the convulsion seized them.

According to Muḥammad b. ʿAmr—Abū ʿĀṣim—ʿĪsā and al-Ḥārith—al-Ḥasan—Warqāʾ—all of them—Ibn Abī Najīḥ—Mujāhid: God's words, "The retribution of a day of gloom," mean the shadows of punishment.

According to al-Qāsim—al-Ḥusayn—Ḥajjāj—Ibn Jurayj—Mujāhid: As for his words, "There came upon them the retribution of a day of gloom," they refer to the time when retribution cast a shadow over the people of Shuʿayb. Ibn Jurayj said: When God brought the first part of the punishment down upon them, great heat came down to them from it. Then God raised a cloud up for them, and a party of them went out to seek shade under it, and found coolness, breeze, and a goodly perfume. Then God poured down retribution upon them from above, from out of that cloud, for that is His word, "The retribution of a day of gloom. Lo! It was the retribution of an awful day."

According to Yūnus—Ibn Wahb—Ibn Zayd: Regarding His word, "There came upon them the retribution of a day of gloom. Lo! It was the retribution of an awful day," God sent them a cloud for shade. Then he gave an order to the sun and it burned everything on the face of the earth, so that all of them went outside to that shade. When they were all gathered together, God took the shade away from them, and the heat of the sun burned them up like locusts in a frying pan. [370]

According to al-Qāsim—al-Ḥusayn—Abū Tumaylah—Abū Ḥamzah—Jābir—ʿĀmir—Ibn ʿAbbās: If any sage tells you what the "retribution of the day of gloom" was, do not believe him.

According to Maḥmūd b. Khidāsh—Ḥammād b. Khālid al-Khayyāṭ—Dāwūd b. Qays—Zayd b. Aslam: They asked Shuʿayb, "Does your prayer command you to make us forsake what our fathers worshipped, or to stop us from doing what we want with our own property?"[347] One of the things Shuʿayb forbade them to do was to debase dirhams, or, as he put it, to cut dirhams. The presence of Ḥammād in the chain of transmitters casts doubt on the truthfulness of this account.

According to Sahl b. Mūsā al-Rāzī—Ibn Abī Fudayk—Abū Mawdūd—Muḥammad b. Kaʿb al-Quraẓī: I had heard that Shuʿayb's people were punished for cutting dirhams. Then I found these words in the Qur'ān, "Does your prayer command you to make us forsake what our fathers worshipped, or to stop us from doing what we want with our own property?"

According to Ibn Wakīʿ—Zayd b. Ḥubāb —Mūsā b. Ubaydah—Muḥammad b. Kaʿb al-Quraẓī: Shuʿayb's people were punished for cutting their dirhams. They asked, "O Shuʿayb! [371] Does your prayer command you to make us forsake what our fathers worshipped, or to stop us from doing what we want with our own property?"

Let us now return to the story of Jacob and his sons.

It is said—and God knows best—that Isaac b. Abraham lived one hundred years after Esau and Jacob were born to him, and then he died at the age of one hundred and sixty. Esau and Jacob buried him at the grave of his father Abraham in the field of Hebron. Jacob b. Isaac lived one hundred and forty-seven years altogether.

347. Ibid., 11:87.

Joseph[348]

Jacob's son Joseph had, like his mother, more beauty than any other human being.

According to ʿAbdallāh b. Muḥammad and Aḥmad b. Thābit al-Rāzayyān—ʿAffān b. Muslim—Ḥammād b. Salamah—Thābit—Anas—the Prophet: Joseph and his mother were given half of all the beauty in the world. When Rachel bore him, her husband Jacob gave him to his sister to bring up.[349] What happened between Joseph and this sister, Joseph's paternal aunt, was related through Ibn Ḥumayd—Salamah—Ibn Isḥāq—ʿAbdallāh b. Abī Najīḥ—Mujāhid: I have heard that the
[372] first misfortune to befall Joseph was the fact that his paternal aunt was Isaac's daughter, the eldest of Isaac's children, and that the belt of Isaac had come into her possession. This belt was supposed to be handed down from generation to generation by age, the eldest child always inheriting it. If someone else acquired it by guile from the person who was supposed to

---

348. The story of Joseph plays an important yet limited role in the Bible (see Gen 37–50 and hardly elsewhere) and in the Qur'ān, where the story is concentrated entirely in *sūrah* 12, which is named for Joseph. For the embellishments in Jewish tradition see *Encyc. Judaica*, 10:202–218; Ginzberg, *Legends*, II, 3–184; V, 324–77; Kisā'ī, 167–192; Tha'labī, *Qiṣaṣ*, 94–125. See also *Shorter Encyc.*, 646–48, s.v. Yūsuf b. Yaʿḳūb.

349. The Genesis account of Joseph begins when he is seventeen, but aggada adds some details about his childhood to explain why his brothers hated him. See Ginzberg, *Legends*, II, 5–8. Here the account begins with his childhood to explain the Qur'ānic reference to his having stolen, but see n. 322, above. Thaʿlabī, 95–96, does not include this account but devotes much space to a discussion of Joseph's beauty.

have it, then he would become absolutely subject to the will of the rightful owner, and the rightful owner could do with him as he wished. Now, no love was so great as that which Joseph's paternal aunt, who had brought him up, felt for him. When Joseph grew up, his father Jacob's soul became fixed on him, and he came to her and said, "O little sister! Hand Joseph over to me, for by God I cannot stand to have him away from me for another hour." She said, "But, by God, I will not give him up." Jacob insisted, "By God, I will not give him up either." She said, "Leave him with me for a few days so that I can look at him and set my mind at ease about him, and perhaps I will feel better about giving him up."

When Jacob left her, she took Isaac's belt and put it on Joseph under his clothes. Then she said, "I have lost Isaac's belt! See who took it and who has it." She looked for it diligently, and then she ordered that everyone in the household be searched. They found the belt on Joseph, and she said, "By God! He is mine. I will do with him what I wish!" When Jacob came to her she told him the story, and he said, "You and that one. If he did it, he is yours; I can do nothing about it." So she kept Joseph, and Jacob could not take him until she died. This incident (in [373]
which it was made to seem that Joseph had stolen the belt) was what Joseph's brothers had in mind when they later said, "If he [one of the brothers] steals, a brother of his stole before."[350]

Abū Jaʿfar said: When Joseph's brothers saw how much their father Jacob loved him during his childhood as well as during his infancy, and how impatient Jacob became when Joseph was not there, they envied Joseph for his position in Jacob's affections. They said to each other, "Verily Joseph and his brother [Benjamin] are dearer to our father than we are, though we may be a troop [ʿ*uṣbah*]."[351] By ʿ*uṣbah* they meant a group, for they were ten in number. They said, "Our father is plainly in a state of aberration."[352]

Then there happened the events which God has related in His book. They asked Jacob to send Joseph out with them to

350. Qurʾān, 12:77.
351. Ibid., 12:8.
352. Id.

the desert to run and play, and they promised to guard him. Jacob told them he would be sad to have Joseph away from him, and feared for him on account of the wolves. They deceived their father with lies about Joseph, and finally he sent Joseph with them. They took him out to the desert, having decided to throw him down a well.

According to Ibn Wakīʿ—ʿAmr b. Muḥammad al-ʿAnqazī—Asbāṭ—al-Suddī: Jacob sent Joseph with them, he who was more noble than they, and when they got him out into the desert they made clear their enmity toward him. One brother began to beat him, and when he asked another brother for help, the other one beat him, too. None of them showed mercy to him, and they beat him until they almost killed him. He began to shout, "O my father! O Jacob! You did not know what the sons of the servant girls[353] would do to your son." When they
[374] had almost killed him and he had begun to shout, Judah, one of the brothers, said to the others, "Did you not give me a pledge that you would not kill him?" So they took him to the well and lowered him into it. When they began lowering him into it he clung to the edge, but they tied his hands and stripped his shirt off. He said, "O brothers, give me my shirt back so that I can cover myself with it in the well." They said, "Call on the sun, the moon, and the eleven stars to keep you company."[354] He said, "Verily, I did not dream that." But they went on lowering him until he was halfway down, then let him fall the rest of the way, for they wanted him to die. There was water in the well and he fell into it, then managed to climb out of the water onto a rock which was at the bottom of the well. When they threw him into the well he began to weep. They called out to him and he thought it was out of pity, but in fact they wanted to smash him with a rock and kill him. But Judah stopped them, saying, "You have given me a pledge not to kill him." And while Joseph was in the well, Judah used to bring him food.

God described how He revealed to Joseph, while Joseph was

353. That is, the four sons of Bilhah and Zilphah, the handmaidens who became concubines of Jacob. Note that various sons of his aunt Leah intervene at various times on his behalf.

354. Referring to Joseph's dream; see Ṭabarī, I, 360.

in the well, that he would one day tell his brothers what they had done to him; the brothers did not know of this revelation to Joseph.[355] This account was also relayed from Qatādah.

According to Muḥammad b. ʿAbd al-Aʿlā al-Ṣanʿānī—Muḥammad b. Thawr—Maʿmar—Qatādah: God said, "We revealed to him, 'You will tell them of this deed of theirs.'"[356] He revealed to Joseph, while he was in the well, that he would tell them about what they had done to him, "while they knew not" of this revelation.

According to al-Muthannā—Suwayd—Ibn al-Mubārak—Maʿmar—Qatādah: More or less the same account, except that he said that he would inform them. [375]

It is said that that meant that they would not know he was Joseph, and this statement is related from Ibn ʿAbbās.

According to al-Ḥārith—ʿAbd al-ʿAzīz—Ṣadaqah b. ʿAbādah al-Asadī—his father: I heard Ibn ʿAbbas saying that, and he got it from Ibn Jurayj.

God described how Joseph's brothers came weeping to their father in the evening and told him that a wolf had eaten Joseph. Their father said, "No, your minds have beguiled you into something. It is best to be patient."[357] Then God described how a caravan came to the well where Joseph was, and how they sent their water-drawer to get water from it. He took Joseph out of the well and told his companions about it, saying, "O good luck! Here is a youth."[358]

According to Bishr b. Muʿādh—Yazīd—Saʿīd—Qatādah: When Joseph was taken out, they said, "O good luck! Here is a youth." The well is in the land of Bayt al-Maqdis, and its location is known.

It has been said that the one who took Joseph out of the well told only one person, a companion of his named Bushrā (which [376] means "good luck"), so that when he called out "O good luck!" he was calling out that man's name. Al-Suddī also reports this.

According to al-Ḥasan b. Muḥammad—Khalaf b. Hi-

355. See Qur'ān, 12:15.
356. Id.
357. Ibid., 12:18.
358. Ibid., 12:19.

shām—Yaḥyā b. Ādam—Qays b. al-Rabīʿ—al-Suddī: The water-drawer's words "O good luck!" refer to the name of his companion Bushrā.

According to al-Muthannā—ʿAbd al-Raḥmān b. Abī Ḥammād—al-Ḥakam b. Ẓuhayr—al-Suddi: The boy to whom he was talking when he said, "O good luck! Here is a youth," was named Bushrā. So it was just like saying, "O Zayd!" (to someone named Zayd).

God described how when the caravan pulled Joseph out of the well they bought him from his brothers "for a low price, a number of silver coins,"[359] because of his brothers' indifference to him. Those who bought him hid him like a treasure from the merchants in the caravan, for they feared that if the merchants knew about him they would demand a share in him. This is what the interpreters have said on the matter.

According to Muḥammad b. ʿAmr—Abū ʿĀṣim—ʿĪsā b. Abī Najīḥ—Mujāhid: The quote, "They hid him as a treasure,"[360] means that those who were actually there when he was pulled out of the well decided to keep him secret as a treasure among themselves, fearing that others in the caravan would want a share in him if they realized for how much he could be sold. Joseph's brothers followed them, saying to them, "Make sure that he does not escape," until they reached Egypt with Joseph. Joseph said, "He who buys me will be happy." The king, who was a Muslim, bought him.

According to al-Ḥasan b. Muḥammad—Shabābah—War-qāʾ—Ibn Abi Najīḥ—Mujāhid: A similar story, except that he said, ". . . for fear that they would want a share in him if they knew about him." And his brothers followed them, saying to the
[377] water-drawer and his companions, "Make sure that he does not escape," until they reached Egypt with him.

According to Ibn Wakīʿ—ʿAmr b. Ḥammād—Asbāṭ—al-Suddī. The quote, "They hid him as a treasure," means that when the two men bought Joseph from his brothers, they were afraid that the rest of the group would say, "We have all bought him, and we are entitled to a share in him." So they decided

359. Ibid., 12:20.
360. Ibid., 12:19.

that if anyone asked them what it was that they had, they would say, "A piece of merchandise for which we traded with the people who own the well." For it is as God said, "They hid him as a treasure."

Joseph's brothers sold him for "a low price"—that is, a bit less than the forbidden price. It is said that they sold him for twenty dirhams, then divided it among the ten of them so that each had two dirhams. The money was counted by number of coins rather than by weight, for it is said that at that time the smallest unit of weight for money was the *ūqiyyah* (the weight of forty dirhams) and coins weighing less than that were not weighed. Some say that they sold him for forty dirhams; others say it was forty-two. It is reported that the man who sold him in Egypt was Mālik b. Daʿar b. Yawbūb b. ʿAfqān b. Madyān b. Abraham the Friend (of God).

This was related through Ibn Ḥumayd—Salamah—Ibn Isḥāq—Muḥammad b. al-Sā'ib—Abū Ṣāliḥ—Ibn ʿAbbās.

As for the man who bought Joseph from Mālik b. Daʿar in Egypt and who said to his wife, "Receive him honorably,"[361] Ibn ʿAbbas reports that his name was Qiṭṭīn.[362]

According to Muḥammad b. Saʿd—his father—his uncle— [378]
his father—his father—Ibn ʿAbbās: The name of the one who bought him was Qaṭafīr (Potiphar), and it is said that his name was Iṭfīr b. Rawhīb and that he was ruler[363] and in charge of the Egyptian treasury. At that time the king was al-Rayyān b. al-Walīd[364] a man of Amalekite stock, according to the account relayed through Ibn Ḥumayd—Salamah—Ibn Isḥāq. Another account gives the full name of the king and Pharaoh of Egypt at that time as al-Rayyān b. al-Walīd b. Tharwān b. Arāshah b. Qārān b. ʿAmr b. ʿImlāq b. Lud b. Shem b. Noah.

It has been said that before this king died he became a be-

---

361. Ibid., 12:21.

362. The biblical name Potiphar appears in a variety of forms in Arabic sources, among them Qittīn, Qiṭṭifīn, Quṭifar, Qiṭfīr, Iṭfīr, and Iṭfīn. See *Shorter Encyc.*, 647, s.v. Yūsuf b. Yaʿḳūb.

363. ʿAzīz, lit. "mighty, honored, proud, precious;" here, the ruler of Egypt but not the king or Pharaoh.

364. Note that he is not referred to as Pharaoh/Firʿawn,which in the Qur'ān has the connotation of an evildoer.

liever and follower of Joseph's religion, and that he died when Joseph was still alive. The king after him was Qābūs b. Muṣ ʿab b. Muʿāwiyah b. Numayr b. al-Salwās b. Qārān b. ʿ Amr b. ʿImlāq b. Lud b. Shem b. Noah. He was an infidel, and when Joseph invited him to Islam he refused to accept it.

Some of the people of the Torah report that, according to the Torah, Joseph was sold by his brothers and brought to Egypt when he was seventeen years old. They say that he remained in the house of the ruler who bought him for thirteen years, and
[379] that when he reached the age of thirty the Pharaoh of Egypt al-Walīd b. al-Rayyān made him vizier. They say that on that same day the Pharaoh died at the age of one hundred and ten, naming his brother Judah his heir. They also say that Joseph met Jacob in Egypt twenty-two years after having been taken from him (by his brothers), that Jacob stayed with him in Egypt with his family for seventeen years, that Jacob named Joseph his heir, and that Jacob had seventy members of his family with him when he came to Egypt. They also say that when Potiphar bought Joseph and brought him to his house, he said to his wife, (whose name, according to Ibn Ḥumayd—Salamah—Ibn Isḥāq, was Rāʿīl)[365] "Receive him honorably. He may prove useful to us.[366] When he grows up and understands things, he may be able to help us in some of the affairs which we have at hand, or we may adopt him as our son."[367] That was because, according to Ibn Ḥumayd—Salamah—Ibn Isḥāq, Potiphar was a man who did not have intercourse with women,[368] though his wife Rāʿīl was beautiful and tender, and had property and possessions.

When Joseph reached the age of thirty-three, God gave him wisdom and knowledge.

---

365. So in Thaʿlabī, *Qiṣaṣ*, 103, with a variant, Bakkā, also recorded. In Kisāʾī, 172, and other Muslim works, it is usua lly Zalīkah, Zulaykah, Zuleikha; see *Shorter Encyc.*, 647, s.v. Yūsuf. The Jewish work *Sefer ha-Yashar* also uses the latter name. See Ginzberg, *Legends*, V, 339, n. 113, n. 111 for other names used.

366. Qurʾān, 12:21.

367. Id.

368. Jewish legends say that Potiphar bought Joseph for a lewd purpose but the angel Gabriel made him an eunuch so that he could not accomplish it. Ginzberg, *Legends*, II, 43; V, 338, n. 101.

According to al-Muthannā—Abū Ḥudhayfah—Shibl—Ibn Abī Najīḥ—Mujāhid: God said, "We gave him wisdom and knowledge"[369]—meaning intelligence and knowledge before prophecy.

"And she, in whose house he was, asked of him an evil act"[370] when he had matured and reached the age of virility. This "she" refers to Potiphar's wife Rāʿīl. "And she bolted the doors,"[371] locking him in with herself, so that she might have what she desired from him, and she began to speak of his charms in order to arouse his desire for her.

Concerning Those Who Said That: [380]

According to Ibn Wakīʿ—ʿAmr b. Muḥammad—Asbāṭ—al-Suddī (As the Qur'ān says,) "She desired him and he would have desired her."[372] She said, "O Joseph, how beautiful your hair is!" He answered, "It is the first thing that will fall off of my body." She said, "O Joseph, how beautiful your eyes are!" He answered, "They are the first things that will melt into the earth from my body." She said, "O Joseph, how beautiful your face is!" He answered, "The earth will eat it." But she kept after him until she had enticed him.

"She desired him and he would have desired her,"[373] and they entered the house and she locked the doors and he went to loosen his trousers, when suddenly the figure of Jacob appeared to him, standing in the house and biting his fingers, saying, "O Joseph, do not have intercourse with her. If you do not have intercourse with her, you are like the bird in the sky who is not caught. If you have intercourse with her, you are like the bird when it dies and falls to the ground, unable to defend itself. If you do not have intercourse with her, you are like a difficult ox upon whom no work can be done, whereas if you have intercourse with her, you are like that ox when he dies and ants

369. Qur'ān, 12:22.
370. Ibid., 12:23.
371. Id.
372. Ibid., 12:24.
373. Id.

come in at the base of his horns and he cannot defend himself."[374] So Joseph tied his trousers up and left at a run, but she overtook him and seized the tail of his shirt from behind and tore it. The tail of the shirt fell off and Joseph left it behind and raced toward the door.

According to Abū Kurayb, Ibn Wakīʿ, and Sahl b. Mūsā—Ibn ʿUyaynah—ʿUthmān b. Abī Sulaymān—Ibn Abī Mulaykah: Ibn
[381] ʿAbbās was asked how far Joseph went in following his desires. He said, "He loosened his waistband and sat with her as one who possesses would sit."

According to al-Ḥasan b. Muḥammad—Ḥajjāj b. Muḥammad—Ibn Jurayj—ʿAbdallāh b. Abī Mulaykah: I asked Ibn ʿAbbās, "How far did Joseph go in following his desires?" And he said, "She lay on her back for him and he sat between her legs removing his clothes."

God turned him away from his desire for evil by giving him a sign that he should not do it. It has been said that that sign was the image of his father Jacob, biting his fingers. Some have said instead that a voice proclaimed from beside the house, "Will you fornicate and be like the bird whose feathers fall out, and who finds he has no feathers when he tries to fly?" Yet others have said that Joseph saw written on the wall, "Do not come near to adultery. Verily it is an abomination and an evil way,"[375] and that Joseph, seeing the proof of his Lord, arose and fled, seeking the door of the house to escape from what she wanted him to do. But Rāʿīl followed him and caught up with him before he left the house, and grabbed him from behind by his shirt, and tore it. Then Joseph and Rāʿīl met her master, her huband Potiphar, sitting at the door of the house with one of Rāʿīl's cousins.

Likewise according to Ibn Wakīʿ—ʿAmr b. Muḥammad—Asbāṭ—al-Suddī "They met her master at the door."[376] He

374. See the very different version in the Jewish aggada where Joseph remains steadfast in spite of all blandishments and threats; Ginzberg, *Legends*, III, 44–50, for a Jewish account similar to Ṭabarī's, with both Jacob and Rachel appearing to stop Joseph, see 53–54. For this reason some of the rabbis blamed Joseph. See *Encyc. Judaica*, X:211.

375. Qur'ān, 17:32

376. Ibid., 12:25.

was sitting at the door with her cousin. When she saw him she asked, "How would you reward one who wishes evil to your folk, if not by imprisonment or a painful doom?[377] He (Joseph) [382] asked of me an evil act, but I refused and defended myself from him and tore his shirt."

Joseph said, "No, rather it was 'she who asked of me an evil act,'[378] and I refused and fled from her. But she overtook me and tore my shirt." Rāʿīl's cousin said, "The evidence for this matter is in the shirt. If it is torn in front, then she is honest and he is a liar. And if it is torn from behind, then she has lied and he is honest."[379] The shirt was brought and Potiphar found it torn from behind. He said, "This is [typical of] the guile of you women. Your guile is very great. Joseph, turn away from this, and you, O woman, ask forgiveness for your sin. Verily you are a sinful person."[380]

According to Muḥammad b. ʿUmārah—ʿUbaydallāh b. Mūsa—Shaybān—Abū Isḥāq—Nawf al-Shaʾmī: Joseph did not want to tell Potiphar of the matter until Rāʿīl said, "How would you reward one who wishes evil to your folk, if not by imprisonment or a painful doom?"[381] Then he became angry and said, "She asked of me an evil act."

There is a difference of opinion about which member of her family it was who pointed out that "if it is torn in front, then she is honest and he is a liar."[382] Some agree with what I have reported from al-Suddī, while others have said that it was a child in his cradle.[383] This version has come down from the Messenger of God by way of al-Ḥasan b. Muḥammad—ʿAffān b. Muslim—Ḥammād—ʿAṭāʾ b. al-Sāʾib—Saʿid b. Jubayr—Ibn ʿAbbās: The Prophet said, "There were four people who spoke when they were small," and he mentioned among them this witness of Joseph's.

According to Ibn Wakīʿ—al-ʿAlāʾ b. ʿAbd al-Jabbār—Ḥam- [383]

---

377. Id.
378. Ibid., 12:26.
379. Ibid., 12:26–27.
380. Ibid., 12:28–29.
381. Ibid., 12:25.
382. Ibid., 12:26.
383. For a Jewish version, see Ginzberg, *Legends*, II, 57;also V, 342, n. 134.

mād b. Salamah—ʿAṭāʾ b. al-Sāʾib—Saʿīd b. Jubayr —Ibn ʿAbbās: There were four who spoke when they were small, and they were the son of the Pharaoh's daughter Māshaṭah, the witness of Joseph, the companion of Jurayj, and Jesus, the son of Mary.

It has also been said that the witness was the shirt itself and the tear in its back.

Concerning Some of Those Who Said That

According to Muḥammad b. ʿUmar—Abū ʿĀṣim—ʿĪsā—Ibn Abī Najīḥ—Mujāhid: Regarding God's statement, "A witness of her own folk testified,"[384] it meant that his shirt was torn from behind, and that was the testimony. So when the woman's husband saw Joseph's shirt torn from behind, he said to his wife Rāʿīl, "This is [typical of] the guile of you women. Indeed your guile is very great."[385] He said to Joseph, "Refrain from talking about the evil act which she was asking of you, and do not mention it to anyone." Turning back to his wife, he said to her, "Ask forgiveness for your sin. You are indeed a sinful person."[386]

Throughout the city of Egypt women talked of what had happened between Joseph and the wife of the ruler, and of how she had asked an evil act of him; the matter could not be hidden. They said, "The ruler's wife is asking of her slave-boy an evil deed. He has smitten her to the heart with love."[387] For her love for Joseph had reached the pericardium of her heart, entered beneath it, and overpowered her heart. The pericardium is the cover and veil of the heart.

According to Ibn Wakīʿ—ʿAmr b. Muḥammad—Asbāṭ—al-Suddī: They said, "He has smitten her with love."[388] The pericardium is a skin on the heart, which is called the tongue of
[384] the heart. Love entered the skin until it assailed the heart.

384. Qurʾān, 12:26.
385. Ibid., 12:28.
386. Ibid., 12:29.
387. Ibid., 12:30.
388. Id.

When the ruler's wife heard of this talk and came to know that they were talking among themselves about the situation between her and Joseph, she sent for them and prepared a support made of cushions on which they could recline when they came to her. They came to her and she presented them with food, drink, and citrons, and she gave each of them a knife with which to cut the citrons.[389]

According to Sulaymān b. ʿAbd al-Jabbār—Muḥammad b. al-Ṣalt—Abū Kudaynah—Ḥaṣīn—Mujāhid—Ibn ʿAbbās: It is said, "She prepared a couch for them and gave each of them a knife."[390] She had made Joseph sit in another room, and when her guests arrived she gave them citrons[391] and gave each of them a knife. This being done she called to Joseph, "Come out here to them!"[392] And Joseph came out to them, and when they saw him they exalted him and were so distracted by his beauty that they cut themselves in the hands with their knives, thinking that they were cutting their citrons. They said, "God forbid! This is not a human being. This can only be a gracious angel."[393]

After they had cut their hands on account of their distraction at seeing Joseph, and had recognized their error in saying, "The ruler's wife is asking of her slave-boy an evil deed,"[394] and in disapproving her action, she confirmed to them that she had indeed asked of him an ill deed. She said, "This is the one on whose account you blamed me. I asked of him an evil act, but he proved continent"[395]—after he had loosened his trousers.

According to Ibn Wakīʿ—ʿAmr b. Muḥammad—Asbāṭ—al- [385]
Suddī: She said, "This is the one on whose account you blamed me. I asked of him an evil act, but he proved continent." She

389. A similar story—usually with citrus fruit but sometimes with bread and meat—is found in old aggadic collections. See Ginzberg, *Legends*, V, 339, n. 118. Goitein, *Jews and Arabs*, 194–95, says that it does not occur in ancient Midrashic texts.

390. Qur'ān, 12:31.

391. See Thaʿlabī, *Qiṣaṣ* 107, "She prepared for them citrus, melons, bananas, pomegranates, and roses. . . ."

392. Qur'ān, loc. cit.

393. Id.

394. Ibid., 12:30.

395. Ibid., 12:32.

said, "After he had loosened his trousers, he remained continent. I do not know what appeared to him. But if he does not do what I order"—that is, have intercourse—"verily he will be imprisoned and brought low."[396] But Joseph chose prison over adultery and disobedience to his Lord, saying, "O my Lord! Prison is more dear to me than that to which they urge me."[397]

According to Ibn Wakīʿ—ʿAmr b. Muḥammad—Asbāṭ—al-Suddī: He said, "O my Lord! Prison is more dear to me than the adultery to which they urge me."

He asked his Lord for help, saying, "If You do not fend off their wiles from me, they will gradually win me over and I will become foolish."[398] God told him that He would answer his prayer, and He averted their guile from him and saved him from committing abomination.

At length the ruler—even though he had seen Joseph's shirt torn from behind, and the scratches on his face, and the women cutting their hands, and even though he knew Joseph was innocent—grew disgusted with himself for having let Joseph go free. It is said that the reason for this was that which was related by Ibn Wakīʿ—ʿAmr b. Muḥammad—Asbāṭ—al-Suddī: "It seemed good to them, after they had seen the signs [of his innocence] to imprison him for a time."[399] The woman said to her husband, "This Hebrew slave has disgraced me among the people, claiming by way of excuse that I asked an evil act of
[386] him. I cannot give any excuse"—that is, because he had restricted her to the house by way of punishment—"so either give me leave to go out and give my excuse, or imprison him as you have imprisoned me." That is the meaning of God's statement, "It seemed good to them, after they had seen the signs [of his innocence] to imprison him for a time."

It is reported that they imprisoned him for seven years.

396. Id.
397. Ibid., 12:33.
398. Id.
399. Ibid., 12:35.

Concerning Those Who Said That

According to Ibn Wakīʿ—al-Muḥāribī—Dāwūd—ʿIkrimah: To imprison him for a time meant for seven years.

When his master the ruler imprisoned Joseph, two young men were sent to the prison with him. They were two of the servants of the king, the great master of Egypt, al-Walīd b. al-Rayyān. One of them was in charage of the king's food, the other of his drink.

According to Ibn Wakīʿ—ʿAmr—Asbāṭ—al-Suddī: The king imprisoned him and became angry at his baker, having heard that he desired to poison him. So he imprisoned him, and also imprisoned the man in charge of his drink, thinking that the latter had helped the baker. He imprisoned them together, for that is God's statement, "For two young men went to prison with him."[400]

According to Ibn Wakīʿ—ʿAmr—Asbāṭ—al-Suddī: When Joseph entered the prison he said, "I interpret dreams." So one of the two young men said to the other, "Come, let us test this Hebrew slave." So they pretended, asking him about dreams, when they really had not dreamed anything. [387]

The baker said, "I dreamed that I was carrying bread on my head, and the birds were eating it." And the other said, "I dreamed that I was pressing wine." They demanded of him, "Tell us the interpretation, for we see that you are one of those who do good."[401]

As to what this "doing good" meant, there is an account relayed through Isḥāq b. Abī Isrāʾīl—Khalaf b. Khalīfah—Salamah b. Nubayṭ: A man asked al-Ḍaḥḥāk about the quotation, "we see that you are one of those who do good." He asked him, "What was his good deed?" Al-Ḍaḥḥāk said, "Whenever a man became ill in prison, Joseph would watch over him. When he needed something Joseph would fetch it for him, and when he found the place too confining Joseph would expand it for him."

400. Ibid., 12:36.
401. Id.

Joseph said to them, "The food which you are given will not come to you"—on this day—"but I shall tell you the interpretation"—while waking.[402] He did not want to interpret for them what they had asked, so he began with something they had not asked. This was because the interpretation of what they had asked suggested something unpleasant for one of them. So he said, "O my fellow prisoners, are many different lords better, or God the One, the Almighty?"[403]

One of the two young men who had been sent to prison with Joseph was named Maḥlab;[404] he was the one who claimed to have dreamed about bread being on his head. The other one was named Nabū,[405] and he was the one who claimed to have dreamed of himself pressing wine. They refused to let him avoid interpreting the dreams about which they had asked him, and at last he said, "As for one of you, he will pour out wine for his lord to drink"[406]—that was the one who claimed
[388] he had dreamed of himself pressing wine. "As for the other, he will be crucified, so that the birds will eat from his head."[407]

Then, when he had given them these interpretations, they said, "We did not dream anything."

According to Ibn Wakīʿ—Ibn Fuḍayl—ʿUmārah, (that is, Ibn al-Qaʿqāʿ)—Ibrāhīm—ʿAlqamah—ʿAbdallāh: When the two young men told Joseph of their dreams, they were only pretending to have dreamed so as to test him. When he had explained their dreams, they said, "We were only playing." He said, "Thus is the case judged about which you asked."[408] Then he said to Nabū—the one he had said would be saved—"Mention me in the presence of your lord"[409]—meaning, in the presence of the king—"and tell him that I am unjustly imprisoned." But Satan made Nabū forget to mention it to the king, which was a misfortune which befell Joseph from Satan.

---

402. See ibid., 12:37.
403. Ibid., 12:39.
404. Thaʿlabī, *Qiṣaṣ*, 108: Mujlib; Kisāʾī, 108: Ghālib.
405. Thaʿlabī: Bayūs; Kisāʾī: Abruhah.
406. Qurʾān, 12:41.
407. Id.
408. Id.
409. Ibid., 12:42.

According to al-Ḥārith—ʿAbd al-ʿAzīz—Jaʿfar b. Sulaymān al-Ḍubaʿī—Bisṭām b. Muslim—Mālik b. Dīnār: Joseph said to the cupbearer, "Mention me in the presence of your lord." And God said, "O Joseph! You have placed trust in one other than Me, therefore I shall lengthen your imprisonment." And Joseph wept and said, "O Lord! The weight of my misfortunes made my heart forget, and I said a word—woe is to my brothers!"[410]

According to Ibn Wakīʿ—ʿAmr b. Muḥammad—Ibrāhīm b. Yazīd—ʿAmr b. Dīnār—ʿIkrimah—Ibn ʿAbbās: The Prophet said, "If Joseph had not said that—meaning what he said [to Nabū]—he would not have stayed in prison as long as he did because he sought deliverance from someone other than God."

As for how long Joseph stayed in prison, it was related by al-Ḥasan b. Yaḥyā—ʿAbd al-Razzāq—ʿImrān Abū al-Hudhayl al-Ṣanʿānī—Wahb: Misfortune struck Job for seven years, Joseph [389]
was left in prison for seven years, and Nebuchadnezzar was punished by being turned into an animal for seven years.

Then the king of Egypt had a dream which terrified him. According to Ibn Wakīʿ—ʿAmr b. Muḥammad—Asbāṭ—al-Suddī: While the king was asleep, God showed him a dream which terrified him. He saw "seven fat kine which seven lean kine were eating, and seven green ears of corn and another seven dry."[411] The king assembled his sorcerers, soothsayers, seers, and prognosticators, and told them about the dream. They said, "Jumbled dreams! We are not knowledgeable in the interpretation of dreams."[412]

Then the youth who had been saved, Nabū, remembered Joseph's request which he had forgotten. He said, "I will tell you the interpretation, so send me forth"[413]—that is, "release me." So they sent him forth and he came to Joseph and said, "O truthful one! Explain to us about the seven fat kine which

410. The aggadic accounts interpret Joseph's longer imprisonment in the same way; he should have trusted in God alone. See Ginzberg, *Legends*, V, 63.

411. Qur'ān, 12:43. See Gen 41:17–21.

412. Qur'an, 12:44.

413. Ibid., 12:54.

seven lean kine were eating, and seven green ears of corn and the others dry,[414] for the king has seen that in his sleep."

According to Ibn Wakīʿ—ʿAmr—Asbāṭ—al-Suddī—Ibn ʿAbbās: The prison was not in the city, so the cupbearer was sent out to Joseph and said, "Explain to us about the seven fat kine, etc."

According to Bishr b. Muʿādh—Yazīd—Saʿīd—Qatādah: He said, "Explain to us about the seven fat kine." The fat ones were seven abundant years, while the lean kine were barren, sterile years. As for the statement, "And seven green ears of corn and others dry," the green ears were the years of abun-
[390] dance, while the dry ones were the sterile, barren ones.

When Joseph had given Nabū this interpretation, Nabū went to the king and repeated it to him. The king realized that Joseph's interpretation was correct. He said, "Bring him to me."[415]

According to Ibn Wakīʿ—ʿAmr—Asbāṭ—al-Suddī: When the messenger came to the king and told him, the king said, "Bring him to me."

When the messenger came to Joseph and invited him to come to the king, Joseph refused to go with him, saying, "Go back to your lord and ask him about the case of the women who cut their hands. My lord surely knows their guile."[416]

According to al-Suddī—Ibn ʿAbbās: If Joseph had gone to the king before the king knew about this affair, Potiphar would have kept after him, saying, "This is the one who sought an evil act of my wife." When the messenger came back to the king from Joseph, the king assembled those women and said to them, "What happened when you asked an evil act of Joseph?"[417] According to Ibn Wakiʿ—ʿAmr—Asbāṭ—al-Suddī, they answered, "God forbid! We know no evil of him."[418] But Potiphar's wife admitted that she had asked an evil act of Jo-

414. Ibid., 12:46.

415. Ibid., 12:50. See the various alternate interpretations in the aggada, Ginzberg, *Legends*, V, 65–66, followed by Joseph's correct one, ibid., 70.

416. Qur'ān, 12:50.

417. Ibid., 12:51.

418. Id.

seph and that he had entered the house with her. Then she said, "Now the truth is out. I asked of him an evil act, but he is surely honest."[419]

Joseph said, "This"—meaning the act of sending back the messenger with letters about the women—"was so that my master Potiphar would know that I did not secretly betray him with his wife, and that 'God surely does not guide the snares of betrayers.'"[420]

When Joseph had said that, Gabriel said to him that which was mentioned in the account of Abū Kurayb—Wakīʿ—Isrāʾīl—Simāk—ʿIkrimah—Ibn ʿAbbās: When the king assembled those women and asked them, "Did you ask an evil act of Joseph?" they said, "God forbid! We know no evil of him." And Potiphar's wife said, "Now the truth is out. I asked of him an evil act, but he is surely honest." Joseph said, "It was so that he [Potiphar] would know that I did not secretly betray him, and that God surely does not guide the snares of betrayers."[421] Then Gabriel said to him, "Did you not desire her even for one day?" And Joseph said, "I do not excuse myself. The soul does indeed drive us to evil."[422] [391]

When Joseph's innocence and faithfulness became clear to the king, he said, "Bring him to me that I may attach him to my person"[423]—that is, take him into royal service. And when Joseph was brought, "and when he had talked with him, he said, 'As of today you are established and trusted.' And Joseph said, 'Set me over the storehouses of the land.'"[424]

According to Yūnus—Ibn Wahb—Ibn Zayd: Joseph's words, "Set me over the storehouses of the land," referred to the many storehouses which the Pharaoh had for food and other things. The Pharaoh turned over all his authority to him, appointing him administrator, and his orders and judgment were valid.

According to Ibn Ḥumayd—Ibrāhīm b. al-Mukhtār—Shay-

419. Id.
420. See ibid., 12:52.
421. Ibid., 12:51–52.
422. Ibid., 12:53.
423. Ibid., 12:54.
424. Ibid., 12:54–55.

[392] bah al-Ḍabbī: His words, "Set me over the storehouses of the land," meant watching over the food supply of Egypt. He said, "I am a skilled custodian. I will be custodian of whatever you entrust to me, knowledgeable in years of famine." So the king appointed him to that post.

According to Ibn Ḥumayd—Salamah— Ibn Isḥāq: When Joseph said to the king, "Set me over the storehouses of the land, for I am a skilled custodian," the king said, "I hereby do so." It is said that he appointed Joseph to Potiphar's post, dismissing Potiphar from it. God said, "Thus We gave Joseph power in the land. He was its owner where he pleased. We reach with Our mercy who We will. We do not fail to reward the good."[425] It is said—but God knows best—that Potiphar died around that time and that the king, al-Rayyān b. al-Walīd, married Joseph to Potiphar's wife Rā'īl.[426] When she was brought to him, he said, "Is this not better than what you desired?" It is said that she answered, "O honest one, do not blame me, for as you see I was a beautiful and graceful woman, comfortable in my possessions and worldly goods, and my master did not have intercourse with women. And you were as God made you, with your beauty and appearance, and I could not control myself, as you saw." They said that he found her to be a virgin[427] and had intercourse with her, and that she bore him two sons, Ephraim b. Joseph and Manasseh b. Joseph.

According to Ibn Wakī'—'Amr—Asbāṭ—al-Suddī: God said, "Thus We gave Joseph power in the land. He was its owner where he pleased."[428] The king set Joseph in authority over Egypt. He was in charge of all selling and commerce. This was the meaning of God's statement, "Thus We gave Joseph power

---

425. Ibid., 12:56.

426. The biblical acount gives Joseph's wife's name as Asenath, daughter of Potiphar. The problem of whether Potiphar, Joseph's master, is the same as Potiphar, his father-in-law, and whether Asenath could be the daughter of Potiphar who was an eunuch, is discussed in Ginzberg, *Legends*, V, 337–338, nn. 100–101.

427. Because her husband did not have intercourse with women; see Ṭabarī, I, 379, and n. 368, above.

428. Qur'ān, 12:56.

in the land. He was its owner where he pleased."

Joseph administered the storehouses of the land, and became established in his office. During the seven abundant years Joseph ordered the people to leave with him all the seeds they [393] harvested from ears of corn (as provision for the lean years). Then the barren years began, and the people suffered from the lack of rain. One of the countries afflicted by the drought was Palestine, and it began to hurt the family of Jacob, which lived there, so Jacob spoke to his sons about the problem.

According to Ibn Wakīʿ—ʿAmr—Asbāṭ —al-Suddī: Hunger became widespread until it struck the land where Jacob lived. So Jacob sent his sons to Egypt (because he knew there was stored grain there) but kept Joseph's full brother Benjamin in Palestine. When Joseph received them in Egypt, "He knew them but they did not know [that is, recognize] him."[429] When he looked at them, he said, "Tell me about yourselves, for I have no knowledge of you." They said, "We are people from the land of Syria." He said, "What brought you here?" They said, "We came to seek food." He said, "You lie. You are spies. How many of you are there?" They said, "Ten." He said, "You are ten thousand. Each one of you is a thousand. Tell me your story." They said, "We are brothers, sons of an honest man. We once numbered twelve, and our father loved a brother of ours. He who was the most loved by our father went to the desert with us and died there."[430] Joseph asked, "On whom did your father rely after him?" They said, "On a brother of ours, younger than he." Joseph said, "How can you tell me that your father is honest, and loves the youngest of you more than the oldest? Bring me this brother of yours so that I may see him. And if you do not bring him to me, then there will be no grain for you, nor shall you approach me." They said, "We will try to persuade his father to send him, indeed we will."[431] Jo-

---

429. Ibid., 12:58.

430. This interrogation of the brothers seems to be a shorter version of the one found in Ginzberg, *Legends*, V, 83–84. For versions similar to this one see Kisāʾī, 180–81; a shorter version is in Thaʿlabī, *Qiṣaṣ*, 114.

431. Qurʾān, 12:60–61.

seph said, "Leave one of yourselves here to guarantee that you
[394] will return." So they left Simeon.[432]

According to Ibn Ḥumayd—Salamah—Ibn Isḥāq: When Joseph saw the sufferings of the people he was charitable to them, and fair; he would not give more than one camel-load to a single man. He was just with the people and generous to them. Among the people who came to him were his brothers, in search of supplies in Egypt. He recognized them, but they did not recognize him, because of what God wanted to achieve with Joseph. Joseph ordered that each one of his brothers have his camel fully loaded, and said to them, "'Bring me a brother of yours from your father,'[433] so that I may load another camel for you and you will go back one camel-load better off. 'Do you not see that I give you the full measure'[434] and no one diminishes it, 'and [that] I am the best of hosts?'[435] I am the best of all those who accept guests in this land, for I am giving you hospitality. But if you do not bring me your brother from your father, I will not measure out any more food for you, and do not come back to my country."

Then he said to the young men who were measuring out the food for his brothers, "Place their merchandise"—he meant the price they had paid for the food—"in their saddlebags."[436]

According to Bishr—Yazīd b. Zurayʿ—Saʿīd—Qatādah: He said, "Place their merchandise in their saddlebags;" that is, their papers. The workers put them in the brothers' saddlebags, but the brothers did not know it.

[395] When Jacob's sons returned to their father, they said what was related by Ibn Wakīʿ—ʿAmr—Asbāṭ—al-Suddī: When they returned to their father they said, "O our father! The king of Egypt showed us such honor that even if he had been another son of Jacob he could not have honored us more, but he took Simeon as a pledge, saying, 'Bring me that brother of yours to whom your father is most attached after your brother

432. Because he had advised the brothers to put Joseph to death. See Ginzberg, *Legends*, V, 86.

433. Qur'ān, 12:59.

434. Id.

435. Id.

436. Ibid., 12:62.

who perished. If you do not bring him to me, I will not measure out any more food for you, nor shall you ever come near me.'"[437] Jacob said, "Can I trust you with him as I once trusted you with his brother? God is better at guarding, and He is the most merciful of all those who show mercy.[438] When you come to the king of Egypt, greet him for me and tell him, 'Our father blesses you and prays for you for what you have done for us.'"

According to Ibn Ḥumayd—Salamah—Ibn Isḥāq: They travelled until they reached their father. Some scholars have told me that their dwelling-place was in al-ʿArabāt[439] in the land of Palestine, in the Ghawr of Syria.[440] Others say that it was in al-Awlāj[441] in the region of al-Shaghb,[442] lower than the two parts of Palestine. Jacob owned desert land with camels and sheep. When Joseph's brothers returned to their father Jacob, they said, "O our father! We are denied grain beyond the load of our camels, and he measured out to each of us only one camel-load, so send our brother Benjamin so that he will be given a measure for himself—we will surely guard him [396] well."[443] Then Jacob said to them, "Can I trust you with him as I once trusted you with his brother? God is better at guarding, and He is the most merciful of all those who show mercy."[444]

When the sons of Jacob who had gone to Egypt for provisions opened their belongings which they had brought back with them, they found that the price they had paid for the food had been given back to them. They said to their father, "O our father! What more can we desire? Here is our merchandise re-

---

437. Ibid., 12:60.
438. Ibid., 12:64.
439. Hebrew, ʿAravah, the depression from the Dead Sea to the Gulf of ʿAqabah.
440. Properly, the Jordan Valley; see Yāqūt, *Muʿjam*, III, 822: "al-Ghawr is the depression [*ghawr*] from the land of Damascus to the land of Jerusalem."
441. Although LeStrange, *Palestine*, 404, has "a place in Syria" referring to Yāqūt, *Muʿjam*, I, 407, the latter seem to have a place in Arabia in mind.
442. Yāqūt, *Muʿjam*, II, 302, refers to it as an estate in the vicinity of Wādī al-Qurā, hence in the Ḥijāz.
443. See Qur'ān, 12:63.
444. Ibid., 12:64.

turned to us. We shall get provision for our folk and guard our brother, and we will have the measure of an extra camel-load[445] besides the loads of our own camels."

According to al-Ḥārith—al-Qāsim—Ḥajjāj—Ibn Jurayj: They said, "We will have the measure of an extra camel-load." Each one of them had a camel-load, and they said, "Send our brother with us and we will add one more camel-load." According to Ibn Jurayj—Mujāhid: A camel-load means the load of a donkey; it is simply an expression. According to al-Ḥārith—al-Qāsim, (that is, Mujāhid): In some dialects they use the word *baʿīr* (camel) to mean donkey.

Jacob said, "I will not send him with you unless you promise me in the name of God that you will bring him back to me, unless you are surrounded"—meaning, unless they all were killed, which would be an excuse. "When they gave him their promise," with an oath, Jacob said, "God is the Warden over what we say."[446]

After permitting them to take their half-brother with them, he ordered that they not all go in by the same gate of the city. He feared the eyes (of the envious) upon them, for they were handsome in appearance and comely in form. He ordered them
[397] to enter by different gates. As we have it from Muḥammad b. ʿAbd al-Aʿlā—Muḥammad b. Thawr—Maʿmar—Qatādah: Jacob said, "Go in by different gates."[447] They had been given form and beauty, and he feared men's intentions toward them. For God has said, "And when they had entered in the manner their father had ordered, it would not have availed them anything against God, but it was a need of Jacob's soul which he satisfied"[448]—that is, he feared for his children from people 's evil eyes because of their appearance and beauty.

When Joseph's brothers once again came into Joseph's presence, he embraced his full brother (Benjamin) to himself.

According to Ibn Wakī ʿ—ʿAmr—Asbāṭ—al-Suddī: And when they went in to the presence of Joseph, he took his

445. Ibid., 12:65.
446. Ibid., 12:66.
447. Ibid., 12:67.
448. Ibid., 12:68.

brother to himself.[449] He recognized his brothers, giving them a place to stay and providing them with food and drink. When night fell he brought them beds and said, "Each two of you should sleep in one bed." When only the boy remained alone, Joseph said, "This one will sleep with me in my bed." He spent the night with him and Joseph began to smell his breath and hugged him to himself until morning came. Reuben said, "We have never seen anything like this. May we be saved from him!"[450]

As for Ibn Isḥāq, we have his account through Ibn Ḥumayd—Salamah—Ibn Isḥāq: When they—that is, Jacob's sons—entered the presence of Joseph, they said, "This is our brother whom you ordered us to bring to you. We have brought him to you. It has been reported to me that Joseph said to them, "You have done well and acted rightly, and you will find the reward for that with me." Then he said, "I think that you are men whom I have wanted to honor." He called his officer in charge of hospitality and said, "House each two men sepa- [398]
rately. Honor them and entertain them well." Then he said to the brothers, "I see that the man whom you brought has no partner with him, so I will take him to myself and his dwelling will be with me." So he housed them two by two in different dwellings, but housed Benjamin with himself. When he was alone with Benjamin he said, "I am your brother, I am Joseph. Do not sorrow for what they did to us in bygone days, for God has been good to us. But do not tell them anything of what I have told you."

God said that when they came before Joseph, he took his brother to himself, saying, "I myself am your brother, so sorrow not for what they did"[451]—"sorrow not" meaning "do not be sad."

When Joseph loaded his brothers' camels with provisions,

---

449. Ibid., 12:69.

450. None of the other accounts include this. At this point (Kisā'ī, 183, and Tha'labī, *Qiṣaṣ*, 116), Joseph and Benjamin sit together at one table. Benjamin tells his brother of his own children whom he has named in memory of his brother's suffering. Kisā'ī has three sons of Benjamin; Tha'labī has ten sons, paralleling the account (and the names) in Ginzberg, *Legends*, II, 97.

451. Qur'ān, 12:69.

providing for their needs and filling their measures, he placed the golden drinking-cup with which he had measured the food in his brother Benjamin's saddlebag.

According to al-Ḥasan b. Muḥammad—ʿAffān—ʿAbd al-Wāḥid—Yūnus—al-Ḥasan: The metal cup (*ṣawāʿ*) and the drinking cup were the same—a vessel from which one drank.

It is said that Joseph placed it in Benjamin's saddlebag, without Benjamin's knowledge.

According to Ibn Wakīʿ—ʿAmr—Asbāṭ—al-Suddī: When he gave them their provisions, he put the drinking-cup in his brother's saddlebag.[452] His brother was unaware of this. When they set out, a crier called out before the caravan had left, "You are surely thieves!"[453]

According to Ibn Ḥumayd—Salamah—Ibn Isḥāq: He loaded camel after camel for them, and loaded one in his full brother's
[399] name as he had done for the others. Then he called for the king's drinking-cup, which was metal— some claim it was silver—and placed it in Benjamin's saddlebag. He granted them a respite until they had left and gone far from the city, then he gave orders about them and they were overtaken and stopped. A caller cried out, "O camel riders! You are surely thieves!" It is reported that Joseph's messenger reached them and said, "Did we not entertain you honorably, give you full measure (of provisions), provide you with good housing, and do for you what we do not do for others? We took you into our own houses and we are entitled to some respect for our property from you." As he spoke to them, they said, "Certainly, what is the matter?" The messenger said, "We are missing the king's drinking-cup, and suspect no one but you." They said, "By God! You know that we did not come to do evil in this land, and we are not thieves."[454]

Mujāhid said that the "camels" (*ʿayr*) were donkeys. I have this by way of al-Ḥārith—ʿAbd al-ʿAzīz—Sufyān—a man—Mujāhid.

---

452. Ibid., 12:70.
453. Id.
454. Ibid., 12:73.

One of the things which Joseph's messenger called out was, "Whoever brings the king's metal cup shall have a camel-load of food, and I shall be responsible for it"[455]—meaning he would be responsible for ensuring that the reward was given.

The brothers only said, "You know that we did not come to do evil in this land, and we are not thieves." They had given back to Joseph the price of the food which he had put in their saddlebags the first time, so they said, "If we were thieves, we would not have returned that to you." It is said that they were known for not taking anything which was not theirs, which is why they insisted upon that.

They were asked, "How should the one who has stolen it [400]
be punished?" They answered, "In our judgment, his penalty should be to be handed over to the one from whom he stole, to be enslaved by him."

According to Ibn Wakīʿ—ʿAmr—Asbāṭ—al-Suddī: The brothers were asked, "And what should the penalty be, if you are liars?" They answered, "The penalty? He in whose bag it is found, let him be the penalty.[456] Take him, he is yours."

Joseph began by searching the others' packs before that of Benjamin. He went through them and finally took the cup out of Benjamin's pack.

According to Bishr b. Muʿādh—Yazīd b. Zurayʿ—Saʿīd—Qatādah: It was reported to us that before he looked into the packs he asked God's pardon, eschewing the sin he accused them of committing until only Benjamin remained, being the youngest of the group. He said, "I don't think this one took anything." They said, "Of course, so consider him blameless." Except that he already knew where the drinking-cup had been put. God said, "Then he produced it from his brother's bag. Thus did We contrive for Joseph. He could not have taken his brother according to the king's law"[457]—that is, according to the judgment and ordinance of the king of Egypt, which did not ordain that a thief be enslaved for what he stole. Instead Joseph

455. See ibid., 12:72.
456. Ibid., 12:74–75.
457. Ibid., 12:76.

took him through a subterfuge which God worked for him, so that his companions handed Benjamin over to him and he satisfied them that the handing over was just.

According to al-Ḥasan b. Muḥammad—Shabābah—Warqā'-Ibn Abī Najīḥ—Mujāhid: God's statement, "He could not have taken his brother according to the king's law," means he could not have taken him except through a pretext which God con-
[401] trived for him and which Joseph carried out. At that point Joseph's brothers said, "If he steals, a brother of his stole before"[458]—they meant Joseph.

It has been said that Joseph stole one of the idols of his grandfather—his mother's father—and broke it. And they condemned him for that.

Concerning Those Who Said That

According to Aḥmad b. ʿAmr al-Baṣrī—al-Fayḍ b. al-Faḍl—Misʿar—Abū Ḥaṣīn—Saʿīd b. Jubayr: The quote, "If he steals, a brother of his stole before," means that Joseph stole one of the idols of his grandfather—his mother's father—and broke it, throwing it on the path, and his brothers shamed him for that.

According to Abū Kurayb—Ibn Idrīs—his father: The sons of Jacob were at dinner with him when Joseph looked at a bone and hid it, and they blamed him for that, hence the quote, "If he steals, a brother of his stole before." When Joseph heard that from them he immediately said to himself, "You are in the worst case, and God knows best the truth of what you claim"[459]—that is, what they said about the brother of Benjamin was a lie, but he did not say so in plain words.

According to Ibn Wakīʿ—ʿAmr —Asbāṭ—al-Suddī: When the stolen object was produced from the boy's saddlebag, they were filled with sadness and said, "O sons of Rachel! Still we suffer tribulation from you. When did you take this cup?" Benjamin answered, "No, rather it is the sons of Rachel who are still suffering from you. You took away my brother and made him die

458. Ibid., 12:77. See above, n. 332.
459. Id.

in the desert. The one who placed the cup in my saddlebag is the one who put the dirhams in your saddlebags." They said, "Don't mention the dirhams lest we be seized for them." [402]

When they were brought before Joseph he called for the cup, struck it, and held it to his ear. Then he said, "This cup of mine tells me that you originally numbered twelve, but you took a brother of yours and sold him." When Benjamin heard that he arose and bowed down before Joseph and said, "O king! Ask this cup of yours about my brother. Where is he?" Joseph struck the cup again and said, "He is alive and you will see him."[460] Benjamin said, "Then do with me what you wish, for if he knows about me, he will deliver me."

Then Joseph went into his chamber and wept, then he washed himself and came out. Benjamin said, "O king! I would like you to strike this cup of yours, that it might tell you the truth about who stole it and put it in my saddlebag." Joseph struck it again and said, "This cup of mine is angry and says, 'How can you ask me who my owner is? You have seen who had me in his possession.'"

The sons of Jacob could not be controlled when they became angry. Reuben said, "O king! By God, leave us alone or I will give such a shout that every pregnant woman in Egypt will drop what is in her womb." Reuben was so angry that every hair on his body stood out and stuck through his clothes. So Joseph said to his son, "Stand at Reuben's side and touch him." Now it was known that whenever a son of Jacob was angry and another son of Jacob touched him, his anger would disappear. (When Joseph's son touched him,) Reuben said, "Who is this? Is there a sprout of the seed of Jacob in this land?"[461] Then Joseph said, "Who is Jacob?" And Reuben became angry and said, "O king, do not mention Jacob. He is Israel of God, the son of God's sacrificial victim,[462] who was the son of the Friend of God."[463] Joseph said, "Then you are honest."

---

460. In Ginzberg, *Legends*, II:98, in addition to the cup, Joseph has a magic astrolabe by which he reveals himself to Benjamin but not to his brothers.

461. For a Jewish variant of this story see Ginzberg, *Legends*, II:107; V:354, nn. 277, 278.

462. That is, Isaac.

463. That is, Abraham.

[403] When Joseph detained his brother Benjamin, his brothers themselves admitted that he had more right to keep him than they did and saw no way to free him. But they began seeking his release by exchanging one of themselves for him. They said, "O ruler, he has an aged father, so take one of us instead of him. We see that you are a person who does kindnesses."[464] Joseph said to them, "God forbid that we should seize anyone but him on whom we found our property; then, truly, we would be wrongdoers"[465]—that is, if they punished an innocent one instead of the guilty one. When his brothers despaired of getting Joseph to agree to their request to take one of them in place of Benjamin, they saved themselves by means of a secret—no one could separate them, nor could any but they associate with them.[466] The eldest of them, namely Reuben (though some say it was Simeon) said to the rest, "Do you not remember that our father made us promise by God that we would bring our brother Benjamin safely back unless we were all surrounded? Before this, we were remiss in the case of Joseph. I shall not leave this land until my father permits me"—that is, permits him to depart leaving his brother Benjamin behind—"or until God judges for me, for He is the best of judges."[467] It is said that by (the words,) "or until God judges for me," he meant that he would fight anyone who tried to stop him from taking Benjamin with him, and God would judge the outcome. "Go back to our father and tell him, 'O our father, your son has stolen and we have handed him over in his guilt. We testify only to what we know, and the king's cup was found

---

464. Qur'ān, 12:78.

465. Ibid., 12:79.

466. Although the unique qualities of Jacob's sons (who could not be separated and who could not associate with others) are mentioned in the aggada, they are not given the prominent emphasis which we find here. Compare the account of Judah's reaction, after his threat to kill Joseph and Pharaoh, to Manasseh's stamping his foot on the ground, when Judah says, "only one belonging to our family can stamp thus!" Ginzberg, *Legends*, II:104–5. Also, Joseph tells Manasseh to lay his hand on Judah's shoulder to allay his fury, and Judah notices "that he was in contact with a kinsman of his," ibid., 110.

467. Qur'ān, 12:80.

in his saddlebag. We are not guardians of the unseen;[468] we promised only to protect him from that against which we have means of protecting him. We could not have known that he would steal and become enslaved for his thievery. Ask the people of the town in which we were and in which your son stole, and those of the caravan with which we came from Egypt, about the story of your son. You will be told the truth about it.' "[469] [404]

When they went back to their father and told him how Benjamin and Reuben had been left behind, he said, "No, it is rather that your minds have beguiled you into something"—which they wanted. He said, "Patience is seemly"—meaning he had no violent grief over the loss of his son. "It may be that God will bring them all to me"—meaning Joseph, Benjamin, and Reuben. Then Jacob turned away from them and said, "Alas, my grief for Joseph!" As God said, "His eyes were whitened with the sorrow he was suppressing,"[470] for he was filled with sadness and anger. When his sons heard this they said, "By God! You will never stop remembering Joseph,[471] or loving him or mentioning him, until your body becomes seriously ill and your brain disordered from loving and remembering him, and you become decrepit and worn out or die." Jacob answered them, "I expose my distress and anguish only to God"—that is, not to you—"and I know from God that which you do not know"[472]—that is, about the truth of Joseph's dream and of its interpretation that Jacob and his sons one day would all bow down to Joseph.

According to Ibn Ḥumayd—Ḥakkām—ʿĪsā b. Yazīd—al-Ḥasan: The question was asked, "How strong was Jacob's emotion for his lost son?" He answered, "As strong as the emotion of seventy bereaved mothers." He asked, "And what did he have as recompense?" He answered, "The reward of one hun- [405]

---

468. Ibid., 12:81.
469. Ibid., 12:82.
470. Ibid., 12:83–84.
471. Ibid., 12:85.
472. Ibid., 12:86.

dred martyrs." He never thought ill of God for a single moment, night or day.

According to Ibn Ḥumayd—Ḥakkām—Abū Muʿādh—Yūnus—al-Ḥasan— the Prophet: the same.

According to Ibn Ḥumayd—Salamah—al-Mubārak b. Mujāhid—a man of al-Azd—Ṭalḥah b. Muṣarrif al-Yāmī: I was told that a neighbor of Jacob b. Isaac visited him and said, "O Jacob! What is this I see? You have become fragile and exhausted, and you have not reached the age which your father reached." Jacob said, "What has destroyed and exhausted me is concern for Joseph, and remembering him with which God has afflicted me." Then God said to him, "O Jacob! Do you complain of Me to My creatures?" Jacob said, "O my Lord! It is a sin I have committed, forgive me for it." God said, "I have indeed forgiven you for it." After that, if he was asked, he would only say, "I expose my distress and anguish only to God, and I know from God what you do not know."

According to ʿAmr b. ʿAbd al-Ḥamīd al-Āmulī—Abū Usāmah—Hishām—al-Ḥasan: From the time Joseph left Jacob's presence until he returned, eighty years passed, and for all that time grief did not leave his heart, nor did he cease weeping until his sight was gone. By God, there is no creature on earth nobler to God than Jacob.

Then Jacob ordered his sons who had come back from Egypt to go there again and seek news of Joseph and Benjamin, saying to them, "Go and find out about Joseph and his brother, and do not despair of the spirit of God.[473] By His spirit he will dispel
[406] from us and from you the grief in which we find ourselves." So they went back to Egypt, and when they entered Joseph's presence they said, "O ruler! Misfortune has struck us and our folk, and we bring only poor merchandise, so give us the full measure and be charitable to us. God will reward the charitable."[474] The "poor merchandise" which they brought with them consisted of spurious, wretched dirhams which could only be taken as a deposit. Some have said it was rings of a sack

473. Ibid., 12:87.
474. Ibid., 12:88.

of ropes or some such thing. Others have said it was butter and wool, while others said it was pine nuts and terebinth fruit. Still others have said that it was very little, less than they had previously used for buying.

They asked Joseph to be generous to them and give them as much food as he had given them the two previous times, and not any less. They said to him, "Give us the full measure and be charitable to us. God will reward the charitable."

According to Ibn Wakīʿ—ʿAmr—Asbāṭ—al-Suddī: In (the phrase), "be charitable to us," the word "charitable" means something between generosity and baseness. It has been said that "and be charitable to us" meant they wanted him to return their brother to them, and "God will reward the charitable."

According to Ibn Ḥumayd—Salamah—Ibn Isḥāq: It is said that when they spoke to him in these words, he was overcome and wept, scattering tears. Then he revealed to them what he had been hiding, "Do you know what you did to Joseph and his brother in your ignorance?"[475] In mentioning his brother Benjamin, Joseph did not mean what he himself had done to Benjamin when he seized him; he meant their having parted Joseph [407]
from Benjamin when they sold him. When Joseph said that, they said to him, "Then you are Joseph!" He said, "I am Joseph and this [that is, Benjamin] is my brother. God has shown us favor"—that is, by bringing the two together after the other brothers had separated them. "He who wards off evil and endures, indeed God does not forget to reward the kindly."[476]

According to Ibn Wakīʿ—ʿAmr—Asbāṭ—al-Suddī: When Joseph said to them, "I am Joseph and this is my brother," they sought pardon and said, "By God, verily God has preferred you above us, and we were indeed sinful." Joseph said to them, "Have no fear this day. May God forgive you; He is the most merciful of all those who show mercy."[477] When Joseph had revealed himself to them, he asked them about his father.

According to Ibn Wakīʿ—ʿAmr—Asbāṭ—al-Suddī: Joseph

475. Ibid., 12:89.
476. Ibid., 12:90.
477. Ibid., 12:91–92.

asked them, "What did my father do after me?" They replied, "When Benjamin vanished from him, he became blind with grief." So he said, "Go with this shirt of mine and lay it on my father's face, and he will recover his sight. Then come to me with all your folk."[478] When the caravan of Jacob's sons departed, Jacob (back in Palestine) said, "I am conscious of the scent of Joseph."[479]

According to Yūnus—Ibn Wahb—Ibn Shurayḥ—Abū Ayyūb
[408] al-Hawzanī: The wind asked permission to bring the scent of Joseph to Jacob before the messenger bearing the shirt would reach Jacob, and it did so. Jacob said, "Truly I am conscious of the scent of Joseph, though you call me a dotard."[480]

According to Abū Kurayb—Wakīʿ—Isrāʾ īl—Ibn Sinān—Ibn Abī al-Hudhayl—Ibn ʿAbbās: About the quote, "And when the caravan departed, their father said, 'Truly I am conscious of the scent of Joseph,'" it means that a wind stirred up and brought the scent of Joseph from a distance of eight nights' journey. And Jacob said, "Truly I am conscious of the scent of Joseph, though you call me a dotard."

According to Bishr b. Muʿādh—Yazīd b. Zurayʿ—Saʿīd—Qatādah—al-Ḥasan: It was reported to us that on that day there were eighty *farsakh*s (four hundred and eighty km) between Joseph in the land of Egypt and Jacob in the land of Canaan; therefore it came a long way.

According to al-Qāsim—al-Ḥusayn—Ḥajjāj—Ibn Jurayj: Concerning his statement, "Truly I am conscious of the scent of Joseph," we have heard that there were eighty *farsakh*s between them when he said, "Truly I am conscious of the scent of Joseph." He had been parted from him for seventy-seven years. By his words, "though you call me a dotard," he meant "though you consider me foolish and an example of decrepitude and declining intelligence." But those of his sons who were with him said, "By God, you are in your old aberra-

---

478. Ibid., 12:93. According to Jewish tradition a seer loses his spirit of prophecy when in a state of grief, hence news of Joseph being alive restored prophecy to Jacob. Ginzberg, *Legends*, II, 116; see also V, 346, n. 198.

479. Qurʾān, 12:94.

480. Id.

tion again"[481]—meaning craziness and error brought on by his remembrance and love of Joseph.

The bearer of glad tidings—the post rider whom Joseph had sent out to bring Jacob word of him—arrived and told of Joseph's being alive and of what had happened with him. It is re- [409]
ported that the messenger's name was Judah b. Jacob.

According to Ibn Wakīʿ—ʿAmr—Asbāṭ—al-Suddī: Joseph said, "Take this shirt of mine and lay it on my father's face. He will regain his sight. Then come to me with all your folk."[482] Judah said, "The time before, I took the blood-smeared shirt to Jacob and told him a wolf had eaten Joseph. Today I shall take this shirt and tell him that he is alive, to gladden his eye just as I saddened him then." So he was the messenger of good tidings.

When the messenger came to Jacob with Joseph's shirt, he laid it on his face and he became able to see again after having been blind. He said to his children, "Did I not tell you that I know from God what you do not know?"[483]—meaning that, from the truth of the interpretation of Joseph's dream in which he saw the eleven stars and the sun and the moon bowing down to him, he knew that which they did not know. Then they said to Jacob, "O our father! Ask forgiveness of our sins for us, for we were indeed sinful."[484] And Jacob said to them, "I shall ask forgiveness for you from my Lord."[485] Some say that he delayed praying for them until dawn, and some say that he delayed it until Friday night.

According to Aḥmad b. al-Ḥasan al-Tirmidhī—Sulaymān b. ʿAbd al-Raḥmān al-Dimashqī—al-Walīd b. Muslim—Ibn Jurayj—ʿAṭā' and ʿIkrimah, the client of Ibn ʿAbbās—Ibn ʿAbbās—the Messenger of God: Jacob said, "I shall ask forgiveness for you from my Lord"—meaning, when Friday night came.

When Jacob and his sons and their families came into Joseph's presence, he sheltered his parents with himself. It is said [410]

481. Ibid., 12:95.
482. Ibid., 12:93.
483. Ibid., 12:96.
484. Ibid., 12:97.
485. Ibid., 12:98.

that they came into his presence before they entered Egypt, because Joseph went forth to meet them.

According to Ibn Wakīʿ—ʿAmr—Asbāṭ—al-Suddī: They brought their wives and families to him, and when they reached Egypt, Joseph spoke to the king who was above him, and he and the king went forth to meet them. When they reached Egypt he said, "Come safe into Egypt, if God wills!" And when they came into Joseph's presence he took his parents unto himself.[486]

According to al-Ḥarith—ʿAbd al-ʿAzīz—Jaʿfar b. Sulaymān—Farqad al-Sabakhī: When the shirt was placed on Jacob's face, he was able to see again, and he said, "Take me with your family, all together." So Jacob was carried with Joseph's brothers. When Jacob drew near, Joseph was informed that he was approaching, and went forth to meet him. The people of Egypt rode forth with Joseph, extolling him. When they approached each other Jacob was walking, supporting himself on his son Judah. Jacob looked at all the horses and men and said, "O Judah! This is the Pharaoh of Egypt!" But Judah said, "No, this is your son Joseph."[487] And when they came together Joseph went to speak the greeting to him first, but was prevented from doing so, for Jacob had more right and privilege to do so than he. Jacob said, "Peace be upon you. Oh one who removes sorrows!"

When they entered Egypt, "he placed his parents on the dais"[488] and sat them down upon it. There is disagreement as to exactly whom it was that Joseph raised to the throne and placed upon it. Some have said that one of them was his father Jacob and the other his mother Rachel. Others have said that the other person was not Rachel but Joseph's aunt Liyyā, for
[411] his mother Rachel had died before that time.

And Jacob and Joseph's mother and all the sons of Jacob fell down prostrate before him. According to Muḥammad b. ʿAbd al-Aʿlā—Muḥammad b. Thawr—Maʿmar—Qatādah: "They

486. Ibid., 12:99. The two sentences are in reverse order.

487. The confusion of Joseph with the king of Egypt occurs in almost all the accounts; see Ginzberg, *Legends*, II:91–94 , the letter of Jacob to Joseph.

488. Qur'ān, 12:100.

fell down before him prostrate,"[489] for the greeting among those people was for one to bow down to the other. And Joseph said to his father, "O my father! This is the interpretation of my dream of old. My Lord has made it true."[490] By this he meant that their prostrating themselves fulfilled the interpretation of his dream which he had had before his brothers sold him—the dream of the eleven stars and the sun and the moon. God had made it true. He said, "He makes the dream true by bringing its interpretation."

It is said that forty years had passed between the time Joseph was shown this dream and the time when its interpretation was fulfilled.

Concerning Some Who Said That

According to Muḥammad b. ʿAbd al-Aʿlā—Muʿtamir—his father—Abū ʿUthmān—Salmān al-Fārisī: Between Joseph's dream and his seeing its fulfillment, forty years passed. It has also been said that it was eighty years.

Concerning Some Who Said That

According to ʿAmr b. ʿAlī—ʿAbd al-Wahhāb al-Thaqafī —Hishām—al-Ḥasan: Between the time when Joseph departed [412]
from Jacob and the time the two of them met, eighty years passed. Grief had not left Jacob's heart and tears flowed down his cheeks, yet no one on earth was more beloved of God at that time than Jacob.

According to al-Ḥasan b. Muḥammad—Dāwūd b. Mihrān—ʿAbd al-Wāḥid b. Ziyād—Yūnus—al-Ḥasan: Joseph was cast into the pit when he was seventeen years old, and eighty years passed between that (time) and his meeting Jacob (in Egypt). After that he lived twenty-three years and died at the age of one hundred and twenty.

According to al-Ḥārith—ʿAbd al-ʿAzīz—Mubārak b. Faḍālah

---

489. Id.
490. Id.

—al-Ḥasan: Joseph was cast into the pit when he was seventeen, was separated from his father for eighty years, and then lived—after God reunited them and Joseph saw the fulfillment of his dream—for twenty-three more years, and then died at the age of one hundred and twenty.

Certain people of the scriptures have said that Joseph entered Egypt at seventeen and remained in the house of Potiphar for thirteen years. When he reached thirty, Pharaoh, the king of Egypt, whose name was al-Rayyān b. al-Walīd b. Tharwān b. Arāshah b. Qārān b. ʿAmr b. ʿImlāq b. Lud b. Shem b. Noah,[491] made him his chief minister. This king became a believer and died. After him reigned Qābūs b. Muṣʿab b. Muʿāwiyah b.
[413] Numayr b. al-Silwās b. Qārān b. ʿAmr b. ʿImlāq b. Lud b. Shem b. Noah, who was an infidel. Joseph called upon him to believe in God, but he did not respond. Then Joseph made his brother Judah his heir, and died at the age of one hundred and twenty years. Jacob's separation from him lasted twenty-two years, while his stay with Joseph in Egypt after God brought them together lasted seventeen years. When death came to him, he made Joseph his heir. Jacob had come to Egypt with seventy men of his family, and when he died he made Joseph promise to take his body back to be buried next to his father Isaac. Joseph did that for him, taking him to be buried in Syria and then coming back to Egypt. Joseph ordered that his own body be taken to be buried with his ancestors, and when Moses left Egypt he carried the coffin with Joseph's body with him.

According to Ibn Ḥumayd—Salamah—Ibn Isḥāq: It was mentioned to me—but God knows best—that Joseph's absence from Jacob lasted eighteen years. But the people of the scriptures claim that it was forty years or thereabouts, and that after Jacob came to Joseph in Egypt he remained with him for seventeen years and then God took him. It has been reported to me that Joseph was buried in a coffin of marble in the waters of the Nile. Someone has said that Joseph lived twenty-three years after his father's death, and was one hundred and twenty years old when he died.

491. See the previous listing, Ṭabarī, I, 378, above.

In the Torah it is said that he lived one hundred and ten years, and that Ephraim b. Joseph and Manasseh b. Joseph were [414] born to him. Nun was born to Ephraim, and to Nun b. Ephraim was born Joshua b. Nun who was the manservant of Moses. To Manasseh was born Moses[492] b. Manasseh, and it is said that Moses b. Manasseh was a prophet before Moses b. Amram. The people of the Torah claim that he was the one who sought al-Khiḍr.[493]

492. See the story of Moses b. Manasseh (Thaʿlabī, *Qiṣaṣ*, 126, has Mīshā), Kisā'ī, 208. Most Muslim Qur'ān commentators associate the story referred to him (see n. 493, below) with Moses b. Amram, but a minority attribute it to this otherwise unknown figure who, according to Thaʿlabī, lived two hundred years before Moses b. Amram.

493. Al-Khiḍr or al-Khāḍir is the popular figure in legend and story who is primarily associated with *sūrah* 18:60–82. The name does not appear in the Qur'ān, but most of the commentators say that he was the "servant of Moses" mentioned there. See *Shorter Encyc.*, 232ff. Compare this with the Jewish story of "R. Joshua b. Levi and the Strange Actions of Elijah" in Brinner, *Relief*, II, 13–16; Obermann, *Elijah*, 387–404.

BIBLIOGRAPHY

(Includes only works cited in translation notes)

Abū Tammām Ḥabīb b. Aws al-Ṭā'i. *Dīwān*. Edited by 'Abduh 'Azzām. (*Dhakhā'ir al-'Arab*, vol. 5.) Cairo, 1970.

A'lām, see al-Ziriklī.

Anklesaria, B.T. *Zand-Ākāsīh; Iranian, or Greater Bundahišn*. Bombay, 1956.

al-Bal'amī, M. *Tārīkh-e Bal'amī* . Edited by M.T. Bahar and M. Parvin. Vol. I. Tehran, 1975.

Baron, Salo W. *A Social and Religious History of the Jews*. 2nd. rev. ed. Vols. I-XVII. New York: Columbia University, 1952–80.

Blachère, Régis, M. Chouémi, and C. Denizeau. *Dictionnaire arabe-français-anglais* Vol. I, Langue classique et moderne. Paris: Maisonneuve et Larose, 1967.

Brice, William C. *An Historical Atlas of Islam*. Leiden: Brill, 1981.

Brinner, see Nissim.

Brockelmann, Carl. *Geschichte der arabischen Literatur*. 2nd ed. 2 vols. and 3 suppl. vols. Leiden: Brill, 1937–49 .

Bundahishn, see Anklesaria.

Dēnkart, see West.

EI₂: Encyclopaedia of Islam. 2nd ed. Vol. I. Leiden: Brill, 1960.

Encyclopaedia Judaica. 16 vols. Jerusalem: Keter, 1971.

Friedländer, I. *Die Chadhirlegende und der Alexanderroman*. Leipzig: B.G. Teubner, 1913.

GAL, see Brockelmann.

GAS, see Sezgin.

Ginzberg, Louis, *The Legends of the Jews*. 7 vols. Philadelphia: Jewish Publication Society, 1909–36.

Goitein, S.D. *Jews and Arabs, Their Contacts Through the Ages.* New York: Schocken, 1955.
al-Khaṭīb al-Tibrīzī. *Mishkat al-Maṣābīḥ.* Translated by James Robson. 4 vols. Lahore, 1963–65.
al-Kisā'ī. *The Tales of the Prophets.* Translated by W.M. Thackston, Jr. Boston: Twayne Publ., 1978.
Lane, E.W. *Arabic-English Lexicon.* 8 vols. London, 1863. Reprint. Beirut, 1968.
Legends, see Ginzberg.
Mishkat, see al-Khaṭīb al-Tibrīzī.
Nissim b. Jacob b. Shāhīn. *An Elegant Composition concerning Relief after Adversity.* Translated by William M. Brinner. Yale Judaica Series, vol. XX. New Haven: Yale University, 1977
Nöldeke, T. *Das iranische Nationalepos.* Berlin and Leipzig, 1920.
Obermann, J. "Two Elijah Stories in Judeo-Arabic Transmission." *Hebrew Union College Annual,* 23, no. 1 (1950–51): 387–404.
Omidsalar, Mahmoud. "The Beast *Babr-e Bayān*: Contributions to Iranian Folklore and Etymology." *Studia Iranica* 12, no. 2(1983): 40–50.
Qur'ān. Verses are numbered according to the Egyptian national edition. The translation, with modifications, is based on Marmaduke Pickthall. *The Meaning of the Glorious Koran.* London: Allen and Unwin, 1957.
Sezgin, Fuat. *Geschichte des arabischen Schrifttums.* Vol. 1. Leiden: Brill, 1967—.
Shāhnāmeh. Edited by Y.A. Bertels. 10 vols. Moscow: 1960–67.
Shorter Encyclopaedia of Islam. Edited by H.A.R.Gibb and J.H.Kramers. Leiden: Brill, 1961.
LeStrange, Guy. *The Lands of the Eastern Caliphate.* London: Frank Cass, 1905.
———. *Palestine under the Moslems.* London: A. P.Watt, 1890.
al-Ṭabarī. *Annales.* Edited by M.de Goeje and J. Barth. 8 vols. Leiden: Brill, 1879–1901. 2nd ed. Cairo, 1939.
al-Tha'labī, Aḥmad b. Muḥammad. *Qiṣaṣ al-anbiyā', al- musammā 'Arā'is al-majālis.* Beirut: al-Maṭba'ah al-thaqafīyah, n.d.
Wehr, H. *A Dictionary of Modern Written Arabic.* Edited by J. Milton Cowan. Ithaca: Cornell, 1961.
West, E.W. *Dēnkart.* Vol. 37, *Sacred Books of the East.* Edited by M. Müller. Reprint. Delhi: Motilal Banarsidass, 1965.
Wolff, F. *Glossar zu Firdosis Schahname.* Berlin: Hildesheim, 1965.
Wüstenfeld, F. *Genealogische Tabellen der arabischen Stämme und Familien.* 2 vols. Göttingen, 1852–53 .

Yāqūt al-Ḥamawī. *Muʿjam al-Buldān*. Edited by F. Wüstenfeld. 6 vols. Leipzig, 1866. Reprint. Tehran, 1965.

al-Ziriklī, Khayr al-Dīn. *al-Aʿlām, Qāmūs tarājim*. 2nd ed. 10 vols. Cairo, 1954.

Index

A

C

N

R

S

T